Are We

Free Yet?

An Interrogative Dialogue About The African

American't Community, Racism &

Discrimination As Social Conflicts, and the

American Law Enforcement System

White Marlin
Media

Copyright 2020 - Michael Donaldson
ISBN - 9781736544921 / 9781736544907
-First Edition -

I cite many works and quotes by learned people in this book, because my opinion is not fact. In an effort not to make the references repetitious, I use modified footnotes to show how the schemata originates, and sustains its infrastructure.

"The individual has always had to struggle to keep from being overwhelmed by the tribe. If you try it, you will be lonely often, and sometimes frightened. But no price is too high to pay for the privilege of owning yourself{Rudyard Kipling}[1]."

Table of Contents

Table of Contents

Table of Contents

Preface

Are we Free Yet?

"You can have peace. Or you can have freedom. Don't ever count on having both at once [Robert A. Heinlein].

⁓

While trying to aid in repairing a house for a friend we encountered too many problems with the repair. Every time we tried to sink a nail the wood was too soft, or it just broke. The other problem is the surface was not smooth it was bubbled, dried and cracked. Since I was new to this type of work, I did not understand the problem and I didn't recognize what was causing the problem.

What I saw was a symptom not the problem and somebody had to tell me. The guy pointed out that the reason the paint and the nails would not do their job was because the structure under repair had damage from termites. Because of the termite damage, nothing we did on the surface was going to repair this particular unit. We had to do a complete overhaul of *The Establishment* structure to ensure that we got not only the termite damage but we also had to treat for termites.

Listening to the media usually has a downside because much of it is untrue, jaded, rhetoric; it is always about setting of stories. The only thing worse than the regular media is personalized shows where the hosts have an opportunity to give their opinion on a subject. One such show gave a discourse on how and why the Black community has so many problems and why and or how a solution should be implemented. I included an excerpt from this well-renowned talk show, which I use to point out the following throughout the entirety of this book.

1. Since I didn't have the skill to make a determination as to what the real problem was I should probably listen to somebody that recognizes the problem and not make the symptoms the target of discourse
2. Find somebody that can determine the problem
3. Learn to recognize the problem not the symptoms
4. Determine a solution from a root cause analysis[2] that addresses the problem and by default will eventually remove the symptoms

What the host never addressed was what caused these problems to exist in the first place. To have anger at the house for a bad paint job makes no sense because the paint cannot adhere to a rotten surface. If you are not a painter or carpenter you may not understand the full gravity of what termite damage entails. If you don't know the full devastation, you have not done a thorough Root Cause Analysis; therefore your solution will also be deficient.

In this case, there is no house standing in a field which both rotted overtime and and developed termites. In regards to the systematic structuring of privileged America: Into a house which was standing;

1. Somebody brought termites
2. Planted them in the foundation of the house
3. Developed a termite colony with the sole intention of making sure that the house would never stand without external supports.

Then a media personality diagnoses a lopsided house with uneven floors as the problem and does not acknowledge;

1. The devastation caused by the termites

                    or

2. Malevolence caused by the persons that planted the termites means that there is no sincerity in their dialogue solution at any rate.

It stands to reason that the people who bought the termites are probably not going to be the solution to the problem.

Let us look first at this discourse from my learned colleague and then we will go through and challenge the paint job and the symptoms by pointing out that you cannot fix the one house with paint you have to do something about the termite damage.

I will start with the insensitive, unintelligent statement used in concluding this diatribe, "It is now time for the African-American leadership, including President Obama to stop the nonsense. Walk away from the world of victimization and grievance and lead the way out of this mess[3]."

African Americans have barely been voting, and eating at the lunch counters for 60 years. White Americans had freedom for almost 100 years (1775-1783), then plunged into a civil war (1861-1865); this without the Termite infestation of systemic oppression, racism, and discrimination. The majority of school shooters have been White, drug use amongst Whites is still more prevalent than other ethnicities, and female Whites dominate the porn industry. Yet this discourse fails to acknowledge them, pretending as those behaviors are not aberrant. There are so many points made by this media personality's discourse that lacks depth, understanding, sincerity, and unmitigated bias.

1.0
Let Freedom Ring

"The great revolution in the history of man, past, present
and future, is the revolution of those determined to be
free[JFK]."

During the time of my enlistment, the Marine Corps
did not allow Marines to call each other Black or White;
only Dark Green or Light Green. Early in my Law
Enforcement career, I realized there was a divide between
Black and White officers. There were snickers and always
a lightly seasoned racial pickling in the station. Off-color
jokes made the tension bearable, but racial tension existed.

Within the first six months of joining *The
Establishment*, I was reminded that I was not welcome. I
had a conversation with another recruit one day during a
training exercise. We started talking about her dating a
married man. She spoke casually about it. I asked her
about dating a Black guy, and she said, "Lord no, my
parents would kill me." Sometimes even morality is Black
and White.

One of the best officers I worked with was quite
proud to be a racist. When asked what he would do if his
daughter dated Black, he would always reply, "I would kill
her and then kill myself. He was a good officer and I never
saw or heard him abuse anybody Black or White. One day,
he remarked that he hated Black people. I pulled my
driver's license out and showed it to him.

"You do realize that I am Black right?" I fired
back.

"No you are not!" He replied.

"Damn! I was wrong all this time," I snorted back.

"No you are not Black, not like them." We were
patrolling the projects that day. 'You have a job, you
joined the service, and you ain't on the corner selling
dope."

I thought about what he said, I sat quiet for a while. "Lucky for both of us then, not all Black people sell dope."

We did not speak of it again. I think he represented a large number of people, who only know of Blacks, what the media shows them. We ate lunch together daily and he even invited our entire squad to his house for Christmas. We laughed about my ability to get past the checkpoints on the way to the house, and I promised not to tell his friends or drink from his glasses.

He had confederate artwork throughout his house. I looked at the pictures, and a glimmer of disdain rose in me until I remembered that my walls bore Buffalo soldiers and Black artwork. I learned a lot about differing opinions and what racism really was from him.

Racism is not just the expression of a belief; it is the imposition of that belief onto another person because they are different than you.

He went into the same houses I went into for years; we fought the same people White or Black, we rode in the same car. Never in that time did the issue of Black and White, come up again.

I even covered for him one day. For some stupid reason he had a bunch of small confederate flags in a box which he left on the car seat when we transported a Black prisoner to jail. All the way to jail the prisoner called us both racial slurs. When the complaint came down from Internal Affairs about the flags, I claimed the flags, and said they were for a school project. It is not as if he was the one using the slurs, and he was a good officer; maybe not a genius.

Are We Free Yet? is a literary dialogue based observations and many questions posed to me about the infrastructure of separation and exploitation in America from the perspective of a Black cop. This questionable infrastructure propelled America to wealth, and maintains her internal conflict simultaneously. Are We Free Yet? is about all the things history reveals that African Americans cannot do as peaceably as their White American counterparts.

This book about the war raging between Black and Blue Americans, originated with questions from friends about cops and current affairs. This purpose of this book is not to simply condemn *entrenched racism* in the Criminal Justice System; instead, it is analytical and offers solutions.

Anyone that denies racism exists is not being honest with themselves. Any Black person in the U.S. who contends there is no oppression, or discrimination, obviously has sided with *The Establishment* and thrives within its comfort is not being honest. It is impossible to see the injustice and inequity within American society say there is no problem. Just because some Black people succeed within an unjust system, does not mean there is no injustice, it just means they were able to overcome it; many were unsuccessful or never had the opportunity.

While I was born Black, and chose to wear Blue, I have no reason to lie for either Blacks or Blues. Many things from both sides are embarrassing, shameful, and unfortunate. However, even more unfortunate is sitting back and pretending racism does not exist, and refusing to acknowledge its negative effect on the Country as a whole.

Environments change constantly based on stimuli and stressors. The difference between the stressor and the stimuli is the perception that one is negative and the other positive. Sitting on both sides of the divide, I frequently answer questions or hear statements that intrigued. It is to these issues I pen this book, in an effort to educate both sides on what is both forthcoming and inevitable and in response to many questions.

This work of literature offers a learned opinion backed up by thousands of hours of observation, experience, education, and the assistance (although sometime unwittingly) of fact, history, and tragedy. These questions (chapters) represent the most frequent or timely questions I fielded. This book covers decades of the African American struggle and experiences on the road to freedom in America; then and now.

Read this book with an open mind. If you cannot read objectively, and see the problems for what they are, then not only might you be oblivious, you may well be part of the problem. President Obama said, "I promise to listen to you especially when we disagree." The truth is essential to freedom. Within the lies strewn throughout history and the media both evil and good, find themselves hidden.

I examined the developing social pattern over several decades. This book may seem an Indictment against the police and at times Black males. I am angry, but not just because of injustice. I am angry at every Black man that committed a crime, or left his kids to fester, and looked at me expecting support because of the color of my skin. I am just as angry at every White cop that committed an injustice or uttered a racial ignorance and looked at me for support because of the color of my uniform. America keeps doing patchwork, because the fact is, no society can survive if it tears its foundation apart, even a good foundation.

Throughout the book, I sometimes come down as a cop, then at times as Black man, and occasionally a Black cop. It is not because I am wishy-washy; it is just that all behavior cannot be explained simplistically. White people did not pick cotton yet they commit crimes. How many Black leaders must point out that the violence within the Black homes and community needs to cease, before there will really be a change. *The Establishment* may not want a change, but it can be encouraged; Ask Malcolm, we can change lives and families, without violence. Freedom gives me the right to agree or disagree, to argue and to even rage; but never to harm another or turn my back on injustice.

I have to thank many officers that for the more than 23 years I served on a Metro Police Department, I had very little to gripe about. While I did not agree with every decision, more than 90% of what I saw the other cops do was above board.

This does not mean that cops did not go to jail during my tenure; I assisted several on their way. I observed hundreds Black males given warnings for arrest worth offenses by White officers. I think if we say Racism is wrong, it must also be wrong to indict an entire profession of people saying they are racist and brutal. Like me; many cops are also Black.

To me, this book is about

- Observations of a Black officer in a predominantly White Criminal Justice System
- The origin and cause of racial tensions in America
- The current effect of these pressures
- How the proper response to interracial situations is an outcry against racism
- How the job of Law Enforcement can be a double-edged sword

I assure you that I have probably arrested more cops than anyone reading this book.

In 1937, The Emmitt Till Anti-Lynching Act was proposed before Congress and was denied. In 2020 The Emmitt Till Anti-Lynching Act was proposed before Congress, passed and was denied by The Senate. In 2021, Under the Biden/ Harris Administration, LGBTQ rights, Asian rights, and Police reform have legislated or proposed. Seeing the inequity, and both the indifference and intolerance towards Blacks, it no longer matters why the caged bird sings. The caged birds now yell in a boisterous voice: Are We Free Yet?

2.0

Discrimination, Racism and Bias

◌◌

"Things like racism are institutionalized. You might not know any bigots. You feel like "Well I don't hate Black people so I'm not a racist, but you benefit from racism. Just by the merit, the color of your skin. With the opportunities that you have, you're privileged in ways that you might not even realize because you haven't been deprived of certain things[Dave Chapelle] ."

2.1
Discrimination, Racism and Bias

"Racism can also be defined as racial discrimination, but the term 'discrimination' itself refers to a broader concept, which entails the unjust or prejudicial treatment of other people on the basis of race, sex, gender, sexual orientation, age, height, physical features or skin color. The two concepts stem from the idea of 'prejudice'[4]."

No work on Racism in America would be complete or stand up to the test of integrity if it failed to give an overview of the foundation of racism in America. In the analysis of racism let us look first at a few things;

- *American War for Independence* - American War of Independence occurred when the thirteen original colonies waged war against Great Britain to show their objection to direct taxation without proper colonial representation.
- *Founding Principles of America*[5] - In order to exemplify American'tisms (Things African Americans can't do in a manner similar to their White counterparts), I pointed out a few founding principles granted to the citizens of the United States of America (Appendix A).
- *Declaration of Causes of Seceding States*[6] -The Declarations laid out reasons for citizens in the seceding states & the rest of the Union, why these particular states withdrew from the Union.
- *The Civil War* - The Civil War in the United States began in 1861, after decades of simmering tensions between Northern and Southern states over the economics of slavery (not its morality), states' rights and westward expansion. The election of Abraham Lincoln in 1860 caused several southern states to secede and form the Confederate States of America.

- *Bill of Rights* - The first ten Amendments to the United States Constitution, the Bill of Rights, amendments to the Constitution, specific guarantees of personal freedoms and rights for Citizens.
- *Racism's Foundation in America* - Lieutenant Richard Henry Pratt, founder, and superintendent of Carlisle Indian School[7] reportedly first used the word 'Racism' in America, giving it a definition. Pratt pointed out, "Segregating any class or race of people apart from the rest of the people kills the progress of the segregated people or hinders their growth. Association of races and classes is necessary to destroy racism and classism."

The *Willie Lynch Ideology* stands undoubtedly and unchallenged as the best literary example of the methods used in American Racism. The documents known as 'The Willie Lynch Letters' contain scathing ideology, singularly set in writing, a set of values so dangerous, they overshadow the values and virtues built into the Constitution. I feel it necessary to include both manifestos from the Willie Lynch Letters to interpret the divisive, reprehensible, insidiously genius system the Willie Lynch Letters describe. The Lynch Letters appear in Appendix B.

As we talk about the foundation, and principles of *Entrenched Racism*, we discuss them from a perspective of policy, not from the aspect of any one person. In other words, we refer to the Lynch ideation as *The Establishment* not a person. For the purpose of this work, I deconstructed the Lynch Letters, and placed portions of them in topical segments to facilitate the dialogue.

I firmly believe one of the most difficult aspects of our discussion on racism is that although racists can agree on a definition of racist behavior they cannot as easily define *Racism*. There are so many that say because it is not codified (any longer) use of the phrase *Institutionalized Racism* is no longer applicable.

As a dangerous but vivid example: A man walks past an alley wherein some dastardly act occurs (rape, robbery, murder, domestic violence, child abuse etc). Most people would agree that this witness is not the perpetrator of these crimes. This however, IS NOT INNOCENCE. Society slowly realized that even beyond basic compassion, there is a need and often a requirement to render assistance to persons in need. About the perpetrator, we all have disdainful things to say, but what if anything is or should be said of the uninvolved spectator?

A racist is simply a person that hates another based on their race; it does not require action; but it definitely can include inaction. Not caring about what happens to a group of humans, because they look different is an ignorant and dangerous proposition.

If you travel into the interior of many countries, you find them to be largely homogenous. East Indians, Asians, Latinos, and Africans are not just regional references. Like the citrus fruit the orange, the use o the terms East Indians, Asians, Latinos, and Africans conjure images of a particular looking skin tone. Conversely, what does an American look like? Until 1620, Americans looked nothing like the first 43 presidents of the country.

James Baldwin gives an observation of the difference between the concepts bias, racism, and discrimination. "...In this country what has happened is a White brother has knowingly murdered his Black, brother White men have lynched Negroes knowing they were their sons, White women have had Negroes burned knowing them to be their lovers. It is not a racial problem it is a problem of whether you are willing to look at your life and be responsible for it." Racism and bias are an ideology, and discrimination is the enacting of that set of beliefs.

I believe much of the anger and resentment encountered discussing racism is due to guilt of inaction, not discriminatory actions. This is why a common response when discussing racism is, "Show me racism." Therein lies the answer, STANDING BY AND WATCHING, OR BENEFITTING FROM RACISM, is also part of the problem Racism could not exist without inaction. Saying I never beat up the woman next door, does not relieve people from the human action of helping her while she is accosted. Not owning a slave is not enough as long as you know where the slaves are and support Cotton Economics[1].

Regarding the use of the term *Entrenched* let us look at a definition of *Institutionalized*; practitioners or progenitors establish (something, typically a practice or activity) as a convention or norm in an organization or culture. Accepted, bureaucratic, conventional, established, establishment, organized, orthodox, societal. For the purposes of this book, we shall use the terms Systematic Disparate Treatment and Entrenched *Racism* in lieu of *Institutionalized,* and *The Establishment* in lieu of *Institution*; by doing this, I hope to avoid useless banter about terms and codification and use empiricism as a basis.

2.2 Racism

In my opinion, racism is the more insidious of the pillars of bias, racism and discrimination. Stephen Vizinczey, seems to agree that the danger in the racist ideation is when (regardless of its morality) we can agree upon it. "As a rule, the most dangerous ideas are not the ones that divide people but those in which they agree." The absurd absolutism of racism encompasses every corner of this American Nation.

While in China, accompanying a party of Black dignitaries I observed a particular phenomenon. By law, Chinese citizens under the age of twenty must learn English in school. As we perused the Imperial City, I noticed many teens sneaking selfies and photo bombing. After a few moments, it dawned on me; they had never seen real live Black people. We posed for several pictures, the kids were friendly, a few walked up and shook hands. One teen-aged girl was being coaxed to take a picture, when she replied, "I cannot, my dad would kill me." She was not going to take a shot even with another female in the group. Maybe it was

---

[1] '©' Indicates terms unique to this book and appear in the glossary of terms.

because we were foreign, or maybe taller; but I think there is a more likely explanation.

We can outlaw discrimination, but we cannot legislate thought processing and hatred. In the same manner, reparations, and Black history month will not alleviate anger, discrimination, and resentment[2].

2.3 Discrimination

The Establishment used a historical Tribal War perspective to ensure the destruction of the integrity of African Tribes; As a result, another system of survival arose. In the New System, African-American Tribes dislike each other because they must to compete for economic survival. *The Establishment* ensures that there is never enough for anything except basic survival.

The chief components making *The Establishment* thrive are;

- Dividing and conquering people

---

2 {[WL11]I have outlined a number of differences among the slaves and make the differences bigger.

[WL12]I use fear, distrust, and envy for control.

[WL13]Take this simple little list of differences and think about them. On top of my list is "age" but it's there only because it starts with an "A." The second is "color" or shade, there is intelligence, size, sex, size of plantations and status on plantations, attitude of owners, whether the slaves live in the valley, on a hill, East, West, North, South, have fine hair, course hair, or is tall or short.

[WL14]Now that you have a list of differences, I shall give you an outline of action, but before that, I shall assure you that distrust is stronger than trust and envy stronger than adulation, respect, or admiration.

[WL16]Don't forget you must pitch the old Black male vs. the young Black male, and the young Black male against the old Black male.

[WL11]You must use the dark skin slaves vs. the light skin slaves, and the light skin slaves vs. the dark skinned slaves}.

- Using fear, distrust, and envy

Disintegrating the tribes and families instantly became a pillar of *The Establishment.* The Field Nigger and the House Nigger verbiage originated as part of this policy, capitalizing on envy. Tribes already bore fear and distrust of each other, enhanced by language barriers, culture shock, brutality, and terror, slaves naturally had problems developing the infrastructure needed to strengthen and embolden themselves.

Woodson expounds on this even further, "If you control a man's thinking you do not have to worry about his action. When you determine what a man shall think you do not have to concern yourself about what he will do. If you make a man feel that he is inferior, you do not have to compel him to accept an inferior status, for he will seek it himself. If you make a man think that he is justly an outcast, you do not have to order him to use the back door. He will go without being told; and if there is no back door, his very nature will demand one[8]."

In the TV show Everybody Hates Chris, while running for class president, the teenage Chris explained to his friend, "Why should they (White people) treat us (Black people) differently if we do not think we deserve it?" *The Establishment* only survives when Blacks remain so focused on survival; they never seek to own property, or are not able to own property. The Sharecropping system never left, now we call it the Credit Bureau/System.

It is not possible to read [WL-13[found on page #20]] and not see the genius or the early ingenuity of '*The Institute*'. [WL-13] articulates almost a dozen criteria upon which to base distrust. It articulates how it is possible for any person to be brought to a new culture, and in then this new culture constantly be bounced back and forth under the weight of social modification socially.

The Establishment's criteria laid out a quilt from beneath which no slave within their own power could ever be able to escape. This foundation of distrust, carried over into the 20th century, would set about the exact same effect things like; discrimination in housing, schools, credit, jobs, the food store, promotions on the job, between light skin and dark skin people on dating apps, and football teams. The effects are subliminal but they are effective. For example how many humans have been bitten by a poisonous spider? Yet because of the media warnings, 95% of people in the world are afraid of poisonous spiders, even ones that have never seen poisonous spiders.

The Establishment brings out a point that most people would not think of; envy or distrust are much better tools than to try and get a slave to like, respect, or admire the slaver. *The Establishment* understood; even in terms of mammies and wet nurses, that there would never come a time that a Black person once held hostage, brutalized, and disenfranchised would ever hold true admiration, respect, or adulation for those who have enslaved them.

The 'Great White Father Over Me Syndrome' was an offshoot of this deceitful mental rift. Survival is a necessity: The prostitute calls the survival motif The girlfriend experience (GFE). This means that the prostitute gives all the attention and everything needed, to appear that they truly care. During the interaction, the care and attention shared makes the client willing to pay more and it makes the whole experience better for everybody. The girlfriend experience also lessens abuse and intolerance from the client; in this case the oppressor or oppressive system.

Everything being equal; despite what *The Establishment* reports, the slave is no less intelligent than the prostitute. Being nice, and showing respect or admiration to 'Massa-boss' on the plantation, helped stop rape, and allows for an extra piece of chicken or an extra piece of fish: in the work place it allows for promotion, hiring, and less firing. Many slaves betrayed other slaves for survival and to feed their families. We now still call these people handkerchief-heads and Uncle Tom's but they came across on the same boat as every other slave.

When dealing with Black males, *The Establishment* combines the Cronus Complex and Stag mentality. Cronus reinforces the importance of the old male to the future.

Simultaneously the Stag says that only by keeping all the females, can he ensure his future. By default, therefore, the old male MUST ERADICATE the younger male.

Killing the young is the most expeditious manner for the old stag to ensure that no young males grow up to threaten the herd (property) belonging to this male. This however, cost the slavers money and as pointed out by *The Establishment,* a waste of resources.

The Establishment's resourcefulness again rears its ugly head with a modernization of the same motive. In lieu of killing, *The Establishment* fostered abandoning the kids, or removing them from the parents. Although this created a symbiotic bond between Black people and children in need of help, it also had the perpetually devastating Roman values of; exploitation, degradation, and mis-education. A reference to ancient Roman is best understood in light of the context. "Slaves were often whipped, branded, or cruelly mistreated. Their owners could also kill them for any reason, and would face no punishment[9]".

"For decades, the share of U.S. children living with a single parent has been rising, accompanied by a decline in marriage rates and a rise in births outside of marriage. In a new Pew Research Center study of 130 countries and territories, it shows that the U.S. has the world's highest rate of children living in single parent households. Almost one quarter of U.S. children under the age of 18 live with one parent and no other adults (23%), more than three times the share of children around the world who do so (7%)[10]".

The statistics bear out the disparity, but they do not offer answers. It begs the question, as to why so many Black children are removed from Black homes for drug related issues, when National statistics clearly indicate a far more pervasive drug addiction problem in the White community. Since the National FBI statistics seem to indicate that arrests in the traditionally drug related crimes, burglary, theft, and prostitution are White led.

The Center for Disease Control and Prevention provides more antithetical data. The data flies in the face of the empirical data visible in familial intervention and incarceration trends. White Americans, and specifically white men, experience the highest rates of Opioid misuse and deaths from Opioid overdose. Even with a 38% increase of overdose deaths in the Black community due to Heroin and Fentanyl[11], Whites still lead in addiction numbers. As of July 2019, the demographic breakdown by race in the United States was as follows[12]:

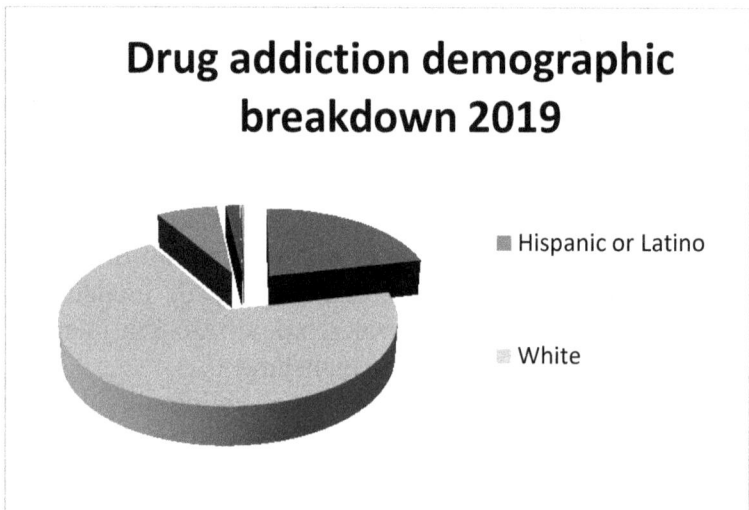

Drug addiction demographic breakdown 2019

Hispanic or Latino

White

[Fig 1]

If White drug addiction exceeds Black addiction, it stands to reason that White parents comprise the highest population if (drug-related) unfit parents (numerically). Why then, is the numbers of Black kids placed in foster care disproportionately high when compared to population?[13]

This information shows that *The Establishment's Abandonment System* still produces results, and the result is unique to America in the number of children removed from stable environments[14].

April 13, 2020

Black Children Continue to Be Disproportionately Represented in Foster Care

Children In Foster Care By Race And Hispanic Origin
(Percent) - 2018

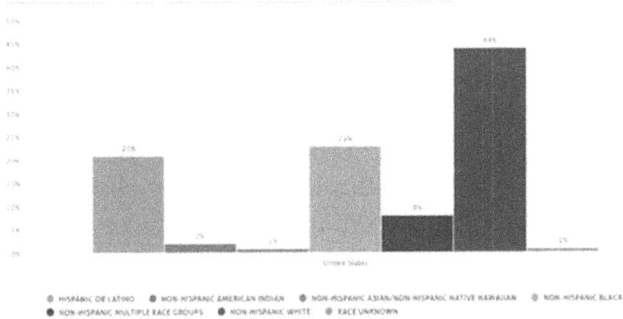

[Fig 2]

Two unintended *Establishment* outcroppings to the are Poor White Trash (PWT), and the Wigger. David Usborne postulated that Wiggers are White who desire to be Black. Usborne is incorrect, the Wigger and PWT are people that *The Establishment simply* pushed from their class into the underworld[3]. Once ousted, these White people found that they had to learn to function by the Laws of the Cotton Field© within which they found themselves living.

What is also phenomenal about this article published in 1993, Wiggers just wannabe Black: White middle-class kids are adopting Black street style and chilling out to rap music, is just like cartoons of mammies, huge lips on Black people, and tails on photos of GIs, this author is basically ridiculing Whites for joining Niggers. Implicit in the article is the undertone that in order for there to be a Wigger, first there must exit a Nigger.

---

[3] Note the reference to an area of darkness.

This 1993 article proves that to *The Establishment* Niggers still exist, and must therefore be monitored and controlled.

The Establishment created another tribe of miscreants, Poor White Trash. *The Establishment* requires Whites have no familiar association or similitude to Blacks: if however, Whites decide they want to be Black (in societal terms do what people consider disdainful and stereotypical), they face excommunication and relegation to live with the Niggers.

Dr. Michael Eric Dyson sums up the effectiveness of this policy, "The Politics of Shade have shadowed Black folk from the time we set foot in North America. Steph Curry's fame has upped the ante: Suspicion surrounds him because of his light skin, and because he has been lauded by both the NBA and media establishments. The subliminal message has become explicit: Curry is a brother we may not be able to embrace because of powers that be embrace him too." Later in the same article, Dyson cites a college professor on the West Coast, proclaimed in his class when I visited his school in 2015, referring to Curry's closest competitor for the award. "James Harden doesn't stand a chance to win the MVP; he's too dark and 'too Black[15]'."

Dr. Dyson calls this 'The Politics of Shade', an ideology developed as a direct result of [WL11, 12, 13, 14, 15] found on page #21. From 1712 to 2015, the politics of shade provided as documentable proof of the viability, stability, and survivability of the Institute of Racism. Only utter futility, or Alumni status at the Racism Institute, would cause anyone to attempt to refute the clear consequences between [WL11, 12, 13, 14, 15] and the politics of shade. Envy and distrust still work between Whites, the dark and the light skinned Blacks: just like *The Establishment envisioned.*

The reason *The Establishment* still exists is that while Slavery was abolished as a policy, hatred of what *The Establishment* created still exists. Baldwin once asked, "If you hate the Nigger so much why did you create him?"

Understand that while racism insists Blackness is the source of Niggerism; Whiteness created the blueprint for American Niggerism. Both the concept of 'Nigger', and the term originated in America. Chinese and Irish faced exploitation in America, but only the Native American and the Blacks suffered systematic destruction.

In regards to the latter two peoples; *Conceptual Niggerism* still exists; that is to say these proud people still exist, but the effect of their reprogramming (as described in the Lynch Letters as the New Natural State) is disparaging, distinct and unpalatable.

Slavery in various forms existed everywhere in the world. Sixty years after WWII, Japanese and Germans freely move about America, yet the Bucks (young Black men) and the Braves (young Native American male) still find that they are American'ts. The Snyder Act in 1924 declared Native American'ts citizens, yet America still has the Bureau of Indian Affairs and Indian Education (Their New Natural State). Blacks in turn received citizenship by the 14th Amendment (Equal Employment Opportunity Commission, Affirmative Action), African American'ts new Natural State.

2.4 Bias vs Racism

Bias is not only more prevalent than people realize, I believe it is also more sinister. Bias lurks around in society masking itself as theory and subtle criteria, yet in fact it is often more damaging than racism. To the matter, a study by U.S. National Library of Medicine National Institute on Health Racial bias in pain assessment and treatment recommendations, and false beliefs about biological differences between Blacks and Whites[16] occurred in 2016. The study focused on the beliefs that Blacks and Whites are biologically different. "In the United States, these beliefs were championed by scientists, physicians, and slave owners alike to justify slavery and the inhumane treatment of Black men and women in medical research. In the 19th century, prominent physicians sought to establish the 'physical peculiarities' of blacks that could 'serve to distinguish him from the White man'. Such 'peculiarities' included thicker skulls, less sensitive nervous systems, and diseases inherent in dark skin. Dr. Samuel Cartwright, for instance, wrote that Blacks bore a 'Negro disease [making them] insensible to pain when subjected to punishment'. Other physicians believed that blacks could tolerate surgical operations with little, if any, pain at all). Well into the 20th century, researchers continued to experiment on Black people based in part on the assumption that the Black body was more resistant to pain and injury. The military covertly tested mustard gas and other chemicals on Black soldiers during World War II, and the U.S. Public Health Service, in collaboration with the Tuskegee Institute, studied the progression of untreated syphilis in Black men from 1932 to 1972."

More ridiculous than the study's thesis, is that it occurred in 2016, and focused on the medical community. If learned doctors and medical practitioners, those that lead science and health related studies, maintain archaic and dangerous bias, why should the less educated, and those that follow education and science be any less ignorant?

Medical students and residents when polled gave responses to the following 15 questions:

- On average, Blacks age more slowly than Whites
- Black people's nerve-endings are less sensitive than White people's nerve-endings
- Black people's blood coagulates more quickly-because of that, Blacks have a lower rate of hemophilia than Whites
- Whites, on average, have larger brains than Blacks
- Whites are less susceptible to heart disease like hypertension than Blacks
- Blacks are less likely to contract spinal cord diseases like multiple sclerosis
- Whites have a better sense of hearing compared with Blacks
- Black people's skin has more collagen (i.e., it's thicker) than White people's skin

- Blacks, on average, have denser, stronger bones than Whites
- Blacks have a more sensitive sense of smell than Whites; they can differentiate odors and detect faint smells better than Whites
- Whites have more efficient respiratory systems than Blacks
- Black couples are significantly more fertile than White couples
- Whites are less likely to have a stroke than Blacks
- Blacks are better at detecting movement than Whites
- Blacks have stronger immune systems than Whites and are less likely to contract colds

My father is a physician, and he tells a very old joke. What do you call the person that graduates last in the class from medical school? doctor. The results of the study in 2016, echo that this is more than a joke; it apparently has a basis in recognizing the failings in the medical community, and that idiots can graduate from medical school.

An interpretation of the findings from the study suggest, "Interestingly, among this sample, the bias emerged because participants high in false beliefs rated the pain of the Black target lower and the pain of the White target higher than did participants low in false beliefs. In other words, relative to participants low in false beliefs, they seemed to assume that the Black body is stronger and that the White body is weaker."

The implications from this study resonate into Uses of Force and the biased beliefs that affect policing and abuses of authority towards Blacks. People that still believe that Blacks and Whites different will continue to treat people differently. The study focused primarily on pain management and prescribing practices but spilled over into every aspect of inter-racial interaction. In much the same manner, people believe that shouting overcomes linguistic barriers, bias lends itself to subversive, discriminatory, or excessive treatment of Blacks. Soon, some learned person may assert that Blacks need less oxygen to live than Whites, and devise a manner in which to circulate air only to White people. This only seems stupid because White people tend to ascribe normal relativistic values when they make determinations; because they plan for interactions with Whites. What would be the response and skepticism, if we conducted a study but instead of Blacks postulated that homosexuals needed less food, and water than heterosexuals?

According to SME Melvin Brown M.S., who has more than 30 years training in Use of Force, Force on Force, SWAT, defensive tactics and is a decorated veteran; racism is intentional; bias is a conditioned part of the OODA (Observe, Orient, Decide, Act) Cycle.

According to Brown, Bias develops based on environment and environment is a part of the OODA Loop. Bias can lead to profiling because of experiences but racism has no valid basis, and is therefore more difficult to eradicate.

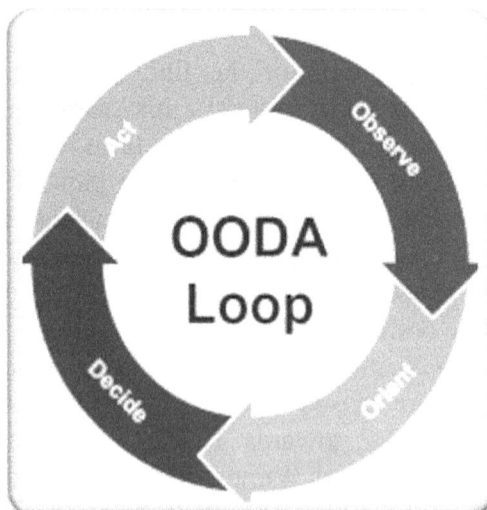

[Fig 3

Often encounters between Blue and Black Americans, which go awry, we credit to racist behavior. However, we must bear in mind that according to [Fig 3] bias is the third stage of the OODA loop termed 'Decide';

and entails a great deal of input from various sources. Bias is difficult to combat because it is subjective and perception driven. Emotional determinations DO NOT REQUIRE VERIFICATION; therefore by the time racism solidifies, the invalidity of bias and experience makes it that person's reality.

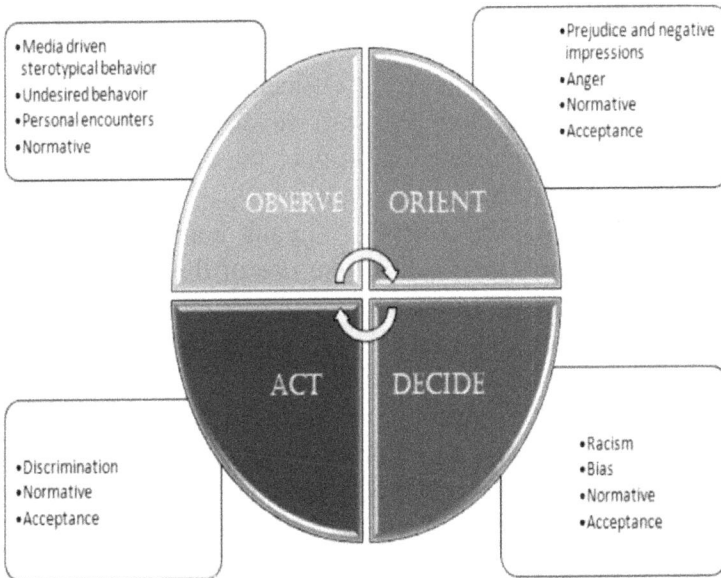

[Fig 4 - ODDA]

2.4 False Narrative vs. Unpublicized Incidents

Melvin Brown, (Formerly one of the 67% male White majority in U.S. law enforcement), points out how the media fuels false narratives thereby diluting the poignancy of legitimate incidents. Of paramount importance to the investigation of the Use of Force is what I collectively call, the Totality of the Facts©. In his qualified opinion, there can be no valid narrative without a Totality of the Facts. According to SME Brown, prejudice proceeding from a false narrative is another form of bias.

The phrase Totality of the Facts has several component parts, NONE OF WHICH CAN COME FROM THE MEDIA;

- Totality of the Facts[1] - Use of Force (absolutely necessary, active aggression, active resistance, aggravated active aggression, authorized weapons and ammunition, conducted energy device, deadly force, defensive force, excited delirium, force-continuum, injury, less lethal devices, lethal weapon, non-deadly force, passive resistance, physical force, positional asphyxia, reasonable belief, restraining force, serious bodily injury, verbal uncooperativeness)
- Totality of the Facts[2] - Officer Subject factors (age, size, relative strength, skill level, injuries sustained, level of exhaustion or fatigue, the number of officers available vs. Subjects, gender)
- Totality of the Facts[3] - Legal basis for the Law Enforcement interaction (the use of the term legal here also means legitimate)
- Totality of the Facts[4] - Officer training factors (See departmental training standards)

Facts not subject to opinion or interpretation are the only objective way to evaluate Uses of Forces, especially fatalities. Opinions based on what is available to be viewed on social media, is valueless. Much as it is in trial, only facts count as evidence; opinion is valueless, as is the newscaster giving the opinion.

Brown's point is that too many events with questionable components make the news when there are many events with no questionable components which are better stories; sadly, they do not yield high enough ratings. One of the most important components not to have in question is are Totality of the Facts component #3, there must be a valid reason for police interaction. If we remove questionable reasons given by police for their interactions, the Use of Force equation clearly indicates police malfeasance.

As an example SME Brown pulled an incident out of his hat; one that I have never heard of. He pointed out the Joseph Lee Pettaway[17] incident from 2018. Although there was a Totality of the Facts[3] component, which is a legal basis for law enforcement interaction, it was questionable. The police responded to a burglary call for service, but did absolutely nothing to investigate or deescalate. The result: a man mauled to death on camera in his own home.

The police had Totality of Facts components:

- A call for service
- A person in the house upon arrival
- Departmental training

But damn, there can be no burglary without information from the homeowner. We know the officers never verified with the homeowner, because she would have verified that Pettaway had permission to be on the property and had been there for more than two weeks, legally making him to be a resident. I am also sure their departmental policy does not condone a dog attack (of an unarmed man) lasting two minutes; that is almost one round in a boxing match.

SME Brown argues that this is one of the most egregious occurrences of racist behavior in modern years. What I find egregious is that I never heard of the incident and it did not stir up national dialogue and outcry from activists for any length of time. Did the Media not find this event worthy of unilateral coverage? Another proof of *The Establishment's* power is that as of October 2020, this event had not been civilly resolved.

In this incident, bias from many sides wittingly or not merged to minimize the magnitude of this injustice. The national media, BLM movement, and the Criminal Justice System have been slow, if they have responded at all.

2.5 White Privilege

The pillars of bias, hatred, racism, and discrimination will never cease to exist in America because they alone sustain White privilege. Someone described White Privilege as, "Inherent advantages possessed by a White person on the basis of their race in a society characterized by racial inequality and injustice."

In order for White Privilege to thrive, by definition there must be someone over which to exert privilege. The purpose of discrimination is to foster, and maintain the security of White privilege.

Many White people honestly are not racists, but how many of them would;

    a. Willingly admit their success is due in large to their privilege

    b. Be willing to abandon their privilege

I would ask this last question as well. Who among Black people, once having established a new empire for their tribe, would abandon Black privilege? How easy would it be to give up Black Privilege? Moreover, why would anyone?

2.6 Black Privilege

I believe there is Black privilege. I believe higher education, religion, financial standing, athletic prominence, and media presence are the only components of 'Black Privilege'. I believe the definition of Black Privilege is 'Transcending skin color by virtue of contribution, or wealth'. I think the comments directed to Tiger Woods about having 'fried chicken and collard greens' for him at the Master's Golf Tournament, is proof positive of the difficulty in transcendence into the world of White privilege.

Whites retain privilege, not just for stability, but for power. Positions of power carry with them influence and the ability to determine resource allocation. According to the NY Times as of Sept. 9, 2020[18];

- 25 people command the largest police forces. 14 are Black or Hispanic
- 29 prosecutors charge people with crimes in those jurisdictions. 12 are Asian, Black or Hispanic
- 24 people led the Trump administration. 3 are Asian, Black or Hispanic
- 9 justices sit on the U.S. Supreme Court. 2 are Black or Hispanic.
- 8 men are military chiefs, 1 is Black

- Of the people at the top of the 25 highest-valued companies, 6 are Asian or Black
- Of the people who head universities ranked in the top 25, 1 is Hispanic
- 15 people direct major news organizations. 3 are Black or Hispanic
- The 5 people who have the most influence over book publishing are all White
- The people who edit the 10 most-read magazines are all White
- 14 people influence most of the music that is produced and played. 2 are Black or Hispanic
- 25 people run the top TV networks and Hollywood studios. 3 are Black or Hispanic
- 99 people own professional baseball, basketball and football teams. 6 are Asian, Black or Hispanic
- 100 people write laws in the U.S. Senate. 9 are Asian, Black or Hispanic
- 50 people are state governors. 3 are Asian, Hispanic or Native American
- 431 people currently write laws in the U.S. House. 112 are Asian, Black, Hispanic or Native American, or otherwise identify as a person of color

2.7 Privilege and Bias

I believe White privilege is the scourge ideology from which much racism and hatred develop. I believe biased based in xenophobia, guilt, shame, and let's face it greed, not only supports the exoskeleton of White privilege they simultaneously maintain its malevolence. Therefore, a large portion of racist discriminatory behavior is self-serving and provides a defensive screen to hide behind.

3.0
Entrenched American Racism, Discrimination, Bias & Social Oppression
[*Est. 1640*]

"Institutions will try to preserve the problem
to which they are the solution [Clay Shirky]

3.1
Racism, Discrimination, Bias and Social Oppression

"Racism is both overt and covert. It takes two, closely related forms: individual whites acting against individual blacks, and acts by the total White community against the Black community. We call these individual racism and *entrenched* racism. The first consists of overt acts by individuals, which cause death, injury or the violent destruction of property. This type can be recorded by television cameras; it can frequently be observed in the process of commission. The second type is less overt, far more subtle, and less identifiable in terms of specific individuals committing the acts. However, it is no less destructive of human life. The second type originates in the operation of established and respected forces in the society, and thus receives far less public condemnation than the first type{Stokely Carmichael}19 ,,

.

As we discuss the foundation, and principles of entrenched racism, discrimination, and social oppression[4]

---

[4]{[WL1] Gentlemen: I greet you here on the bank of the James River in the year of our Lord one thousand seven hundred and twelve. First, I shall thank you, the gentlemen of the Colony of Virginia, for bringing me here. I am here to help you solve some of your problems with slaves.

[WL2]Your invitation reached me on my modest plantation in the West Indies, where I have experimented with some of the newest and still the oldest methods for control of slaves.

[WL3]Ancient Rome's would envy us if my program is implemented, Lynch not only referred to the brutality, and perpetuity but of the effectiveness of Slave Management as an institution in America, remember the discussion is in terms of policy, the terms '*Willie*', '*Willi'ism*', and *The Establishment* for the remainder of the book refers to the thought and methodology of American Racism and Systematic Disparate Treatment, not the actual documents themselves.

According to the Lynch construct, there were obvious problems arising in the management of the slaves. The colonists combined their former government's methods; the same methods of oppression and exploitation they rebelled from and sought to employ methods known to be oppressive. The colonists sought to recreate, in their

---

[WL4]As our boat sailed south on the James River, named for our illustrious King, whose version of the Bible we cherish, I saw enough to know that your problem is not unique.

[WL5]While Rome used cords of wood as crosses for standing human bodies along its highways in great numbers, you are here using the tree and the rope on occasions.

[WL6]I caught the whiff of a dead slave hanging from a tree, a couple miles back.

[WL8]Gentlemen, you know what your problems are; I do not need to elaborate. I am not here to enumerate your problems; I am here to introduce you to a method of solving them.

[WL9]In my bag here, I have a foolproof method for controlling your Black slaves. I guarantee every one of you that if installed correctly it will control the slaves for at least 300 years.

[WL10]My method is simple. Any member of your family or your overseer can use it.

[WL12]These methods have worked on my modest plantation in the West Indies and it will work throughout the South.

[WL15]The Black slaves after receiving this indoctrination shall carry on and will become self-refueling and self-generating for hundreds of years, maybe thousands.

[WL21]If used intensely for one year, the slaves themselves will remain perpetually distrustful of each other.

[WL22]Gentlemen, these kits are your keys to control. Use them. Have your wives and children use them, never miss an opportunity}.

newly freed land, the effectiveness of the oppressive system from which they fled.

A flaw in the mentality of the slavers was they thought God honored their institution, and saw it as a God given right and privilege. This mentality embraced by *The Establishment*, reminded the slavers that previously, God gave man dominion over the earth. To them slaves are not people; they are the bounty of the earth - mere wealth generating property. *The Establishment* craftily maintained the ideology that the slave is just another animal, an extension of the wealth of the kingdom.

The Establishment's dispassionate discarding of slaves reinforced their animalistic standing in the society. Like slaughtering hogs, slaves were just meat hanging in the sun. Elitism breeds racism, it is just called class, or cast in modern times. Likening slave owners to Romans instilled a mindset that they were free to govern their own destiny, control their property, and enjoy the economic fruit from the yield of their livestock. Rome after all was a free Republic, *The Establishment* also laid down the ideology that made the Civil War inevitable.

How loathsome any human that experiences pleasure and familiarity with the smell of rotting human flesh. How powerful a smell to the other animals, that even this human perceived the fragrance miles from the tree where the carcass hung.

The Establishment teaches that the slaver's methods are for the Black slaves. At the time, there were still Native American slaves, possibly even Chinese slaves but *The Establishment's* methods adopted were expressly for the Blacks.

Is it not ironic that in 2020, illegal Latinos, Asians (even the ones that bombed Pearl Harbor not too long ago), Indians, and even Middle Easterners post 9/11, find acceptance, though American still wages wars with them[5]?

---

[5] The 2000 U.S. census states that racial categories, "Generally reflect a social definition of race recognized in this country. They

These people are not actually of European decent, but they are grafted into *The Establishment;* sadly not to make their lives better, but they serve the purpose of allies in furthering the plan for *Entrenched racism,* and maintaining White as the majority demographic in the country[6].

The Establishment was better than Nostradamus when it came to predicting the success of the program. Racially motivated confidence relied on history and racism to succeed, after all, *The Establishment* never used world history to prove that Blacks were incapable, or less intelligent. *The Establishment* did not use science; they used the inerasable mark of race and color to ensure that *The Establishment* would last as long as people are Black. All *The Establishment* needed to do was convince people, that those with Black skin, never deserved to be treated as equals.

The Establishment's expertise in the King's English becomes evident via the usage of the word *shall*[WL15]. The word *shall,* connotes a strong assertion, future tense, used as insistence or a command in many legal documents. *The Establishment* therefore guarantees perpetuity of the model via the Theory of Cultivated Ignorance [Fig 4].

How best to remind White of Black's lower value than; television, music, and billboards. Why is it that billboards for welfare and public assistance most often feature Black people? Why is it that the news report in neighborhoods where a crime has been committed, the person that is interviewed was never the person in the

---

do not conform to any biological, anthropological, or genetic criteria." It defines "White people" as "people having origins in any of the original peoples of Europe, the Middle East, or North Africa. The Federal Bureau of Investigation uses the same definition.
https://en.wikipedia.org/wiki/Race_and_ethnicity_in_the_Unite d_States_Census, 2020.

[6] Europe, the Middle East, and North Africa, and Hispanics are classified   as White for statistical and Criminal Justice purposes.

neighborhood that can read; it is the village idiot? Why is it that for years Black media roles were limited to prostitutes and criminals? Why is it that Blacks are stereotyped in the media, and Blacks are also condescended for group activities and behavior that when done by other ethnicities, nobody takes notice? Black Spring Break is a big deal, but nobody cares about San Padre Island. Blacks selling drugs horrific; White using drugs no big deal.

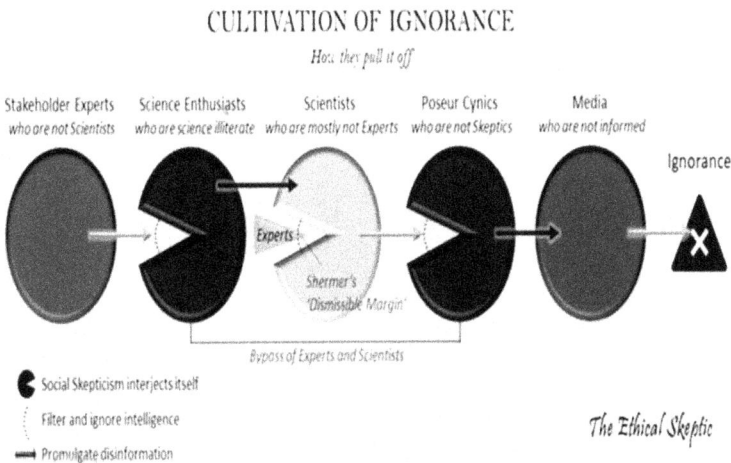

CULTIVATION OF IGNORANCE

How they pull it off

Stakeholder Experts | Science Enthusiasts | Scientists | Poseur Cynics | Media
who are not Scientists | who are science illiterate | who are mostly not Experts | who are not Skeptics | who are not informed

Ignorance

Experts

Shermer's
'Dismissible Margin'

Bypass of Experts and Scientists

Social Skepticism interjects itself

Filter and ignore intelligence

Promulgate disinformation

The Ethical Skeptic

[Fig 4$^{2.0}$]

Karl Marx and Sigmund Freud provided powerful accounts of systematic ignorance[21]. The Theory of Ignorance is a simple one as indicated in [Fig 3]. If you take an idea and cultivate it to people who through education, either moral influence or sheer necessity to survive, you can train a person to believe anything.

This pervasive methodology perpetuates racism. All *The Establishment* had to do was convince the Black man that he was not worth anything so Blacks would never forget. *The Establishment* also reasserts this fact to Whites.

Cultivated Media Ideation© is how you constantly reinforce that the value of dark people to society, is of a lesser tier. White people are doctors, lawyers, and teachers and the question is what do Black people do other than make kids and catch football? That is the perception. Multi generational indoctrination via media, school, church, and enforced by the police, created a schism, and a scar from which America has yet to heal.

Throughout the course of the entrenchment of racism in America, the White family developed disdain for the Black family and vice versa. Males from both sides of the track saw/see each other as enemies; they share this common thread. Both the White males and the Black males fight for dominance. The White male wishes to retain ownership and power, and the Black male fights reversion to disenfranchisement and being powerless.

Racism has a simple ideation, they are Black; so hate them, and no one needs ever ask why.

3.2 Oppression / Apart - hate

"After the United States abolished slavery, Black Americans continued to be marginalized through enforced segregation and diminished access to facilities, housing, education - and opportunities[22]."

Sometimes during conversations with White people, they asked things like, "Why did you have to bring that up, or why can't Blacks just get over it?" I find this peculiar that many cite their ancestry, to show that they succeeded from Ellis Island.

The other more important reason this response is not only counter-intuitive, but lacks depth is that this would imply that racism, discrimination, and oppression no longer exist. The people that supported discrimination did not all die.

The relics of years gone by;
- Black Codes and Jim Crow
- The Supreme Court and Segregation
- Housing Segregation
- Segregation during the Great Migration
- Segregation and the Public Works Administration
- Red-Lining
- Housing Segregation
- Segregation in schools

- Boston busing crisis

have simmered but not gone out. Statistics still show disparities in lending, school funding, hiring, and firing.

The media conveniently blames President Trump for racial woes within the country's borders. However, where were the anti-Trump people that claim we need to make a difference when Treyvon Martin needed help?

A poll by Gallup in 2017 attempted to poll White racial resentment during Obama years using eight questions including the following four questions:

1.   In general, do you think that Blacks have as good a chance as Whites in your community to get any kind of job for which they are qualified, or do not you think they have as good a chance?

1.   In general, do you think that Black children have as good a chance as White children in your community to get a good education, or do you think they have the same chance?

2.   Do you think that Blacks have as good a chance as Whites in your community to get any housing they can afford, or do you not think they have as good a chance?

3. Are Blacks in your community treated less fairly than Whites who are in the following situations?

- On the job/at work
- In neighborhood shops
- In stores downtown/in the shopping mall
- In restaurants/bars/theaters/other entertainment places
- In dealing with the police, such as traffic incidents

The numbers do not reflect a great divide or enlightenment within the White community.

- Pre-Obama 82% of all respondents resented Blacks
- During-Obama 75% of all respondents resented Blacks

Yes, Trump catered to his voting masses, but according to Gallup's numbers; racism, dislike, and antipathy for Blacks existed in 75% of responding voters polled, Democrats and Republicans; before Trump took office.

3.3 Integration

Many things changed in American during Desegregation, because the law changed. As people acclimated to new laws, there were numerous acts of violence across the country.

Desegregation began in 1954, 10 years later Dr. ML King pointed out how little things had changed in the country. Then as a response to apathy in the equalization of citizens, the American Black Power Movement emerged. Black Power as a revolutionary ideation emphasizes racial pride, economic empowerment, and the creation of political and cultural institutions.

Look at *The Establishment* and ask what enlightenment caused the same government that branded Malcolm X and Martin as radical and dangerous, to support and provide security for the Blacks to march on Washington? A similar epiphany occurred in Memphis March 18th 1968; Dr. King's point was that White Memphians were willfully indifferent to the suffering of the city's Black working poor. *One day these Whites would suffer for their blindness*, he warned[23].

Desegregation is always the last ditch effort an oppressor offers to stave off a revolution. While Blacks were not the majority, there is still an uncertainty between Whites as to which side they will enter during another internal conflict between Whites and Blacks. The conflict would not be considered a Civil war because like the Native American, African American'ts are still considered a subculture: therefore a Revolution.

Although *The Establishment* did not fear a physical revolution, there was a great deal of support and sympathy towards Blacks by White who heard the I Have a Dream speech. *The Establishment* was not willing to risk an all-out revolution, it would be too costly, and as we discussed before; someone has got to pick the cotton.

The Establishment decided to pull off the Greatest American Coup. In order to maintain control, and avoid a race war the following had to occur;

- JFK [the power] had to die
- RFK [the law] had to die
- Malcolm X [the heart of the revolution] had to die
- Martin Luther King Jr. [the soul of the revolution] had to die

Then, while America watched in horror, terror, and grief *The Establishment* cleverly snatched the reformation and the Black Power Movement out from under the African American'ts.

Prior to desegregation, there was a surge and definite emergence of Blackness in America. Blacks established buying power, business economies, education flourished, and professionals developed and Black America became a vital part of the country's ebb and flow.

Post-integration, emerging Africans again became American'ts. This time the message was not the yelling, 'Nigger go home!' Integration's phrase Hollywood made famous - 'Guess who's coming to dinner?' Black Power became outdated; yet again Blacks are just chocolate chips in the batter.

3.4 A Funny Thing Happened on the Way to the Capitol

The Posse Comitatus Act is a United States Federal law (18 U.S.C. § 1385) signed on June 18, 1878, by President Rutherford B. Hayes limited the powers of the Federal government in the use of Federal military personnel to enforce domestic[24]. This was a great move from the leadership, in that it stops professional soldiers from enforcing policy. The reason Posse Comitatus is important is that it prevents dictatorships from forming with the borders of the U.S.

In lieu of the military, the National Guard exists as a tool to enforce domestic order when Law enforcement is insufficient, or defiant. In two iconic moves, the Lynch Pendulum swung both ways.

On June 10, 1963, President John F. Kennedy federalized National Guard troops and deployed them to the University of Alabama to enforce its desegregation.

[Fig 5]

CNN's photo depicts the other end of the spectrum when the National Guard stands against Black citizens

exercising displeasure.

[Fig 6]

I do not think the Government was wrong in either instance, however I believe the anger and the fear commensurate with the Black Lives Matter Movement of the 2020's is fueled by inequality shown by *The Establishment*.

How are African American'ts not to ask <u>Are We Free Yet?</u> when staggering inequities fly in the face of reason, decency, and justice. The staggering hypocrisy of *The Establishment* begs the question, as to how White Americans fail to understand what Black Americans decry. If Blacks in America are free, why is there still the disparity between Law Enforcement responses to its citizenry?

Five dead, nation's Capitol looted, and defecated upon[25/26]: Where are the Uses of Force from Law Enforcement January 6th 2021? Where is the copious amount of mace, the masks ripped off, flash-bangs, and people trampled by horses? It is not as though Trump rallies did not have a history of violence.

What is inexplicable is why the National Guard was deployed in an aggressive posture for only one of two similar protests at the U.S. Capitol and why at the Inauguration, they had orders to stand down, and take no action? The world watched the hypocrisy of White America turn in on itself, when the government failed to respond to the protestors with its usual fervor.

Look at the total Law Enforcement response to the swarming of the U.S. Capitol building on January 6th 2021. There is no way to feel free and equal if you are treated like step children; or in the case of African't Americans stepped-on kids.

[Fig 6a]

A person describes the dilemma best in an Instagram Post supported by the NY Post, where one of many cops was determined to be a participant in the raid on the capitol January 6th 2021.

When the protesters and the people who are suppose to stop them ARE THE SAME PEOPLE!

[Fig 6b]

How are Black Americans supposed to feel when constantly reminded that many of those empowered to enforce the law themselves feel above or not beholden to the law?

As pointed out previously, the sheer inefficiency of injustice is a financial burden on the American economy. Not only is *The Establishment* wasting money oppressing its citizens, the collateral civil penalties, and lost income for oppressed people relegates the U.S. to a less desirable posture in the global market economy. What pulled the U.S. out of the depression was industrializing its citizens. Currently, 18% of the U.S. economy stands restrained by *entrenched* inequity, oppression, and discrimination.

America received a wakeup call January 6th 2021; the Great Experiment reached another boiling point in its divisive history; a nation divided cannot stand. January 6th 2021, White people got to see that Blacks are not the only people facing problems caused by the ineffectiveness and toxic environment pervasive with the American Law Enforcement community.

This information would also fit well into the chapter on Media influence. The Media while claiming ratings from BLM movement tumult severely downplay the brutality against White supporters within the BLM movement.

Even White people trying to exemplify the America of the fairytale, find themselves at odds again with the entrenched firewalls of oppression, suppression, and discrimination.

The Establishment found a ground swell hiding in the wake of what has been called Trumpism. Trump's rally cry, "Let's make America great again!" was by many biased and racist Americas as Let's Make America White Again. Despite the cost of subverting enlightenment and civil empowerment, the cost of inappropriate Law Enforcement responses mounts.

Interesting statistics about the cost of police brutality[27];

- Police officers are indicted in fewer than 1% of killings, but the indictment rate for civilians involved in a killing is 90%
- On average, in the United States, a police officer takes the life of a citizen every 7 hours
- 52% of police officers report that it is not unusual for law enforcement officials to turn a blind eye to the improper conduct of other officers
- 61% of police officers state that they do not always report serious abuse that has been directly observed by fellow officers
- 43% of police officers agree with this sentiment: "Always following the rules is not compatible with the need to get their job done"

- 84% of police officers have stated in a recent survey that they have directly witnessed a fellow officer using more force than was necessary
- The estimated cost of police brutality incidents in the United States is $1.8 billion

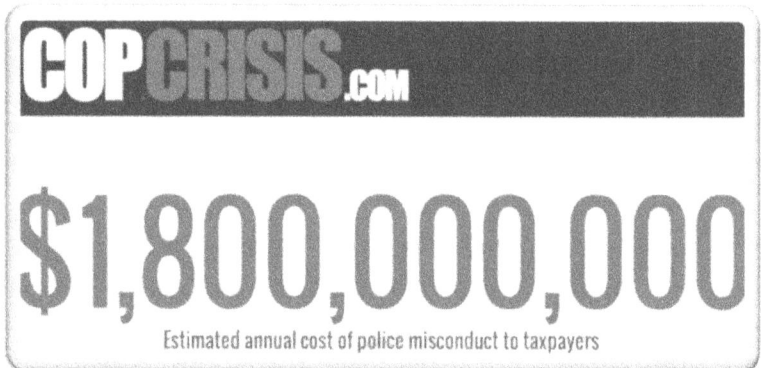

COPCRISIS.COM

$1,800,000,000
Estimated annual cost of police misconduct to taxpayers

[Fig. 7[28]]

Civil unrest will continue to escalate as police brutality spills out of the minority neighborhoods, and into the lives of mainstream White Americans and American interests.

3.5 White Fright©

Media driven fear and hype about the dangers of Black people find solace in the statistics in [Figs 47-50]. These statistics and the Media splashes of Black violence, and Black on Black crime gave rise to and fuel White Fright.

While the insidious *The Entrenched Racism Media Support System* continues to fuel White Fright, we look at the U.S. cities with the highest murder rates in 2020. What the numbers bear out is that it is NOT the concentration of Black people which creates the danger[29/30] it is the caliber of the individual.

Data from murder statistics shed light on the grotesque bias promulgated media. Skewed data in the media steers bias to racism and racism to discrimination.

Percentage of population by race

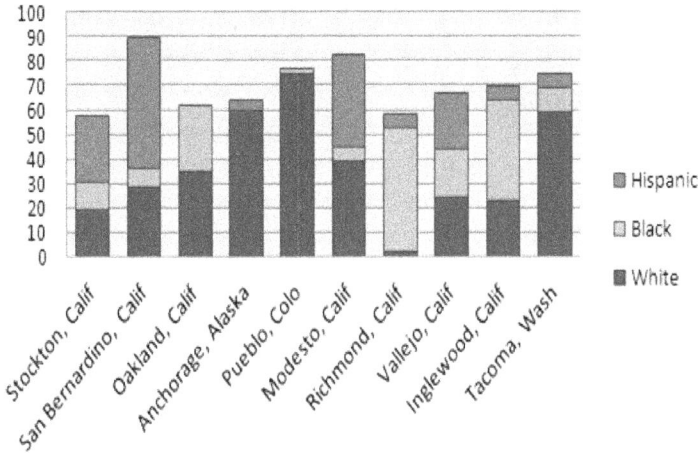

[Fig 8]

1. Stockton, Calif[31] - largest ethnic groups in Stockton, CA are White (Hispanic) (27.6%), Asian (Non-Hispanic) (21.9%), White (Non-Hispanic) (19.3%), Black or African American (Non-Hispanic) (11.5%), and Two+ (Hispanic) (8.08%). NaNk% of the people in Stockton, CA speak a non-English language, and 86.8% are U.S. citizens.

2. San Bernardino, Calif[32] - Hispanic (53.3%) followed by White (28.5%) and Black (7.9%).

3. Oakland, Calif[33] - White: 35.48% Black or African American: 23.75% Other race: 16.94%

4. Anchorage, Alaska[34] - The 5 largest ethnic groups in Alaska are White (Non-Hispanic) (60.1%), American Indian & Alaska Native (Non-Hispanic) (14.6%), Two+ (Non-Hispanic) (7.44%), Asian (Non-Hispanic) (6.17%), and White (Hispanic) (4.24%). NaNk% of the people in Alaska speak a non-English language, and 96.7% are U.S. citizens.

5. Pueblo, Colo[35] - White: 75.47% ,Other race: 11.32%, Native American: 5.07%, Two or more races: 4.55%, Black or African American: 2.66%, Asian: 0.84%, Native Hawaiian or Pacific Islander: 0.09%

6. Modesto, Calif[36] - w-38.4, h 38.1, b 5.85, asian 13.9

7. Richmond, Calif[37] - 50.6% were Black or African American, 40.8% White, 2.3% Asian, 0.3% Native American, 0.1% Pacific Islander, 3.6% of some other race and 2.3% of two or more races. 6.3% were Hispanic or Latino (of any race).

Vallejo, Calif[38] - The 5 largest ethnic groups in Vallejo, CA are White (Non-Hispanic) (24.2%), Asian (Non-Hispanic) (23.2%), Black or African American (Non-Hispanic) (20.4%), White (Hispanic) (12.5%), and Other (Hispanic) (9.76%). NaNk% of the people in Vallejo, CA speak a non-English language, and 90.5% are U.S. citizens.

8. Inglewood, Calif[39] - The 5 largest ethnic groups in Inglewood, CA are Black or African American (Non-Hispanic) (41.1%), Other (Hispanic) (23%), White (Hispanic) (22.8%), White (Non-Hispanic) (4.04%), and Two+ (Hispanic) (2.22%). NaNk% of the people in Inglewood, CA speak a non-English language, and 83.9% are U.S. citizens.

9. Tacoma, Wash[40] - The 5 largest ethnic groups in Tacoma, WA are White (Non-Hispanic) (58.7%), (Black or AfricanAmerican (Non-Hispanic) (9.71%), Asian (Non-Hispanic) (9.09%), Two+ (Non-Hispanic) (7.75%), and White (Hispanic) (6.16%).

***Query who is doing all the killing in these cities where the numbers of Blacks is low** (N.B. Anchorage and Pueblo have a negligible amount of African American'ts)?

My Black Side

Repeatedly during this discussion, the issues of race and ethnicity appear integral to the problems cited. There is no way to avoid the conclusion that in the American condition, racial enmity is so interwoven into the fabric, it has become indistinguishable from wrong. Subliminal fear and disdain for American'ts is as American as Apple pie.

The officers I worked with, who were the most integrated mentally, were the officers that spent extensive time during their formative years socializing with different cultures. The ones closest to peoples of colors were athletes, played on teams or served in the Armed Forces, and learned to trust and communicate with each other as equals.

My Blue Side

Pack mentality works both ways. Studies and experience shows that packs of people who share traits (age, race, gender, social media likes, sports teams, political parties) react differently to authority than the individual component parts when alone. Cops are no different.

When dealing with groups of people, pack mentality heightens the risk exponentially for everyone. For cops, multiple targets create nuances that many officers cannot handle easily. Each additional person brings to the field of interaction the potential attack and weapons.

Civilians always ask the same thing; Why do cops always assume the worst? It is not the worst it is pragmatic. Cops exist to take away people's freedom to exert their varied individuality. Since taking away people's freedom is an unpopular task, the reality of interactions is that most people do not want to face exposure to consequences; so they are innately fearful, resentful, or hostile. This does not mean that all people are dangerous; but they all wish to exercise their right to life, liberty and the pursuit of personal happiness.

In the case of African American'ts, they want nothing to do with the police, so there is always an undercurrent. Upon perceiving this undercurrent, the blue-pack becomes a Wolf Pack. It is logical to assume similarity amongst a group of comrades. Consequently, the guilt of one, we attribute to all until proven innocent.

3.6

Are There Societal Perspectives and Expectations on Either Side?

"The reality of Barack Obama being the president of the United States, quite possibly the most powerful nation in the world, means that the image of power is completely new for an entire generation of not only Black American kids but every population group in this nation{Kehinde Wiley},"

※

The irony of the American dream is that the only two tribes that did not immigrate to America for the dream still cannot enjoy its fullness. Native Americans lived the American dream until near the end of the 14th Century. Then one day their history ended, and a new, lighter, chapter ensued.

Like any self-respecting tribe, Native Americans fought against the invaders; they lost their way of life. The invaders, coming from a more hostile environment, complete with disease, war, and tribal feuds were more experienced and more extreme in their methods of violence. The European war clans had a history of mutilation, pillaging, and sadism, their behavior came with them to America.

The next tribe to come to American en masse found themselves dragged here for mercantile purposes, and by design left out of the American dream; despite helping to build the foundation. The violence of Europe spilled into the Americas, beginning with the vile expeditionary practices by Columbus.

Whatever tribes left Europe came to the Americas, and reformulated. However, instead of the Normans, the Saxons, the Gauls, and the French etc, the tribes formed new tribes and new tribe colonies - a new Union.

Look carefully at the incensed verbiage in Declaration of Causes of Seceding States[41.] The Southern

Colonies (Tribes) who together repelled the British and subdued the Native Americans now felt betrayed by the Northern component of the alliance tribes.

The verbiage is clear; 'We plundered this place together and split it by agreement. Now the North is trying to violate that agreement of the American Dream, and steal the Southern part of the dream'.

The Civil War between the White tribes in America purports to have been the bloodiest years in White American history with some 600,000 persons counted as lost. The resulting White Tribes post Civil War union, fully expected to enjoy the fruits of their plunder - The American Dream. This is the American Dream they created for others like them, and those who wished to join them; unless you are an Afro or Native American't.

Why were the 13th, 14th, and 15th Amendments necessary? Because the American'ts were not American citizens, therefore they could not partake of the American Dream[7] by law.

According to a survey about the American Dream, White, Blacks, and Latinos when asked about the American Dream, the responses were interesting, a relatively low number of Blacks still considered themselves American'ts.

Currently living	White	Black	Latino
The American dream	51%	43%	55%
Not living the dream but believe they can	17%	39%	28%
Not living the dream and don't believe that they can	32	19%	17%

[Fig 9]

---

[7] Appendix A.

However according to the information in [Fig 10], the barriers listed disproportionately affect Blacks according to National trends and statistics. The numbers come from a poll inquiring as to what Americans say is the top barrier to achieving the American dream is;

- Decline in work ethic
- Decline in moral/value standards
- Personal debt
- Rules favoring the wealthy
- Lack of economic opportunity
- Economic inequality
- Big government
- Decline in the middle class
- Cost of health care
- High government spending

[Fig 10]

It appears to be universally agreed upon that the American dream requires some struggle, and includes various barriers. The trouble for Blacks is that they never received a fair chance to achieve the American Dream. Without landownership as a basis for family wealth, Black start at zero economically, and that makes wealth acquisition difficult for anyone. Many people still consider them African American'ts.

My Blue Side

Bias must be a real thing; there have been policies about it since at least 1996 following the decision in Whren. Can selective enforcement and pretextual stops be abused for less than honorable purposes? Of course, they can as can be religion, medicine, and parental privileges. I can personally attest that drug enforcement would come to a screeching halt without pretextual stops. Pretextual stops as a policy have nothing to do with race; they target behavior, and people.

My Black Side

Of course there is abuse of authority and racially biased policing, how could there not be, with the country's racial divide. There is a solution, but it is not defunding. We dialogue about the best solution in the chapter on Citizen's Oversight Committees. *The Establishment* is flawed, the solution complex but bastardization of the American society is the direct cause of the tumult within the American border.

3.7
Why Aren't White Officers Afraid Of White People?

"If White people want outrage for the death of Zachary Hammond, then make noise and try to achieve public change. But that would require you to stop victim-blaming murdered suspects of excessive police violence. That would require you to stop crowd-funding murderous officers. That would require you to stop blindly and unilaterally defending police officers. And that would require you to do the hardest thing of all: admitting that Black folks haven't been lying or exaggerating when we've said that there is a real problem with policing in America{Lincoln Anthony Blades} ."

Simply put; White officers do not fear White people because White people like officers. Vesla Mae Weaver in her article states that the experiences of White and Blacks who call the police are vastly different. Blacks report that they often feel unwelcome or even looked at with suspicion. Whites, on the other hand Weaver says, "May even gain a sense of personal efficacy in seeing the state perform its basic function of protecting them[42]."

10 things we know about race and policing in the U.S.[43], provides this list;

1. Majorities of both Black and White Americans say Black people are treated less fairly than White in dealing with the police and by the criminal justice system as a whole

2. Black adults are about five times as likely as White to say they've been unfairly stopped by police because of their race or ethnicity (44% vs. 9%)

3. White Democrats and White Republicans have vastly different views of how Black people are treated by police and the justice system
4. Nearly two-thirds of Black adults (65%) say they've been in situations where people acted as if they were suspicious of them because of their race or ethnicity, while only a quarter of White adults say that's happened to them
5. Police officers and the general public tend to view fatal encounters between Black people and police very differently
6. Black Americans are far less likely than White to give police high marks for the way they do their jobs
7. Around two-thirds of police officers (68%) said in 2016 that the demonstrations over the deaths of Black people during encounters with law enforcement were motivated to a great extent by anti-police bias.
8. White police officers and their Black colleagues have starkly different views on fundamental questions regarding the situation of Blacks in American society
9. Majority of officers said in 2016 that relations between the police in their department and Black people in the community they serve were "excellent" (8%) or "good" (47%). However, far higher shares saw excellent or good community relations with White (91%), Asians (88%) and Hispanics (70%)
10. An overwhelming majority of police officers (86%) said in 2016 that high-profile fatal encounters between Black people and police officers had made their jobs harder. Sizable majorities also said such incidents had made their colleagues more worried about safety (93%), heightened tensions between police and Blacks (75%), and left many officers reluctant to use force when appropriate (76%) or to question people who seemed suspicious (72%).

My Black Side

Black people are not overly fond of the police. Sadly, many Black parents teach their kids to disdain police officers and paint them in the light of the enemy or a boogeyman.

I read my illustrated books, So You Want To Be A Policeman, and So You Want To Be A Fireman at many churches, schools and libraries. Sales however were jaded. To date, despite the little Black kids who said they want to be cops when they grow up, less than 4% of my in person sales were to Black patrons.

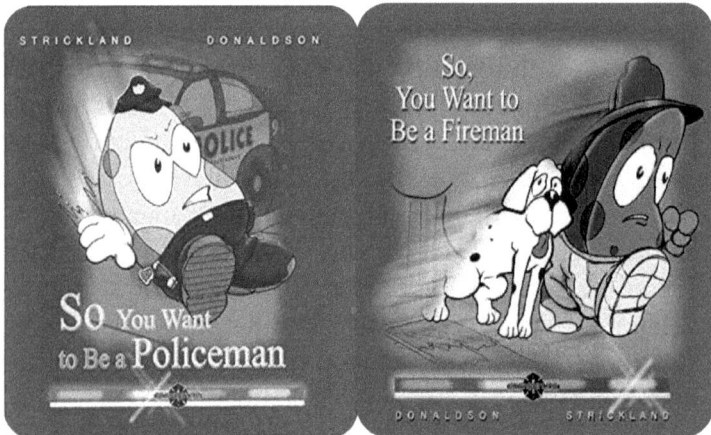

[Fig 11]

Look at the list of 10 things we know about race and policing in the U.S., there are no reasons listed creating a need for cops to fear Whites; White people see them as an integral part of maintaining their privileged White way of life. Many White people also see cops as their defense against encroachments from the other side of the tracks.

My Blue Side

I think this question is misleading, White people do not only welcome White officers. Law Enforcement works for their way of life, so they accept all comers. As a result, most officers, even the Black ones have a differing view and are treated differently by White people.

3.8
Future Hoodlums of America

"To have once been a criminal is no disgrace.
To remain a criminal is the disgrace[Malcolm X]."

An analysis of people incarcerated and arrested indicates that familial ties are key to understanding criminality. Fox Butterfield contends, "10 percent of families account for two-thirds of criminals[44]. This makes sense since most early behavior patterns emanate from home. I believe this theory contributed to the inception, and support for Planned Parenthood efforts towards minorities. Even though the 10% is not necessarily predominately Black.

I believe however that the Heritage Foundation has the correct answer, - <u>The Real Root Causes of Violent Crime: The Breakdown of Marriage, Family, and Community</u>. Patrick Fagan[45] reports, "The scholarly evidence, in short, suggests that at the heart of the explosion of crime in America is the loss of the capacity of fathers and mothers to be responsible in caring for the children they bring into the world. This loss of love and guidance at the intimate levels of marriage and family has broad social consequences for children and for the wider community."

My Black Side

The Establishment engendered a Frankensteinian experiment in human engineering. Black Cotton is the result of painstaking creativity by *The Establishment*.
- The rise in violent crime parallels the rise in families abandoned by fathers
- High-crime neighborhoods are characterized by high concentrations of families abandoned by fathers

- State-by-state analysis by Heritage scholars indicates that a 10 percent increase in the percentage of children living in single-parent homes leads typically to a 17 percent increase in juvenile crime
- Rates of violent teenage crime corresponds with the number of families abandoned by fathers
- Types of aggression and hostility demonstrated by a future criminal often is foreshadowed in unusual aggressiveness as early as age five or six
- Future criminals tend to be an individual rejected by other children as early as the first grade who goes on to form his own group of friends, often the future delinquent gang

How long did you think the Black Cotton would happily remain in the underbelly of society? The 60's was Black's greatest economic attempt to exit the underbelly. The BLM movement is the latest attempt; it is a social attempt. According to historical trends, the next evolution, or revolution will be based almost entirely on violence. The Black Stallion may yet return and take the day.

Violence and delinquent behavior does not plague the Black community, it is a problem everywhere;

- Worldwide some 200 000 homicides occur among youth 10-29 years of age each year, which is 42% of the total number of homicides globally each year
- Homicide is the fourth leading cause of death in people aged 10-29 years, and 84% of these homicides involve male victims[46]

The major difference between Black youth and most other groups in the U.S., is cited earlier, "In 2014-18, the share of families headed by single parents was 75% among African American families, 58% among Hispanic families, 37% among White families and 21% among Asian families[47]."

Remember this book is about showing the ongoing *entrenched* effect of racism. The obvious result of breaking the families apart is a destroyed Black infrastructure. More than that, it also speaks to why social programs have limited effect, as do many other governmental programs.

These above statistics also mean that for events where two parents are required; Black youth are 75% less likely to successfully engage in those activities. It is as simple as,

- Not tonight, you cannot....because I have to work
- No we cannot...because we cannot afford it

There is compelling information about the widespread *entrenched* effect in the article, 40-facts-two-parent-families[48]. Because of the length of the information, I included it In Appendix C. I believe Appendix C contains vital information as to why we need to do the following things to rebuild the Black infrastructure;

- Reinforce Christian values, specifically marital values
- Stop just handing out condoms and encourage meaningful relationships
- Stop promoting trampishness amongst Black females
- Stop advocating drug use {yes, Marijuana is a drug}
- Stop telling Black youth not to join the Armed Forces, or other first responder occupations
- Encourage and financially support education
- Requiring the reading of physical books (not on cellphone or tablet)
- Repair the rift between Black men and women
- Increase Black male involvement in early education
- Instill positive civic values

Without a male and female led Black family, the future of the Black community is guaranteed to remain abysmal; without the Black family, we will remain Black Cotton.

My Blue Side

Someone said that the best indicator of future behavior is past behavior. This is a basic tenant in the hunting and apprehension of criminals. People say a lot of stupid things like; families can be predisposed to crime; criminals are not responsible for their actions, etc. the empirical data, make more sense. People become what they are trained to become. Families generally commit crimes, because that's what they teach their kids to undertake.

There would be no future criminals if they did not learn criminal behavior in their youth. Without a positive base, reinforced middle, and applauded finish - there will always be criminals. Criminals are the losers in society who use their environment as an excuse for crime. If you look at the figures from the Crime Bureau, theft of food is not the predominant criminal infraction; greed is the cause of most crime.

Not having the same things as everybody else is not poverty. Since greed (a selfish) motivation is the predominant cause of crime, it makes sense that greed is also the main cause of police corruption. The Federal Welfare System subsidizes Americans to the tune of $1,811 billion annually.

According to Statista[49] Blacks have a higher percentage of low income members of any U.S. group, but not a great deal more than Hispanics.

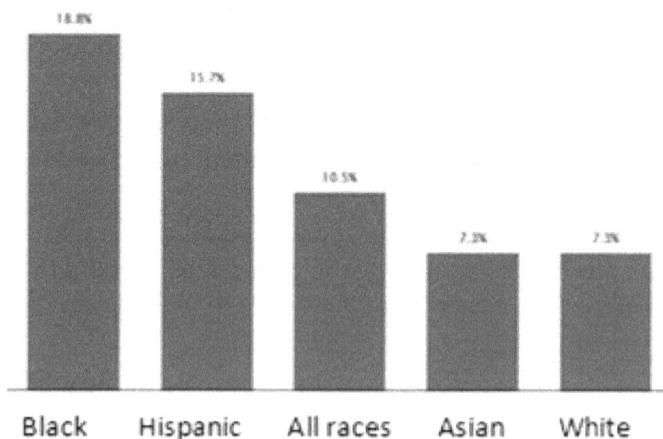

[Fig 11a]

Yet as we delve deeper we read that the Washington Post reports[50], "Whites without a college degree are the largest group of people lifted out of poverty by the government safety net."

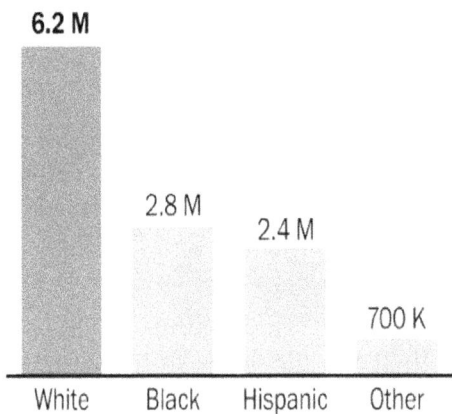

6.2 M

2.8 M

2.4 M

700 K

| White | Black | Hispanic | Other |

[Fig 11b]

	All Americans In Category (Millions)	Americans In Poverty (Millions)	Poverty Rate
White, not Hispanic	194.6	14.2	7.3%
Black	43.0	8.1	18.8%
Asian	19.9	1.5	7.4%
Hispanic, any race	60.6	9.5	15.8%

While the poverty rate for the population as a whole is 10 5% the rate varies greatly by race. Blacks have the highest poverty rate at 18 8% and Non-Hispanic whites the lowest at 7.3%.

The Poverty rate for Blacks and Hispanics is more than double that of non-Hispanic Whites.

[Fig 11c[51]]

Blaming poverty for crime is inaccurate; most crime does not involve survival needs like food and water.

In my opinion, the main thing cops crave is power. Greed and the need to attain, not explain, and maintain their power leads some cops over the line. Any challenge to power threatens not only the power structure but stimulates an emotional response from the officer. If the humanity of the officer is not a challenge to the job, there would be no reason to have policies regarding deportment and discipline.

Cops and soldiers more than any other profession rely on discipline and self-discipline as part of their profession. Cops and soldiers have more rules than any other profession; because;

- The nature of their work
- The authority the operate under
- The need to be objective and let something other than emotions dictate actions
- The personal toll of their duties
- The mount of scrutiny they endure
- The devastation they can cause

Not even the brain surgeon has the level of stress and scrutiny the LEO endures. 8.5 hours per day, every action, decision, and reaction an officer makes is subject to scrutiny and reprisal. Unlike the suspect, the patient is not trying to harm the officer.

According to the United States Institute for Peace[52], The most common forms of police corruption were making false reports and committing perjury, protecting illegal gambling, theft of drugs on the street, theft of seized property, receiving discounts on purchases, and selling information about police operations.

People pretend surprise at police corruption, yet cops are just citizens who perform a service; a service no one really wants them to perform yet is essential. The reason we keep producing corrupt cops, is that *The Establishment* is corrupt. *The Establishment* makes allowances for their watchdogs when they make mistakes, as long as they bite the enemy when required to do so.

Rest assured, there are more corrupt cops in America's future. As long as society turns a blind eye to corrupt politicians, lawyers and judges, corrupt cops must exist; they need each other to survive.

4.0

Are

Perceptions

Good or Bad

"We see the world, not as it is, but as we are-or, as we are conditioned to see it. {Stephen R. Covey }53,,

4.1
Why Do The Police Seem To Be Intimidated By Intelligent Black People Or Get Irritated By Questions?

"Because they have different priorities than you do. {Justin Freeman},,

My Black Side

It seems as though sometimes the police think that Blacks should not ask questions. Or who are Blacks to question? The questions seem to come across as challenging their authority instead of trying to ascertain information. This is often a cultural issue; Black people express themselves in different methods; vocal inflection is a large portion of Black expression. However, something else that is part of Black idiom is an instantaneous determination of cynicism, derision, and arrogance. Nobody wants to be put off and spoken to like a silly, ignorant child even if they act like one. If you did not speak down to the White woman who cursed at you then why are you speaking down to the Black person? Because I happen to be Black shouldn't matter to the manner in which you treat me. Last time I checked there was only one set of laws in America; the colored drinking fountains days are past.

Freeman adds that the arrogance imparted by many officers in their dealings with the public is due to the necessity to be the authoritative influence in the situation. Unfriendliness often presents this posture better than chumminess[54].

Some cops act as though citizens do not have a right to plead their case or challenge an interpretation of the law. Asserting rights are not the same as challenging authority, rights are not competitive. My rights actually give the police authority. Police would have no authority without my rights, because my rights come from the same document, granting them authority.

On occasion, cops have the wrong information or draw the wrong conclusion. Most people would rather discuss the matter with the officer before the arrest than having to be released from custody and taken back home. Because cops have Discretionary Authority over misdemeanors, people also hope to dissuade cops from arrest, even when wrong.

The police do not actually determine who calls dispatch. It is unfair to characterize the police as racist if they happen to have calls for service where the suspects are Black.

My Blue Side

I do not think the police are intimidated by intelligent people; we just get sick and tired of getting the same stupid questions over and over and over again. Yes, people have rights. We know that people have rights. We spend months in the academy learning to protect people's rights, and of what those rights actually consist.

Apparently, people do not spend enough time listening to the civics lessons; things like do not beat your wife, do not shoot your kids and do not steal other people's property. The only reason cops would be standing and talking to you is because you will or probably have done something illegal.

Therefore, I really do not feel like talking to you in a manner befitting a person who is not a criminal. You say you are not a criminal then get a dictionary definition of a criminal, which is a person who commits a crime. My job was very simple; if you commit a crime; I put you in a jail cell. If you do not agree with the law, take it up with the people you voted for because I had nothing to do with writing it; my job is just to enforce it.

4.2
What About Drugs In The Community?

"If you want to fight a war on drugs, sit down at your own kitchen table and talk to your own children[Barry McCaffrey]."

My Black Side

It is obvious that since the 60's drugs were systemically allowed to flood the inner cities as a control mechanism. It had to be a control mechanism because the only way for it to get into the inner city was to come through ports that are controlled by the government, interstates controlled and managed by the government, and into the cities which are also controlled and managed by the government. If you think of how many law enforcement agencies (also controlled by the government) have to be avoided in order for drugs to hit the street; something is amiss. Moreover, who told all the drug dealers where to find Black communities especially when these drugs come from Colombia, Mexico, and Afghanistan? There is no map in Columbian schools of the ghettos in the U.S.A

Do you think the same company that gave the Native people blankets with Smallpox would not allow drugs to overtake the Black community to control the Black community and make money? You are sadly mistaken. Drugs in the Black community is just New Cotton Economics. I keep reminding you that somebody has to pick Cotton.

Drugs in the Black community backfired however. Black Cotton meshed in with the Green Cotton. Drug-based Cotton Economics was not functional until the White component entwined. Drugs became an easy way for everybody to make money; Black, White, or Latin American. If you know all the source countries, how difficult can it be to stop loads of Narcotics from getting into a country with borders, surveillance detection gear, and spy satellites?

The question becomes do you hate a certain type of people so much that you would destroy even White people just to get them gone?

My Blue Side

Yeah I'm going to have to call BS on this one. I spent more than 18 years as a vice Detective and I've heard that stupid argument over and over again that Black people don't own planes etcetera, etcetera, etcetera. Not exactly sure what the hell it has to do with selling crack at home selling weed, from your own apartment, getting your girlfriend and her children evicted from government funded property because you won't stop selling dope in the apartment. I do not know exactly what it has to do with White dudes in Columbia or some other place bringing drugs to America.

Yes *The Establishment* allows drug trafficking[55]. *The Establishment* makes billions of dollars every year in net proceeds from both allowing drug sales and from fighting the drug war. However, since the Black community are the ones footing the bill for drug trafficking, and it seems to be destroying our community more than the White Community, why not fool 'The Man' and not sell dope? I guess Black on Black shootings are Eliphalet Remington and Samuel Colt's fault as well. Either Black lives matter; or they do not.

4.3
Why Are There So
Few Minority Police?

"Still getting asked if I struggle with being Black and Blue. I'm not a crayon folks. There is no conflict. I wear my ethnicity and badge with pride, honor and integrity. But both are controlled by my soul and will. [Deon Joseph]"

Share of law enforcement by race/ethnicity

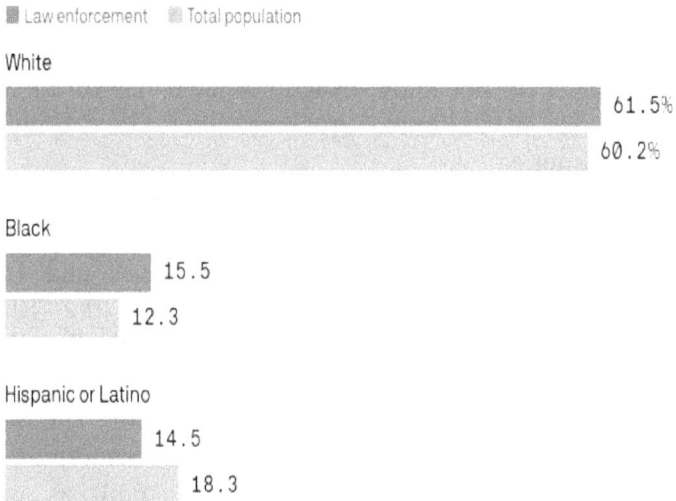

Law enforcement   Total population

White

61.5%

60.2%

Black

15.5

12.3

Hispanic or Latino

14.5

18.3

[Fig 12]

According to a 2018 data from Courtenay Brown, Stef W. Knight, even with higher numbers of minority officers there are, More Black police officers, yet the killings persist[56].

DataUSA[57] offers the following information on diversity within the Law Enforcement community. "65.5% of Police officers are White (Non-Hispanic), making that the most common race or ethnicity in the occupation. Black officers 12.8% is the second most common race or ethnicity in this occupation'

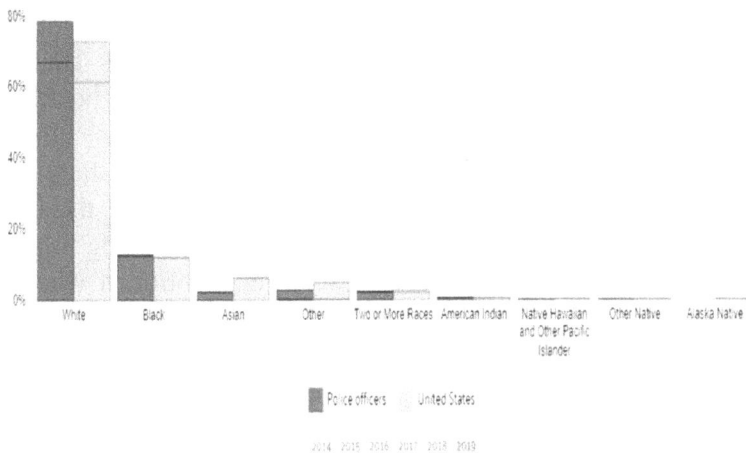

[Fig 13]

I think stereotypes play a huge part in minority representation; the perception is that you are a sellout if you are a cop. Whether or not you experience it personally or not, there is a history of a discriminatory, oppressive, system enforced by police officers. Therefore, entering into a law enforcement position is an ominous ideation toward the police in the minority community.

My Black Side

Sadly, because of bad policing, bad tactics, sheer ignorance, and most recently malice; the Black community has more examples to use to as why Black people should not be cops. I personally do not agree and that is why I became a cop, but doing so ensured that I was called a sell-out and Uncle Tom, the majority of my career. I did not mind the ones I arrested calling me a 'Tom', or the ones whose dope-dealing husbands I took to jail; but I don't understand why the non arrested people who saw me respond to a call for service, were mad when I arrested the perpetrator because they happened to be Black.

Why is it that in the Black community that we expect and tolerate Black on Black crime, as long as the suspect is Black?

We must also consider that the Black cop often becomes a pariah amongst their peers. Females Blacks seem to have less of a problem, but remember the hostility is between the males more so anyway.

Because of the cultural unpopularity there is perception that you are a sell out and traitor, and the low pay of the job does not appeal to as many young Black males. Law Enforcement almost never mentioned when I speak at schools or churches, as a job of choice.

The problem is far more ingrained and insidious than racism, fear, or bias. The euphemisms people use to describe *The Establishment* {*The Establishment*, the man, company, big machine} is better understood as a Civilization. The reason that the killings persist even with more minority officers is that the reason for the killings is NOT singular. The superficial reasons we cite, racism, sexism, fear, and greed, fail in comparison to the reality of the root cause.

The Secret Societies do not run the world as is assumed, the converse is true. Secrets run the world and are maintained by watchdog societies. No one group controls the entire system; it is a Syncretism. Syncretism is the merging of several originally discrete belief systems or traditions. The United Syncretism in the Americas is difficult to combat, and often times describe because there is no one basis for this civilization. The violence persists because the Law Enforcement profession is the domestic arm, which collectively corrals and herds the populous into the next phase of Civil Development.

If Blacks and Latinos are increasingly responsible for shooting deaths of citizens, the question is what do they all have in common? They are implementers of the systemic indoctrination and civil development utilized by *The Establishment* in whatever stage the U.S. undertakes to exist.

My Blue Side

I do not agree with Mitchell Hartmen, that minorities, due to their smaller number, will not get to make decisions in the inner city. There is not a different set of laws for Blacks and Whites now-a-days. It does not matter the color of the commander; politics play more of a role in deciding these factors than the police administration.

Obviously, Black supervisors and workplace diversity affords more sensitivity and more varied interactions, but I think too often the lines blur between what a cop is and what cops do as a function.

Hartmen correctly points out that many Latinos also have a bad taste in their mouth caused by the corruption of Law Enforcement agencies in their respective communities or countries, and that criminal background, educational hurdles, and credit issues create entry into police academies.

Ironically, even with all the illegal Latino immigration, Blacks are still victims of police violence more than Latinos.

4.4
Statistics Pertaining to Blacks and Latinos?

"Among minorities, the rate of police killings for Latinos is second to those of African-Americans[58]."

"While their rate of imprisonment has decreased, the most in recent years, Black Americans remain far more likely than their Hispanic and White counterparts to be in prison. The Black imprisonment rate at the end of 2018 was nearly twice the rate among Hispanics (797 per 100,000) and more than five times the rate among Whites (268 per 100,000)[59]."

My Black Side

The Law of Supply and Demand also applies to Green Cotton. We discussed previously that somebody has to pick cotton. In modern times, **somebody has to be the cotton**. The Criminal Justice System generates more than $300 billion dollars every year[60]. The Criminal Justice System consists of fines, civil and criminal seizures, money charged for the incarceration, housing, and care of inmates, training, rehabilitation programs, DCS, probation and parole officers, drug test, GED testing, and a host of other subordinate programs that exists only because of the Criminal Justice System.

A simple definition of utilitarianism or pragmatism is taking a practical approach to a problem or coming up with a practical solution to a dilemma. Money needs to be made. Money is going to be made. There are only so many ways to make money off the same people. It is like a timeshare, how many times can you resell the same piece of property?

In modern times, Latinos are the easiest to pick on. They enter the country illegally, which means their future is severely limited so they can easily be thrown away. You do not kick them out of the country because that costs money; incarcerate them; incarceration generates money. Latinos therefore, become part of the New Cotton System. People that are disenfranchised, uneducated, or unmotivated systematically become ineligible for careers, ending up as throwaway people.

Throwaway people function like slave-day field hands, thereby elevating Blacks to sharecroppers. Somebody has to supply both sets of people with tools. Every year Whites, Blacks, and Latinos graduate from high school, there are only so many jobs and even fewer good jobs. If you are *The Establishment* and you had to pick somebody to give those good jobs to, you would find people to perpetuate *The Establishment,* which seems to indicate mostly White people. *The Establishment* therefore creates a status-quo, by capitalizing on (victimizing) the useless eaters.

My Blue Side

After twenty years of observed evidence, I can emphatically state that often times Blacks and Latinos also are prey for lawyer's experimentation. The Trial lawyer makes significantly more money than their counterpart. The way to become a trial lawyer is to go to trial. In order to get a trial someone has to be facing incarceration. Since the largest portions of adjudicated cases are plea bargains, the remaining cases for trial should be cases where conviction is uncertain. Not so. Year after year, I sat in court suffering unwinnable trials, and ludicrous not guilty pleas. Some lawyer whispered to the poor, dumb wretch that they could beat a case where they are on video committing the crime.

The unscrupulous lawyer does not face jail, what does he care. Word in the jail spreads that this lawyer is going to fight and get the client off. It does not happen, but the lawyer accomplishes several career-building trials, leaving a wake of starry-eyed convicts to wear matching shoes and jumpsuits.

For example, when people sold the undercover officer drugs, and they were probation eligible, I would agree to lessen their actual time in jail if they got their GED. One day, one of these low-life lawyers got irate with me in court and said I was violating their client's rights. They never asked the young Black man, would he rather truncate his sentence by three years. They declined the offer and informed the client of the longer sentence. The offer was never even conveyed to the client; THAT IS RACISM and New Cotton Economics at work.

But you know who his momma blamed; the old punk ass-Black cop. It was entirely my fault because I arrested him for selling drugs in a school zone.

4.5

Black perspectives on
Law Enforcement?

"Did you ever stop to think why cops are always
famous for being dumb? That's simple because
they don't have to be anything else {Orson Welles} ."

The dichotomy is not unique to me in regards to
Blackness and Law Enforcement, but as vague as the views
on Law Enforcement are, the solution is even less clear.

"When it comes to policing and crime, Black
attitudes escape simple explanations. In polling, Black
people often express disgust at police racism yet support
more funding for police. A 2015 Gallup poll found that
Black adults who believed police treated Black people
unfairly were also more likely to desire a larger police
presence in their local area than those who thought police
treated Black people fairly. A 2019 Vox poll found that
despite being the racial group with the most unfavorable
view of the police, most Black people still supported hiring
more police officers. And more recently, a June 2020
Yahoo/News/YouGov survey taken after the killing of
George Floyd found that 50 percent of Black respondents
still said, "We need more cops on the street," even as 49
percent of Black respondents said when they personally see
a police officer it makes them feel "less secure[61]."

My Black Side

The purported Black perspective on the police is
interesting because the media is asking people who feel
preyed upon, to give their opinion of the predator that
accosts them. People do not like the police in many
communities because the police are considered annoying.
The police are there to remind us of the fact that we are not

behaving in a manner that society expects. Between White people and Black people there is a different sociological expectation. Culturally, it has been decided that White people are free to come and go about as they please. However, there is a stereotypical interaction between the police and African Americant's. The African Americant's automatically assume that the police are there to instigate trouble with them and there is a common belief among some that there is always going to be trouble from Black people.

I too have been stopped by ignorant police officers, but I would not say are racist. I think that term in is an over utilized misnomer. In this particular instance, I made a turn onto my street. My son and I were driving wearing hoodies. As soon as he drove past the officer, I told my son to watch him get out and follow us. As expected, the officer pulled in behind us and followed us down the street; he took enough time (I'm assuming) to run the tags. This is why he should not have stopped me because he would have determined that I lived in the area. However I made a left turn. While making a left turn he activated his blue lights to which I pulled over, as I always do. I turned on the interior light in my vehicle and I pulled my driver's license out before he ever got to my window. I put my hands on the steering wheel in plain view with my driver's license so there was no movement after that officer got out of his vehicle.

I was a cop and I understand that traffic stops are some of the most dangerous activities cops undertake. In a car, there is no way to know what or who you have; mass murderer, or angry soccer mom. Not only does the officer know who is in the car, the occupant does not know the reason for the stop. The mental state of the occupant is a complete unknown, therefore the level of danger is high.

When the officer walked up, I said, 'What seems to be the problem officer?' He said I made a wide left turn and cut across the shoulder of the road. To which I calmly replied okay but you and I both know that didn't happen considering I'm also in law enforcement and I didn't cross the shoulder of the road as there is no Gourd (stripped) Area; I was within my lane on this one lane Road. He just looked at me as I handed him my driver's license. He said if another car had been coming, I would have been over into their lane of traffic. I said that is not true either, because you initiated your blue lights before I actually turned off the street, which means the infraction that you say I committed, had to occur on the Main Street. About the side of the road which is where you're saying I committed the infraction, that's neither here nor there. You and I both know you stopped me because we are riding two deep, in hoodies in the middle of an area devoid of a whole lot of Black people.

He did not write the ticket. But if he had, I would have signed the ticket and gone to court. I definitely would not have got into an argument, or refused to sign it; that would have led to something far worse, than an inconvenience. I was also armed, so I needed to take that into consideration for both of us. I would much rather sue, and complain than post bond, push up daisies, or needlessly shoot a cop.

My Blue Side

I understood what he was doing but I also understand why Black people would be pissed. I do not think he was racially motivated. I think he was motivated by a common practice done among officers that is more a form of bias and a matter of profiling, but it is not malicious. For the sake of not being repetitive, we will cover all of that in the chapter on profiling.

I think Blacks in America will always have a different view of law enforcement. For so long the law has been an oppressive force in the African American't historical experience, and historically, cops are a major part of that bad experience.

Police officers go to restaurants during work often, and because of limited salaries cops go places that tend to service officers at a discount, which some people say is unethical but we are not discussing that at this time. Many

White businesses give cops a discount of 10% or 50% sometimes. Sometimes cops eat free if you take breaks in places in their Zone. Asians and Indians never give cops a break on anything where I worked. Hispanics will sometimes give you a break of half price.

What is my point? I think that if you are not a business owner, or property owner, the police are annoying to you because the only time you will really interact with them is when there is an infraction. But business owners and property owners like cops because cops keep what they own and work for safe. This in turn keeps them safe because their restaurant is safe while the cops eat.

I think Blacks sometimes react to *The Establishment* by taking it out on the representatives that we encounter most frequently. The officer is the only *entrenched* representative, you can curse out and argue with on a regular basis. Because Blacks do not want the officer there and frankly the officer may not want to be there either there is a personality conflict. Personality conflicts do not have to be racist or racially motivated but they certainly can occur between two races.

Even amongst Black people, or White people, Chinese people or any other races, when arguing, people resort to insults and emotionalism. Therefore, invariably in a heated debate, a difference between gender, age, race, socioeconomic standing, or even physical ability, will result in some type of unpleasant name-calling.

4.6
Is Fair To Be Mad At The Police If They Arrest Your Kids?

"We can't pick out certain incidentals that don't go our way and act like the cops are all bad...Do you know how bad some of these neighborhoods would be if it wasn't for the cops?{Charles Barkley} ."

My Black Side

"Although Black kids represent less than 14 percent of all American youth under the age of 18, Black boys make up 43 percent of the male population in juvenile facilities, while Black girls comprise 34 percent of incarcerated girls. Native Americans, who represent less than 1 percent of the U.S. youth populace, constitute 3 percent of all girls and 1.5 percent of all boys in juvenile detention facilities[62]."

There is no denying that statistics bear out systemic disparate treatment, or some form of Social Abortion©. While raw statistics do not prove racism, there also however, no significant explanation for why two of the smallest minorities in the country, constituted almost 50% of the total number of people incarcerated in the U.S.A in a given year. The assertions of racism and discrimination can certainly be made.

Even the staunchest supporter of the police would sound incredibly stupid asserting that Blacks and Native kids are just 'bad seeds' as a justification. Even more dastardly, is the fact that I had trouble finding any type of official or legit rationalization; could this be because no one thinks there even needs to be a justification for disproportionate incarceration numbers?

I am torn however, because my personal experience does not jibe with statistics. In the 1300 officer department I worked in for more than 20 years, approximately 78% of that department was male White. Although there were some real jackasses that work there, I can honestly say by and large if my child was justifiably arrested by the majority of them I would not be angry at the officer, nor automatically think them racist.

By the same token, if a Black officer arrested my child for no valid reason I would be pissed. Nobody should be arrested fallaciously Black or White.

I am more disappointed than I am angry because I know these individuals personally and most of them are professional, majority of the time; if one or two of them took it upon themselves to do something as unprofessional as 'throw a charge on somebody', they deserve to go to jail.

In one instance, I had the opportunity to arrest an 18 year male Black offender. He ended up knocked to the ground, because he reached in his pocket and tried to pull something out very quickly. Not knowing if it was a weapon or it could have been drugs, it was safer for me to simply put them on the ground and secure him than it was for me to either shoot him or get shot. When I finally took him into custody and all the smoke cleared, it turned out he had absolutely nothing to do with what we were investigating in terms of a narcotics transaction.

The prevailing thought at the time was, since I put my hands on him I needed to arrest him for something. I on the other hand do not believe in throwing charges on people; so I did not. Ironically although he had no charges from my incident, he was a career armed robber and was actually going to be indicted for about 13 robberies that he committed since becoming an adult.

My point is *The Establishment* is jacked up. There are many jacked up cops. Sometimes, what happens is just a jacked-up situation. All too often though, it seems like jacked up situations seem to happen to Black people. It also begs the question, why isn't the Criminal Justice System just as jacked up towards White people?

My Blue Side

As a guest speaker at a church, I began a presentation by making a simple statement, "You might be a bad parent if your child has more mug shots than family photos." Professionally my blue side believes that this has more to do with the impropriety in criminal justice statistics than just racism alone.

I went to court one day and saw this young man sentenced for a robbery, taken from the custody of his parents and become a ward of the State. When asked by the judge if he had anything to say, he looked around and said, "No sir ain't nobody here for me to say nothing to." Prior to the judge sentencing him, an individual who walked through the courtroom several times in a sweat suit, reminiscent of the 1980's stood up and said, "Bring it home, no limit soldier," threw his hands up in the air and walked out. The Juvenile Judge asked the young man who the individual was, or if you knew the man, to which, the young man replied yeah that was his dad. The juvenile judges lowered his head, and said, "I understand." Obviously, robbing people is a jail worthy crime, but you have to ask yourself why being a lousy parent is not a jail worthy crime?

People mistakenly believe that the police interact with citizens only because they target people; this is not the case. Calls for service, count for the majority of time during the shift. Sadly, certain areas of the city have higher calls for service than others. Large numbers of people hanging out in the streets, unsupervised, afford themselves the opportunity to encounter enforcement at a higher frequency. Proportional to the higher arrest, and the higher number of people hanging out, is the need for higher numbers of officers for officer safety purposes. It is a snowball effect.

If people call the police, then there are options in terms of arrest that are not as smooth as people believe. At any time, a private citizen can call the police and affect an arrest on another citizen using the police as a vehicle. In other words if a kid steals ice cream, the store-owner can call the police. The officer actually cannot prosecute under the law because the misdemeanor did not occur in the officer's presence. Therefore, the storeowner has to prosecute; police officers just provide paperwork or transportation. The public seems to be by and large unaware of this scenario because they believe that because the officer puts the suspect in their vehicle, the officers are actually the ones effectuating the arrest. The officer is actually just taking the juvenile into custody; the private citizen is making the arrest.

I had an apartment complex in my zone and all of the office staff was female White even though the majority of the residents were not. In the office, there was routinely a plate of free cookies for people to come in and take what they wanted. One day I got a call from the office staff on my cell phone and they asked us to come and make an arrest in the complex. Upon arrival, I found four children under the age of 13 sitting in the office two males and two females, all Black. The office manager was upset. She was about 55 years old female White. She explained the issue at hand, that the children in custody were apprehended in the act of stealing cookie dough. The office manager said she brought the cookie dough to the office to make cookies and she wanted them prosecuted.

I thought about this call for service. Then I asked the office manager if the cookie dough in question was the cookie dough used to make the cookies given away free in the office. To which she said yes. I then questioned further because I wanted to be certain, I inquired whether she wanted me to arrest them for stealing the cookie dough for the free cookies? To which she said yes. I did not arrest the children. I told them not to come back, and do not come back and get more cookies I'm not even sure if you can be arrested for stealing cookie dough for free cookies because you don't really have a value for; the object in question has to have value.

I am not certain what to call this other than ignorance. It may well be racism, it may be subliminal, it may be a bias. I do not know what was wrong with her, but

I do know that the only crime that would have been committed that day would have been to arrest those children for stealing free cookies.

I hope that I do not know anybody that would have arrested those kids. I did not opt not to arrest them because they were Black (like me), I did not arrest them because it was stupid. As I told her, in about 45 minutes she would be giving away the cookie dough to anybody who would walk in the building, why on earth would she want to arrest those kids for eating it? She said she just wanted to teach them a lesson. I did teach them a lesson. I called their moms. I assure you the mothers did more than the Court System would have done.

Someone said it was not my place to decline the arrest. I disagree; a cop's job is to enforce the law. The theft law requires an item to have value in order for there to be a theft. Free is a null value. My Blackness had nothing to do with this, my professionalism did. Had there not been a decent human/professional cop, those Black kids would have been arrested. Black kids also matter to Black cops.

This is a shining example, the difference in how White people see police versus Black people. This lady saw the police as her lesson teachers; she meant to make those little Black kids not take her free cookies. That is not a police officer's job. All that would do was make the Black people in the complex angry.

4.7
Do You Really Believe That Black Males Are Targets?

"I have no hatred for cops. I have hatred for racists and brutal people, but not necessarily the cops. The cops are just doing what they're told to do[Ice T]."

⁓

My Black Side

In my heart, I sadly hang my head to this question, and say yes, but not for the reason you think. As we discussed before, the police officer is a pawn of a brutal system. The economics of the situation is sound, the Black female, exists to make fledglings. As discussed previously, anything that stands in the way of cash crops is an impediment.

Poor, hungry, docile people ('useless eaters') are a cash crop everywhere in the world. This is what slaves have always been; a cash crop. You cannot simply kill off the Black males; they carry the Black Cotton Seed©. Impotence is the key; geld Black males socially.

- Amos and Andyism
- Stereotypical niggerisms
- Encourage him to make babies, then leave them
- Incarcerate him for not paying child support for the baby he fails to raise
- Hand out condoms and encourage teen pregnancy, steering young Black minds away from education
- Systematically use the Criminal Justice System brand to keep him in menial labor[63]
- Discriminatory housing, lending, or hiring

No matter how much I try to understand the manner of a system that hands out verdicts and sentences, how can any literate person explain probation for hanging a 16-month-old Black kid and dragging another (minority) man

10 blocks, while destroying the (minority) man's son's leg with her car?

Whatever this is, racism or some other schism; the evidence is too invasive to ignore. People of a certain color are not given the same protections and privileges as those who are of a more acceptable color. Some people are still American'ts.

[Fig 14[64]]

My Blue Side

I remain silent on [Fig 14] due to shame. An officer actually grabbed the child in the mall, roughed him up and arrested him. I will say there is more wrong in this jurisdiction than that officer; I dare say he is a byproduct of this obviously Plantation-like jurisdiction. As long as men have eyes - skin color will play a part in injustice.

The arresting officer obviously thought it was ok and the fact that the court ever heard the case is proof of African-American'tism. This picture of a 12 year old standing before the court system having been dragged there by an officer while the lynching-White lady is seated speaks volumes of the type of humanity prevalent within the U.S. Criminal Justice System

5.0

Subliminal

Fear

"Of all the liars in the world, sometimes the worst are our own fears {Rudyard Kipling} ."

5.1
Subliminal Fear

"Racism is a much more clandestine, much more hidden kind of phenomenon, but at the same time it's perhaps far more terrible than it's ever been[Angela Davis]."

Entrenched Racism is more costly than realized. The War of Independence interestingly enough took place to stop Whites from feeling the weight of a master's whip. What made them turn around, brutalize and enslave the Natives and the Blacks? The Operant Condition took hold. A slave, once *properly conditioned*, can never be free again. The Americas are just an extension of Willie's modest plantation[8] concept.

The Establishment uses intriguing terminology in the WL Letters. In the phrases, 'in my bag', 'my program', 'my method', 'my list', *The Establishment* allows us to see

---

8 [WL19]{You must also have your White servants and overseers distrust all Blacks.

[WL20]It is necessary that your slaves trust and depend on us. They must love, respect and trust only us

[LMAS1]It was the interest and business of slaveholders to study human nature, and the slave nature in particular, with a view to practical results. I and many of them attained astonishing proficiency in this direction.

[LMAS2]They had to deal not with earth, wood and stone, but with men and by every regard they had for their own safety and prosperity they needed to know the material on which they were to work.

[LMAS3]Conscious of the injustice and wrong they were every hour perpetuating and knowing what they themselves would do. Were they the victims of such wrongs? They were constantly looking for the first signs of the dreaded retribution}.

the inner workings of their devious mind. Free from the Crown, America willingly created a system based on servitude and colonialism under the whip of one thought - Greed.

The Establishment, like any egomaniac, requires all under its voice to adopt their words. In teaching Whites to conform, *The Establishment* transferred it's loathsomeness into the waters from which both Whites and Blacks drink, is what we see still flourishing and the impetus behind the movement. Bearing in mind that the police came on line to protect property owners and collect taxes from the have-nots; the tension between the warring factions continues to ebb and flow[65].

The police officer senses an instant uneasiness when dealing with Black males, and vice versa. Because I was Black, and a cop, my street name was Oreo. The contention was that I was Black on the outside and White in the middle. Although I served most of my career in drug enforcement, the majority of the people I arrested were 'quality of life' offenders. In other words, these people were making living conditions for their neighbors and fellow African Americans hellish. If, by my actions of removing the violent, drug dealing, abusive males that I arrested I am a sell-out, what does that make the guys I charged?

The Establishment wants Black people to be mad at cops when they take away their perceived meal ticket, or their prize stag; the Black male. African Americans forget Black cops are subject to the same Racism they face.

Existing both as Black and blue was not easy but I walked the line with my head up. I locked up anyone deserving: regardless of color; but I personally demanded respect. The officers I worked with showed a mutual professional respect for me or we both disdained each other. No averting my eyes, or holding my tongue, but in the more than 20 years, I experienced a few occasions of overt racist behavior operating within the job.

While there was much grumbling over the years, and even the occasional head butts thrown, I was lucky. I worked on a small team of 12 people that changed my way of thinking. 8 of the 12 were White, but I always felt welcome. I also felt empowered while within this family. I did not feel accepted because I was accepted by the White members, but instead because I was able to wield the full power of *The Establishment* to help people that looked like me and where in need.

Just as the world rallies behind the BLM movement, I had my family that stood with me, and I with them. I endeavored to ensure that the Black people arrested were treated the same as the White people. In order to do this, in order to ensure equality, it required authority. Authority from the Blue, gave me the ability to assist Blacks as a free man, free to think, free to act, or free not to act.

This is the insidious nature of *The Establishment*'s system, it changes the way White people think about others, and encourages people not to think for themselves. Just because a person is Black, should not be a basis for a decision, but too often it is the only basis.

"History shows that it does not matter who is in power or what revolutionary forces take over the government, those who have not learned to do for themselves and have to depend solely on others and never obtain any more rights or privileges in the end than they had in the beginning.[66]"

Sheer brutality and terror created a variety of socio-psychological conditions for the slave[67]. Stockholm Syndrome, Battered Women's Syndrome, PTSD, ASD, isolation from others, guilt, and Post-Traumatic Slave Syndrome[68] rank among the list of issues generated through racism and discrimination.

There is no flinching in *The Establishment's* discussion of psychology and human nature; while delineating humans from slaves. Slaves in *The Establishment* model are not simply second-class citizens they are not human.

The taking of slaves is an old and accepted tradition throughout history and the world. American slavery commenced in 1619 and officially ended in 1865 with the 13th Amendment to the U.S. Constitution. *The Establishment* therefore did not found slavery. *The Establishment* simply establish it in the Americas. The proficiency that the Lynch Papers speak of is in the application of behavior modification principles to a people having been studied extensively.

Human behavior modification principle models have terminology. The Lynch Papers did not use the same, terminology but the essence of the research is the same[69]. Christian Jarett describes 10 traits amassed from hundreds of hours of observation and surveys. *The Establishment* had no clinical study tools to employ, instead *The Establishment* had captives, no rules governing experimentation, and decades of historical experience.

From Jarrett's list, I find the following characteristics of human nature most interesting;

- *The Establishment* view minorities and the vulnerable as less than human
- *The Establishment* experiences Schadenfreude (pleasure at another person's distress)
- *The Establishment* is blinkered and dogmatic
- *The Establishment* is vain and overconfident
- *The Establishment* promotes moral hypocrites
- *The Establishment* favors ineffective leaders with psychopathic and dark personality

If these traits are characteristic of persons with or without education, it is obvious that socio economic status coupled with skin tone subliminally set the stage for human interaction. Dissection is the word which comes (from Latin *dissecare* "to cut to pieces") is the meticulous process of disassembling a subject for the purpose of research. Different terms, but this is to what *The Establishment* alluded. Whether *The Establishment* was the researcher or it was cumulative information; the Papers do not mention, but the fact-finding/training process was complete.

Aman Sharma[70] gives a breakdown of common *dissecare* methods used to 'study human nature.'

a. OBSERVATION 'Naturalistic' Method - Useful in the study of children, mentally ill animals, and unconscious patients. The researcher observes the subject in its natural (slave) settings, and situations. The slave/subject will not understand or be aware that he is being studied; therefore, the behavior will be natural.

b. EXPERIMENTAL METHOD - This is the most objective way of studying the behavior. There will be other external unwanted variables that the researcher controls preserving the experiment. The researcher/slaver can study any stimuli negative or positive, in men, women, and children duplicating the experiments between dark and light skin slaves. General experiment steps often tier out as:

- Identification of the problem
- Formulation of hypothesis
- Designing the experiment
- Testing the hypothesis by experiment
- Analysis of results
- Interpretation of results

c. CLINICAL METHOD/CASE HISTORY METHOD - This method relies on detailed history of the indoctrination, and the methods of slave management from various periods.

d. SURVEY METHOD - Used at the onset of the speech, by virtue of the fact cited that they invited *The Establishment* in as a guest lecturer.

e. GENETIC METHOD - Selective breeding of plants and animals showed progress, and inevitably held promise for the slavers. Weak, tepid slaves were a waste of money, they required food and gave little yield. Also known as The Developmental Method allows for genetic testing and matches to produce a superior breed of slave. Ironically this method was supported by the U.S. Constitution in Article 1, Section

9, affectionately known as The Slave Trade Clause (Article I Section 9, Clause 10)[9].

f. TESTING METHOD - The author refers to scientific objective testing, methods not available to *The Establishment*. *The Establishment more* than likely used subjective methods to study;

- Attitudes (other slaves forced to watch horrific events)
- Interests (noting which behaviors slaves gravitated towards when not punished)
- Abilities (for example throwing slaves in water weighted down to determine maximum carrying loads)
- Intelligence (set a slave on fire and see what the other slaves do about it)

There is no better description of the reason for the existing tension between the Blacks and the Blues other than 'fear of a Dreaded Retribution'. The benefactors from Racism/discrimination/elitism are pondering, not because they are actively engaged in what they know to be wrong, but more so because they are unsure of how much longer the victims will remain docile. The tension is a direct result of the oppressors, 'constantly looking for the first signs of the dreaded retribution.'

The Dreaded Retribution will be violence not unlike Haiti unleashed against the slavers and the mixed children of the slavers[71]. Sadly, neither the Blacks nor the Blues realize they are both still victims of the Lynch Syndrome[72] and Willie Lynch Behavior©, and the clashes are results of both ideologies.

Perpetuation of the indoctrination (Willie Lynch Syndrome) and maintaining the status quo accounts for the

---

[9] The Migration or Importation of such Persons as any of the States now existing shall think proper to admit, shall not be prohibited by the Congress prior to the Year one thousand eight hundred and eight, but a Tax or duty may be imposed on such Importation, not exceeding ten dollars for each Person.

assassinations of so many Black leaders physically, economically or socially[73]. When any leader says and believes none of the *entrenched* rhetoric, they must be extinguished before the fire blazes through the withering dried grass of the Black community.

Malcolm X said he I believed that there will ultimately be a clash between the oppressed and those that do the oppressing. I believe that there will be a clash between those who want freedom, justice, and equality for everyone and those who want to continue *The Establishment*s exploitation.

The Un-Kunta©, or Anti[nigger]© is the vindicator of the enslaved. This free, unassimilated former victim will set about freedom to the masses. The natural aftermath of the chained animals escape is an aggressive posture. The animal will fight anything perceived as a threat or in the way of it experiencing its freedom.

There is nothing so toxic to the freed slave as the overseers tasked to maintain their servitude. Nowadays the Law Enforcement professionals we call cops play the role of the overseer cast by the Aristocracy. The law enforcement role places the police in the forefront of the Black anger; for now, the police are as high up the organizational ladder as Blacks can reach.

5.2
Black Men And The Police

"There are fundamentally two ways you can experience the police in America: as the people who call when there's a problem, the nice man in uniform who pats a toddler's head and has an easy smile for the old lady as she buys her coffee. For others, the police are the people who are called on because of them. They are the ominous knock on the door, the sudden flashlight in the face, then barked orders. Depending on who you are, the sight of an officer can produce either a warm sense of safety and contentment or a plummeting feeling of terror{Christopher L. Hayes}."

My Black Side

It is time to get personal. My first semester in a prominent HBU was frightening. The culture shock was bad. I immediately felt out of sorts. I did not understand why in a university full of people that looked like me I felt like an outsider. One day, an attractive young woman and I sat and spoke at length about nothing important. For some reason, still unknown to me, she pondered, "Why don't you talk Black?"

Perplexed, I looked at her. Her skin was actually lighter than mine was; she too was working on her Baccalaureate Degree and we both wore pants that were too tight. I politely asked her what she meant. She remarked that I spoke White. I replied, "My father paid good money for my education, and I enjoy reading. And for the record I am Black; therefore if I speak it stands to reason that I am speaking Black." Perhaps the problem for her was that I was not Black enough. I grew up around successful affluent Black people; but this was the first time I did not feel Black enough. I soon aligned with the Black men in my dormitory, watched what they watched, listened to Public Enemy and fell under the influence of their anger.

I returned home during Thanksgiving and at the table, a discussion of current affairs arose. My father asked me what I planned to do as a profession. I said lawyer or politician. The plan was to join the police department and serve for three or four years, then go inside and be a freedom fighter like my father. I ranted on about the racism and discrimination alive in the country and how Whitey was keeping Blacks down. I was angry. My father said something I did not expect. The first unexpected thing he did was to raise his voice, "Now wait a minute," he said, "I don't know where you got that bitterness and rhetoric from but you did not learn it here. Take it back where it came from."

He was right; I had not experienced racism personally, although I am Black. I simply had a different experience; thus far. I was mad because I felt uneasy not being part of the struggle, not feeling angry, not feeling oppressed. I did not understand why anyone at the largest Black University with the largest endowment felt angry, disenfranchised, or disenchanted. How were we being oppressed, we were in college?

But as I listened to the stories and to begin to watch TV, I realized two things. There was an undercurrent of tension between the races, and here: in this county, I was just as Black as the next guy.

I chanced upon a poem, an expression of rage; suppressed as my feelings were, it was definitely still rage. But it stuck with me; it expressed better than anything I had read or heard and expressed what Black American men think of the police.

"I had said I wasn't going to write no more poems like this.

I had confessed to myself all along, tracer of life, poetry trends that awareness, consciousness, poems that screamed of pain and the origins of pain and death had blanketed my tablets, and therefore, my friends, brothers, sisters, in-laws, outlaws, and besides -- they already knew.

But Brother Torres, common ancient bloodline brother Torres is dead.

I had said I wasn't going to write no more poems like this.

I had said I wasn't going to write no more words down about people kicking us when we're down, about racist dogs that attack us and drive us down, drag us down and beat us down. But the dogs are in the street. The dogs are alive and the terror in our hearts has scarcely diminished. It has scarcely brought us the comfort we suspected.

The recognition of our terror and the screaming release of that recognition has not removed the certainty of that knowledge -- how could it? The dogs rabid foaming with the energy of their brutish ignorance stride the city streets like robot gunslingers, and spread death as night lamps flash crude reflections from gun butts and police shields.

I had said I wasn't going to write no more poems like this; but the battlefield has oozed away from the stilted debates of semantics beyond the questionable flexibility of primal screaming the reality of our city, jungle streets and their Gestapos has become an attack on home, life, family and philosophy, total.

It is beyond the question of the advantages of didactic niggerisms. The mother***ing dogs are in the street. In Houston, maybe someone said Mexicans were the new niggers. In LA, maybe someone said Chicanos were the new niggers. In Frisco, maybe someone said Orientals were the new niggers. Maybe in Philadelphia and North Carolina they decided they didn't need no new niggers.

I had said I wasn't going to write no more poems like this; but dogs are in the street.

It's a turnaround world where things are all too quickly turned around. It was turned around so that right looked wrong.

It was turned around so that up looked down. It was turned around so that those who marched in the streets with bibles and signs of peace became enemies of the state and risk to national security so that those who questioned the operations of those in authority on the principles of justice, liberty, and equality became the vanguard of a communist attack. It became so you couldn't call a spade a motherf*king spade.

Brother Torres is dead, the Wilmington Ten are still incarcerated Ed Davis, Ronald Regan, James Hunt, and Frank Rizzo are still alive, and the dogs are in the mother-f**king street.

I had said I wasn't going to write no more poems like this I made a mistake[74]."

The point of the poem is that the Black male feels anger towards the establishment for its oppressive posture. 'The Police, the brutish robot gunslingers' are the enforcement arm of the establishment; therefore they represent the rawest form of racism. The feeling towards the police is the feeling any slave felt towards the whip…they hate it more than they fear it.

According to Robert Decoy[75] the White man created the word Negro as a transition, because he implied that he could make a Nigger grow. The purpose of 'Seasoning[76] a slave' was to make good slaves, or good Negros. This good negroism is defined by doing your best to help support *The Establishment*.

My Blue Side

Sadly, my 20 plus years of Law Enforcement had a divisive effect on the people I encountered. Virtually 100% of the young Blacks and about 60% of older Blacks, and an unknown number of White saw me as a good Negro. This is ironic because I established myself as an Anti-nigger[c] upon to entering Police Academy. Ironically my academy class was tagged by the media as the 'most ethnically diverse' in that large agencies history.

I spoke out on the news speaking about the Rodney King[77] and Reggie Miller[78] incidents, and voicing my opinion about the 78% White police force I was to join. In another incident, complained on one of the instructors in the academy for saying in 1993 to put Negro on the arrest report. I had to defend my point against the entire cadre; (minus the only Black staff member, they were not invited to the lynching). I ended the discourse by saying, "Fine let me teach the course, I'll use B for Black and H for honkey. They were offended, I told them that was how I felt, "I have not been a Negro since 1960 and I will be damned if I am going to be one now."

Word spread of my uppityness, so much so that before I left the academy, my training officers had been warned about me and the issue preceded me to several assignments in the following years. I guess they perceived my irritation as Anti-niggerism[c]. Maybe they were just unprepared for a free-d Black man to join the department. Maybe they were expecting a good slave to be in my seat.

While in the academy one of the other Black recruits approached me in the locker and suggested I drop the racist remarks complaint, and just go silently into plantation service. One of the other men that looked like me, and was to be oppressed like me, suggested I be a good negro, and not make it harder for him. I looked him in the eye, "You be a Negro, I am a free man." He spent his career practicing good negroism, making no waves, excelling at nothing, making no enemies and no arrests.

One of my White partners, and friends after years said they were surprised at how much of an Uncle Tom I was being a Black cop. I was surprised at their comments. It is hard to be free in a system that assumes you are a good negro.

One of the benefits of using Africans as slaves instead of the Native Americans was that there was never a doubt in anybody's mind that a Black person in America during the time of slavery was property. The Native Americans kept escaping, and they knew the land and blended in with the free tribes. Their indelible Mark of their skin was all they needed to see to assume that this person was a slave; apparently, that mentality still exists to this day.

Later in my career, I had the occasion to have to defend a female White that was assaulted by a Black officer. When I did, I ended up having to cross the lines between White and Blacks several times. The Black officer's supervisor was White; however, the Black officer was protected by a captain that was Black.

The Black Captain took it upon himself to punish me for not taking care of the Black officer. My posture was it had nothing to do Black and White; no man should put his hands on any woman. Here I was a Black officer catching hell, trying to do the right thing; because this Black officer had another Black officer to protect him. The Black Captain was more concerned with me not siding with Whitey than doing the right thing. Ironically, White people came to my aid against the Black Captain.

Racism and hatred is a natural by-product of the racial indoctrination spread in America against all men and women of color.

5.3
Jooking (Shucking)

"It is a defensive performance that produces a stereotypical image that is by the audience but disbelieved by the performer[18]."

"Shucking (and jiving) is another unique form of masking that Black males have used successfully since slavery. Shucking is a communication style that conforms to racial stereotypes yet cognitively rejects them at the same time. Stanback and Pearce define shucking as 'Talk and physical movements that construct a temporary guise or façade designed to accommodate The Man. Shucking produces, in the moment of an encounter, whatever appearance *The Man* would find acceptable'."

Kochmean says the function of shucking is to work on 'members of the establishment' in a way that results in the Black male gaining some advantage[18]. I have been around young Black men my whole life and one of the things that is cultural is what we would call 'chicken'. 'Chicken' is using a series of stutter steps, aggressive head movements pantomiming as if you are going to fight or throw something at the person and or punch him: This is a way of expressing self it is peacocking. Shucking is just kind of a way to play and roughhouse without actually making contact.

The problem with this is it becomes a means and a method of expressing self because you're not supposed to touch each other or you're not supposed to be fighting or you may have to lose a fight so you learn to express yourself this way to make yourself look 'Larger than Life'.

My Black Side
As a Black man, I say the same thing as my blue side. I have been pissed off by the police too and I have

been stopped by the police unjustly DWB as they say. There is one thing you want to be careful of when dealing with a cop that stops you for Driving While Black (DWB). **Anybody stupid enough to stop you just because you are Black is probably stupid enough to do something else like hurt you because they are afraid.**

My Blue Side

'Jooking' works to the Black male's detriment when dealing with people that are not from the Black male's culture, not interested in hearing the Black male's perspective, or may simply be intimidated. If the Black male presents as aggressive with full plumage, then what emanates from the cop more than likely will be a defensive posture. In other words, it is not so much fear as it is a natural response to the plumage and all the outspread feathering action. The reason animals use plumage is to make themselves look intimidating; hoping to either frighten the prey away, or avoid or escape the fight.

It makes sense that individuals posturing can sometimes cause the police to believe that you are planning aggression, thereby causing a violent response. Their violence therefore is not intended to be malicious, it is preventative or reactive. This does not mean that their response is unwarranted; any response out of fear that is unjustified is not warranted but here is the problem. It is hard to determine exactly what a police officer should or should not fear. The law on self-defense does not specify; it uses the phrase *something that would reasonably cause a person to fear.* If a person's behavior or pantomimes causes a person to reasonably fear attack them, they are going to respond in self defense.

In the case of the police, the rationality also applies to escape, resist, arrest, or stop. If the police reasonably think that because of a behavior, you are going to flee, fight, or resist handcuffing, the behavior is going to elicit a response that you are not going to enjoy.

As a cop, I have preemptively taken suspects to the ground because of the manner in which he closed his fists, pulled them back, or lunged toward me with his head or his chest. Cops would love to give everybody the benefit of the doubt, but at the end of the shift, they want to go home even more.

It should be more important for you to stay safe than it is for cops to try and figure out what you're trying to do as well as monitor your safety. If you do not want to be touched by the police then resisting arrest is the worst thing you can possibly do. Whether by passive resistance, verbal resistance, or active resistance, if you do not want the police to touch you, any type of resistance is only going to increase the chances of being touched in a manner that you do not desire.

Simply put; the best way to evade, avoid, or resist arrest is not to break the law. However, if you do break the law it still makes more sense to be charged and adjudicated for a lesser charge. Do not to add resisting arrest and the potential physical damage or death to something silly. Face up to the consequences of the actions you undertook.

5.4
Are the Police
Afraid of Black Males?

"People don't know that the very reason the police were made was to oversee slaves; they would be called overseers, and if a slave got out of line or tried to break away and escape, these were the people to hold them in and bring them back[Robert Glasper]."

❧

My Black Side

When people ask this question, it behooves me to sit down with them and ascertain what or who they mean when they say the 'police' do they mean the person or the *Establishment*?   Only people can experience fear, an Institution cannot. Cops are human just like everyone else.

The police came on line to serve property owners. Policing as an institution does not actually serve a moral purpose; it is functional. The Law serves the moral purpose. The function of the police is to enforce the Law; which at times means taking or protecting the lives of people.   By-and-large however, the police serve the functions of Law and Order Enforcement.

Regardless of Glasper's contention that the police were originally overseers it is imperative to understand that the cliché, 'To Protect and Serve' is incomplete, it should read to 'Protect and Serve Society', not people.

Law enforcement as an institution is not racist; it serves at the pleasure of whoever is in charge at the time. If the police were all racists, they would have all resigned during the 8 year Obama administration. Nevertheless, it behooves us to understand that if the Masters are racists then by default, the police come across as racists that serve racist agendas.

The Establishment however is a different story. Of the cops working when George Wallace barred the kids from entering, it would be interesting to know how many worked the day the U.S. Marshals walked the little girl inside[79].

[Fig 15]

Now it is time to consider Glasper's hypothesis regarding the role of the overseer. Overall, the Police Officer is a unique individual, they do not come from a hive they are not Artificial Intelligence or Clones. Cops are people; they grew up in America. Because of *The Establishment's* devilish model, the 'Criminal Justice System' is dirty, of which cops are a fundamental branch.

I do believe and bear witness to the behavior of many cops. I believe many of them suffer from *The Establishment* effect as well. It stands to reason that if I contend that *The Establishment's* absurdities have a pronounced effect on the Black males' stature and standing, the effect must also affect attitudes of White males.

The Establishment continually drives wedges between the races and fosters both unrest and inequity. Even Rev. Jesse Jackson admits he fears Black males[96].

At the age of 21, people filled with foreboding, lies, and conjecture become old enough to be hired on as police officers. The shining metal star placed upon the proud peacocking breast of the officer DOES NOT IN ANY WAY ALTER THIS PERSON'S MENTALITY. 6 months in the police academy informs, possibly even guides; but it does not change. Only experience and interaction change attitude.

According to Data US[97], 69% of all U.S. Law Enforcement is White (non-Hispanic). Therefore; by default, this means that 69% of all Law Enforcement practitioners have been inundated by stereotypes, and prejudices, bias, subliminal fear producing stimuli from literature and the media.

Many officers spend their careers serving in high crime areas, or areas where they are not welcomed. Statistically, Projects, Trailer Parks, and Reservations (The poor and disenfranchised) have higher calls for service than other areas. Unfortunately, the natural propensity for dealing with negativism is to respond negatively. Officers stuck in a zone or an area of responsibility where the people are a constant irritant and they reject police presence not because you are corrupt but they simply don't want their lifestyle interrupted, become adversarial.

Cops from the projects, trailer parks, and reservations all use the same terminology; "These people, those people, they always have crime, they always kill each other, or they are always beating each other up". Cops from the projects, trailer parks, and reservations disassociate the people in these lower tears from people they do not work around; this is bias. This disdain for unpleasant people of a particular characteristic is a natural propensity in the human creature.

The anger is exacerbated when the police officer goes on a call already disinterested or irritated by the fact that they have to deal with this occurrence repeatedly. The occurrence could be the incident, the type, crime, or the people committing a crime. If an officer is sick and tired of going to a trailer park to deal with rednecks that keep fighting each other; when they get the call, their attitude changes. Unlike the regular call where you may have a clash of cultures: with bias, you have a clash of angers.

Black men are angry with *The Establishment* and those perceived as *Entrenched Henchmen*; the police. Cops are angry because they do not get any support from the communities in which they work. Often officers get virtually zero support from their Administration because of politics and they are left to deal with bad situations, in uncomfortable surroundings, working with people that do not want them there.

So you have a mad cop, and a mad individual. Before the interaction between the police officer and the suspect even occurs, anger is already on the scene. If you watch the videos of police officers when they get out in certain neighborhoods, the police officer is yelling and screaming at people and the people yelling and screaming back at the police officer. Under normal circumstances, this yelling and cursing is expected from society, but people do not expect the police to respond in this manner, they want professionalism.

I do think permissive police misconduct represents the fear of Black men by society, I think when you employ and encourage violence towards a particular group, there is a vested survival instinct at work.

My Blue Side

I witnessed a lot of interaction between Black men and officers over the years; I would say I did not get the perception that officers were afraid of Black men. Many officers seem to have a disdain or bias against for Black men but it does not seem to be fear. One officer that I worked with got into some type of altercation with a fellow officer and his punch line was, "I did not assault this individual because he was Black, it just happens to be a bonus." I do not know if this person was a racist but his quip was extremely ignorant. I think there is a lot more ignorance that there is animosity between the races. I think that people who do not spend time with other people have a propensity to be judgmental and even dislike each other, but I would not classify that as fear on its face.

I do believe however, that there is an uncertainty and uneasiness between many White officers and male Blacks because the officer has been inundated with rhetoric that would give the perception that the male Black is volatile, unstable and unpredictable. Therefore, when facing males of different ethnicities the one that poses the greatest perceived threat is the one that you were told poses the greatest threat.

This does not mean that a White supervisor walks around roll-call saying, "Black guys are dangerous, Black guys are dangerous, Black guys are dangerous." But statistical and empirical evidence from the average everyday Patrol officer gives the distinct impression that if there's going to be a running suspect, a fighting suspect, or a shooting suspect the odds are exacerbated in lower-income neighborhoods; probably Black. The numbers of calls for service are higher in the lower-income areas. It therefore makes sense that if you go into a lower-income neighborhood; perhaps one called Dodge City, for example, called such because of the number of shootings in this area, and the people in this area are of a particular ethnocentric variant, you might believe them to be dangerous. I do not know if this is racism; paranoia maybe, but I do not know if I would call it racism or fear.

In addition, because the police do not actually determine who calls the police it is unfair to characterize the police as racist and fearful. If the police happen to have calls for service where the suspects are Black. If you receive ten shooting calls in a day and seven happen to be in Black neighborhoods and 3 are in White neighborhoods how is it the officer's fault if they have to respond in the Black neighborhoods; with a higher number of responses?

This is because of the higher number calls in these particular neighborhoods. All of these things have to be taken into consideration before we point fingers and say instantly that the police were wrong.

Last point on this, when an officer does respond for service, if the people that greet or meet the officer are hostile, loud, or threatening the officer is now outnumbered and feels peril even before they have to contend with the gunman. What reasonable person would not act from an elevated level of awareness and possibly force?

5.5
The Police and Black Men

"Because White men can't police their
imaginations, Black men are dying[Claudia Rankine]."

❧

My Black Side

I have noticed that officers often speak to young Black men differently than they speak to other people. It is not always negative, it is not always derogatory, but I do find it is ironic slang terms come out quickly when the police are talking to young Black males. "He's a brother," or "You know; see what I'm saying," or "We got to keep it real." Some think this is an attempt at diffusion but it rarely works.

The use of street terms when speaking seems not only unnatural; I think it creates uneasiness between the two. In my opinion, this is the equivalent of slanting your eyes, or yelling at Latinos. The declination to speak standard english implies that you are speaking to a non-native speaker. If this is not the case, then the dialect is a pantomime of stereotypical idioms.

It is difficult for any police officers including myself to deal with people who do not like them. Black males have a pronounced disregard for police officers in my experience, and a lot of it has to do with their perception of unfair treatment. Many of the complaints are about the disparate treatment in incarceration. Many of the complaints are not about jailing Black people so much as White people are routinely not jailed for similar incidents.

Statistically, both nationally and locally, there are a disproportionate amount of traffic stops and Terry stops involving minorities, especially male Blacks; for this there is no legitimate rationalization. If you say that cops stop cars because drug users, bank robbers, burglars, and rapists use cars; statistically more of these people are White than they are Black. However, more traffic stops seem to target

Blacks than Whites. I do not have an answer for that except there is something wrong with the Criminal Justice System. Quotas may also have something to do with the anecdotal data. Sadly days off, take home cars, and actually getting your own zone have long been dependant on arrest stats. I'm not going to brandish everything as racism because I believe it taints true racism when you do that.

People are not required to be professional and courteous when dealing with the police but the police are required to be professional and courteous. The perceived authority of the police officer threatens only a person that is breaking the law. Authority is not a carte blanche to speak in a discourteous inflammatory manner via inflection or vocal tone to a citizen. The badge on your chest is supposed to shine as an example of what the officer represents.

If you do not want to be a shining example of what you represent then take off the badge and go get a security guard job some place. This applies obviously more to uninformed officers than to plain clothes officers but it goes across the board.

My Blue Side

I was asked have I ever spoken down to anyone. Well of course, I have. Verbal Judo was taught at the Academy, for use to de-escalate or control situations. Frankly, I have used harsh language with lots of people and that was the extent of their injury; no pepper spray, no taser, no pistol-whipping: nothing. I resolved many situations via the use of some bad language or vocal inflection. Because of the manner in which they were spoken to, no physical force was necessary. One may think this discourteous, but in my opinion it is a preferred methodology to arresting them or pepper spraying them. I believe that if you asked, the majority of people I cursed out would agree, that they preferred no physical force.

Yes there are racist cops, cops that hate gays, cops that hate women, and cops that hate anything else they can think of, but this is by no means the majority of cops.

I think it is ignorant of anybody to say that it is racist if the police are called and you are pissed off about what happens when cops get there. If the police officer jumps the gun and punches the Black dude in the face, fear or stupidity is more often the cause than racism. As we discussed, throughout the book when you mentioned the term racism you bring an ideation into the scenario where just because the person is Black the cops do not like them. I think that is an inappropriate assertion, and too sweeping an indictment.

Nobody likes unpleasant, unreasonable, aggressive people. If you are White and you are unpleasant, unreasonable, and aggressive, nobody is going to like you. If you are Black and you are ignorant, stupid, and aggressive; nobody is going to like you either. What you therefore have is two people who do not like each other standing in the middle of the street arguing but one of them has a badge and a gun the other one does not. It does not make it right, authority it just makes it the way it is; but that does not make it racism either.

Ignorance, bias, and unprofessionalism are not racism.

5.6
Why Are You Mad At Me?

"What I want to know is how the White man, with the blood of Black people dripping off his fingers, can have the audacity to be asking Black people [why] they hate him[Malcolm X]?"

The Establishment reminds Whites to be ever reminiscent that Blacks are not people they are Niggers. The term Niggers to *The Establishment,* then means something lower than property, worth less than a horse, yet more valuable. You can beat niggers to death, no would dare do that to a horse.

If the male with their strength and worth means nothing, what value can the Black woman have? She carries the Black Cotton seed and is the broodmare/toy. She also serves as the carrot to keep the Black studs at bay.

The Black male may not stay to be father or husband, but he is never late for a honeymoon. The Black woman is the Control Element in the experiment[80], she sweetens the pie. Without a bit of sugar, the stallion had nothing to look forward to but the fields. Slavers therefore allowed the obedient studs, plenty of *sugar*. The studs learns to bed every woman he can; and the mare lies with anyone she needs to. Either way, they are both victims, as they lay bare before each other basking in the nakedness of bondage©.

By design, the adult Black male resents juveniles (even his own child), seeing him as a threat and a nuisance. The mother must weigh the future of her child against her future. Remember, *The Establishment* only allows for one in her life[10].

10[MN1]{For example take the case of the wild stud horse, a female horse and an already infant horse and compare the breaking process with two captured nigger males in their natural state, a pregnant nigger woman with her infant offspring. Take the stud horse, break him for limited containment. Completely break the female horse until she becomes very gentle, whereas you or anybody can ride her in her comfort. Breed the mare and the stud until you have the desired offspring. Then you can turn the stud to freedom until you need him again. Train the female horse whereby she will eat out of your hand, and she will in turn train the infant horse to eat out of your hand also.

[MN18]When it comes to breaking the uncivilized nigger, use the same process, but vary the degree and step up the pressure, so as to do a complete reversal of the mind.

[MN19]Take the meanest and most restless nigger, strip him of his clothes in front of the remaining male niggers, the female, and the nigger infant, tar and feather him, tie each leg to a different horse faced in opposite directions, set him afire and beat both horses to pull him apart in front of the remaining niggers.

[MN20]The next step is to take a bullwhip and beat the remaining nigger male to the point of death, in front of the female and the infant. Don't kill him, but put the fear of God in him, for he can be useful for future breeding.

[NM1]We breed two nigger males with two nigger females. Then we take the nigger males away from them and keep them moving and working. Say one nigger female bears a nigger female and the other bears a nigger male. Both nigger females being without influence of the nigger male image, frozen with an independent psychology, will raise their offspring into reverse positions.

[NM2]The one with the female offspring will teach her to be like herself, independent and negotiable (we negotiate with her, through her, by her, we negotiate her at will.

[MN3]The one with the nigger male offspring, she being frozen with a subconscious fear for his life, will raise him to be mentally dependent and weak, but physically strong, in other words, body over mind.

[MN4]Now in a few years when these two offspring become fertile for early reproduction we will mate and breed them and continue

Enigmatically, the Black male develops anger and a severe resentment for all authority other than mom's. The male are not as foolish as hoped, for they perceive the disservice their environment imparts. They now flounder in the new natural setting they find themselves within, a setting where they are collected and despised because they represent a cash crop to *The Establishment*. *The Establishment* thrives off their bewilderment.

"Mind control (also known as brainwashing, coercive persuasion, mind abuse, thought control, or thought reform) refers to a process in which a group or individual systematically uses unethically, manipulative methods to persuade others to conform to the wishes of the manipulator(s), often to the detriment of the person[81]". The reversal of the mind, we call Stockholm Syndrome. If we brutalize a man until he learns to accept that this is what he deserves, his lot in life. The man can be taught to appreciate the care master gives him. Historically the alternative was assault, dogs, fire hoses, hanging in a tree, or a cross shaped nightlight; the typical response to this reversal of the mind is despondent-indifference.

The Establishment can no longer tar and feather, but it can humiliate (Clarence Thomas, Vanessa Williams), *The Establishment* can now fire him for kneeling during the Anthem (Kapernick). *The Establishment* can lynch him in his uniform (Ron Van Cleef). Or *The Establishment* can just shoot him (Malcolm, Martin). If Blacks still do not get the message, blow the Black bastards off the face of the earth.

How many non-brainwashed Black people does it take before *The Establishment* blows up a city block? Eleven.

According to Lindsey Norward[82], "Longstanding tensions between MOVE, a Black liberation group, and the Philadelphia Police Department erupted horrifically. That

---

the cycle. That is good, sound, and long range comprehensive planning}.

night, the city of Philadelphia dropped a satchel bomb, a demolition device typically used in combat, laced with Tovex and C-4 explosives on the MOVE organization, who were living in a West Philadelphia row home known to be occupied by men, women, and children. It went up in un extinguished flames[83]."

[Fig 16[84]]
["Row houses burn after local officials dropped a bomb."]

[Fig 17]
[May 13, 1985]

In true *Willlie Lynch* style, Mayor W. Wilson Goode, the first Black Mayor of Philadelphia (The City of Brotherly Love) proved that no free thinking Blacks would be allowed to continually disrupt *Establishment* business. The House and Field slaves clashed. The House-nigger had the support of *The Establishment*, so the he tied legs to horses and set them ablaze, just as recommended in the Lynch manual.

The Establishment (happily) paid about $15 million in damages via lawsuits, but this was just a ROI (return on investment). *The Establishment* invested in Goode, and he delivered; "Eleven people were killed, including five children and the founder of the organization. Sixty-one homes were destroyed, and more than 250 citizens were left homeless[31]."

Fewer people died this time as opposed to Wilmington Massacre of 1898 where a violent overthrow of a duly elected government, by a group of more than 2000 White supremacists against the Fusionist biracial government in Wilmington[85] led to the death of more than 60 people. no plane was used as in the Tulsa Massacre in 1921[86], where the attack, carried out on the ground and from private aircraft, destroyed more than 35 square blocks of the district-at that time the wealthiest Black community in the United States, known as 'Black Wall Street'. More than 800 people were admitted to hospitals, and as many as 6,000 Black residents were interned in large facilities, many of them for several days and approximately 10,000 Black people were left homeless,

In the decades since May 13, 1985, other than gangs how many other Black organizations have gone up against *The Establishment* using force? I think Goode made their point.

Psychological warfare works, ask José Campos Torres[87]. Six officers[88] beat up Torres after arresting him for drunk and disorderly. Due to his injuries, the jail required that he go to hospital prior to booking. The same officers met at the bayou in the area officers called 'The hole.' According to records, Officer Denson said, "Let's see if the wetback can swim," and then shoved Torres into the bayou. Three days later, his body was found. His death was ruled a 'drowning homicide'. The officers received probation in State Court and 1 year suspended sentence in federal Court on a Civil Rights violations charge. Jose and MOVE may not be around for breeding, but the next stallions in line, got the message. Comply or drown, suffocate, and burn.

My Black Side

A few lines from a Latina student in a movie describes more about why Blacks are angry than I could say in another book, "It's all about color. It is all about people deciding what you deserve. It's about people wanting what they don't deserve; about Whites thinking they run this world no matter what. See I hate White People because I know what you can do. I saw the White cops come into my house and take my father to jail, because they felt like it. And they can; because they are cops and they are White[89].

This is the despair Blacks convey, they are not fighting a person, they are fighting the idea of Whiteness. Whiteness is a universal paradigm. This particular paradigm crosses nations without a word; yet rules the world. How can you compete against the wind?

7.7 "At least I said my Piece!"

This is why it a frequent occurrence during arrests for Blacks to 'mouth off' to the police no matter what the cost. For the most part that is as high as their power of reprisal reaches. I cannot defeat White, but my spirit and my mouth are indomitable.

My Blue Side

Sometimes there is not really a blue side, because the behavior is so outlandish. I will say this however, the state election process is pivotal, as is civic involvement.

The Establishment will protect itself and those within its walls the best way it knows how. Violence made this country, and will maintain it; that is the cost of American survival. In 1993, the world watched while *The Establishment* extinguished the lives of 76 White People that decided to go against the rules. Almost a decade after the mayor detonated a bomb within city limits to kill Black people; the Federal government destroyed a compound with White women and children housed within its walls.

This is equality, dead bodies from either side, attributed to a *Establishment* elected to keep a certain way of life alive. Black people are on the frey of *The Establishment*, but we cannot watch starry eyed and think that *The Establishment*; the same *The Establishment* that fought a Civil War, orchestrated the death of JFK and RFK, and killed the Waco 76, would be squeamish about bombing, gassing, tasing, or shooting a few Black troublemakers. It is unreasonable for Blacks to want equality, but only when it is positive.

The Establishment has enough to manage; the last thing they concern themselves with is the welfare of people they disdain. White people may not like poor White people or Blacks but I guarantee they hate Black criminals.

America is White people's dream, it became a hellish nightmare for the Natives and then Blacks found themselves grafted into the nightmare. Blacks are here now. Black people have the right to enjoy some of the dream they are victims and constructors of; or at least somebody should be able to tell them why.

5.7
False Reports

"These tensions are rooted in the very same depths as those, from which love springs, or murder, the White man's unadmitted - and apparently, to him, unspeakable - private fears and longings are projected onto the Negro {James Baldwin} ,,

[Fig 18]

It took me a while to properly diagnose what s behind the current trend of false reports filed against Blacks. Baldwin never spoke more poignantly than when he ask why White people do fear that which they created - The Nigger? As we discussed Whiteness is not only uniform but is has been the staple of the *entrenched racism*, and the Police became its henchmen

Starting in 2007 White American started losing the buffer of safety afforded by their - 'Robot gunslingers'. It was not that Blacks were gaining ground, White people felt the sting of losing ground. MAGA, was not just a rally cry for the new president, it became a, hiding place for fearful

Whites. The fearful White is the White person that only has achieved their standing by virtues of their Whiteness. Remember, according to *The Establishment*, even the Wigger and PWT are better than Blacks. They are not better because of skill, but because of skin. As White America loses its faith in the power of the police to keep their Whiteness intact, they stepped in in a vain effort to fill the gap.

What does this have to do with Baldwin's statement asking if White people hated the Nigger so much why did they create him? Nothing because Nigger is not a real thing.

The Doppleganger is a ghost or apparition' so is the Nigger. The Nigger-ganger© is a real thing. The Nigger-ganger is the demonized Black male that every White person fears. The Niger-ganger is the murdering, raping, blood and flesh eating, White woman raping creature of bedtime stories. Whites sold the lies that Blacks were dangerous Pit bulls, for so long they believe their own lies. If you trained your dog to only do one thing; attack and id has no loyalty to you, when it finally gets loose, you are not sure what it is going to do to you now that it has a chance.

I wager that this is exactly the fear the South felt once the slavers were freed. I wager that their fear fueled their violence. The old adage might makes right when in fear right takes flight, is what White privilege hinged its survival upon.

CNN aired a story about a Black man asking a White woman in the park to put her dog on the leash as required by Park rules. The Cooper incident gives a plethora of evidence to support what we see and do not see in the media and on social media. She exemplifies Baldwin's statement."

My Black Side

If you watch the CNN video[90] and listen to her voice and the choking dog, she is in abject fear. Her fear is real: it is misplaced, but undeniably real. This is another side effect of the media's hate mongering stories. The Black man in the park, as large as he was, did not threaten her in any way, or her dog. Yet she distinctly told the police that by filming her, he was threatening her and her dog. The age old cry, 'Save me from the darkie.'

Upon asking the man to stop filming her, she informed him that she would BLATANTLY LIE TO CAUSE AN EXPEDITED RESPONSE and tell the police he threatened her life (Referred to from now on as a $2C^{2©}$) response. This is the age old American cry, 'save me from the darkie'. Rather than leave; rather than disengage, this woman faced peril (according to her) rather than accept instructions from a Black man. How dare he tell her what to do?

Watching the video, she encroaches upon him, and threatens him with $2C^2$ police action. How afraid of this man could she be if she is willing to walk right up to him? Her actions and her language assuaged all fears of murder and rape - rationalisms, she disconnects from 911 and walks up to him and asks him to stop filming her. Her White privilege overrode her common sense.

Ironically, the $2C^2$ action when reviewed by an employer resulted in the termination of the woman, citing a company policy and posture against racism. Black people did not raise the alarm in this case, White peers used the terminology. Trevon Martin, and Ahmaud Arbery were both $2C^2$ Reports. How can Black people be free when they suffer from lies still?

My Blue Side

$2C^2$ Reports; as in this case are not a distraction, they are a travesty. $2C^2$ lies cause injury, and potentially lives. This woman intentionally requested her call for service elevate from Code 2 to Code 3. Responding officers, White and Black received an update that the suspect threatened this White woman's life.

[Fig 24] and our Use of Force information should immediately trigger an understanding of the dangers of what she did. This man, this large Black man with a cell phone in his hand has been branded to the police as threatening to kill a White woman in the park. Even if she was not White, officers responding to the threat of lethal force are going to arrive on the scene poised to present a lethal solution.

Sadly, the problem she claimed did not exist. This is an instance wherein the cop's responses would never pass public scrutiny. Officers arriving would see a large Black man pointing something Black at them and an unarmed intimidated White woman and possibly fired upon him. Any Use of Force would be unjust because the man was not restive, nor threatening anyone, he in fact was the only one of the two in compliance with the law.

I do not know if the woman was charged with filing a false report, but she should have been. She actually filed a $2C^2$ report. This is a report not based in racism, but shrouded in subliminal fear, and panic, which stemmed from both Media hate mongering and the indoctrination of the American public regarding race relations.

7.9 2C2 Reports

$2C^2$ Reports occur frequntly. Among the most common is calling a theft a robbery. People do not realize that there is a legal differentiation and a different police response to a robbery versus a theft. The explanation is the theft is a property crime, and robbery a crime against a person and society.

$2C^2$ Reports are not new; they have been getting Black men challenged for decades. White women screaming rape when caught in infidelity used the $2C^2$ Report to save their own skin. The kids stealing free cookie dough was a 2C2 Report, "I think they had a gun," is a common $2C^2$ Report.

The most common Police initiated $2C^2$ Report is the, 'You match the description of a suspect.' And it has been used and abused for decades.

Not all civilian $2C^2$ Reports stem from discrimination, but most of them originate from resentment and/or racism. Cop $2C^2$ Reports are often utilitarian, giving cops a reason to initiate contact in situations where they normally would not have access. This is often systemic, but not always racist.

A recent good decision by many jurisdictions made $2C^2$ reports *Hate Crimes*, and prosecute people for lying. Look out Karens and Kens you are next.

5.8
What Type Of Black People Intimidate You?

"Millions of Americans shrugged off their fear of the Corona Virus when restaurants opened. But there is another type of contagion that still keeps some of White America paralyzed: Fear of Black men in public spaces[91]."

Aamna Mohdin[92] contends that White fear is just a cover for racism. "White people regularly call the police on Black people who are doing nothing wrong; not only because of misplaced fear, but as a method of regulating access to shared spaces. Calling the police in these instances is about having "The power to say you don't belong here."

Kevin Kruse accurately points out that desegregation, (To include White Flight) only created, "A new division in which the public world was abandoned to Blacks and a new private one was created for Whites."

My Black Side

My assertion is that White Fright is a cover term, and that it covers the true intention to use whatever authority is available to enforce racism. This covering action is what creates discrimination.

My Blue Side

As we discuss idioms, we see that the deliverers of the White Fright are cops. The reason cops seem so discriminative, is that White people use them to facilitate their discrimination. Perhaps the term *robot gunslinger* is appropriate, because cops spend most of their careers responding to allegations (input, programming) from other people.

Officer's choices to stop a Black family from buying toys, or to investigate Black people barbequing on a golf course, makes the cops look like Nazis when in fact it is just Chapter 2 of the Birth of Nation saga called; Maintaining the Nation©. The police have no choice but to respond to Starbucks when they call for service. Even if the officer shows up to say that this is not a police matter, dispatch cannot make legal determinations, therefore the officer's appearances are mandatory. The problem occurs when the police attempt to maintain order and the guys at the store won't leave. Regardless of personal beliefs, once a lawful order is given, the crime becomes failure to comply, not the original offense.

Upon arrest, the police gained the name, racist, because they had to act. What if it was not Starbucks, instead it was at a Black owned business. What if it had been one of Dr. Shaquille O'Neal's 155[+] businesses and the same instance occurred? Would the responding officers have still been racists? What if I responded to the call; am I then a sell out because someone refuses to leave private property?

Whether or not the owner had a legitimate reason to ask a person to leave is not a matter for the police, the law says they can demand anyone off their property. Much like your home, if you want a person to leave for any reason, their failure to do so is a violation of law. 'Maintaining their Nation' is not an indication of police malice, racism or abuse of power; it is an ongoing example of *entrenched racism*.

6.0

Media

Influence and

Stereotypes

"Your time is limited, so don't waste it living somebody else's life. Don't be trapped by Dogma which is living with the result of other people's thinking. Don't let the noise of others' opinions drown out your own inner voice. And most important, have the courage to follow your heart and intuition. They somehow already know what you truly want to become. Everything else is secondary[Steven Jobs] "

6.1
Media Influence and Stereotypes

The only thing worse than the lies the
Media spreads, is the truths that they share

～

In my opinion, the most important word in journalism is not truth it is Ratings. Having appeared on the news numerous times in my professional career, I can definitively say that the news reports only that which they think sells stories. It does not matter if it is true, slanted, jaded, inaccurate, or just downright wrong. The news, because of the Sunshine Law and because the press is not really held to a rigid standard in terms of civil and libel unless they make out right allegations; they can say whatever they desire[93].

We must at all times remember that a media / journalism / mass communication major has a four-year college degree in telling stories; not telling the truth.

Many of the stories on the news are not worth actually telling unless you put a spin on them. For example, a man robs a bank (about 5000 reported each year to FBI) and is then shot to death by the police. No big deal, the man who robbed the bank according to statistics is more likely going to be a male White. According to statistics the person shooting this individual is probably also going to be a male White. Officer shoots Black suspect as he flees from bank robbery, that headline sells stories; but it is misleading it is inflammatory and it actually changes both the entire discourse and truth of the matter.

My Blue Side

The civilian fails to realize that the police are empowered to shoot dangerous people fleeing a crime, not because they are fleeing the crime but because as many policies state, 'if left un-apprehended, this person will continue to be a danger to society'. But my question is this; under what circumstances do you not want the police to shoot a bank robber? If a Chinese guy robbed the bank is it okay to shoot him? If a White guy robs a bank is it okay to shoot him? What if those same three guys rob three banks at the same time, and all three of them did exactly the same thing. They threatened to harm the customers and tellers if they did not hand over money. Then when the police came they pointed a gun in the general direction of the police who shot them all. Which one of those stories would make the headlines? Which one of those stories is different? Most importantly in which one of those stories did the police do anything wrong? What if the robber wore a mask and no one knew he was Black, until after the shooting. Is it still racism? Should the police call ahead and ask before they shoot?

My Black Side

Black people, we need to be a little bit more careful of trusting information that comes from the same people that said we had tails, swung from trees, had big pink lips, and descended from monkeys. If the media portrayed that of Blacks then what changed, and what do they think of Blacks now; we are still just as Black. If you were mad because Shaft had a White girlfriend then what makes Blacks think that the Media feels more comfortable with it now?

This is the same media that when there is a story in a Black neighborhood or the projects, finds the lowliest of persons to give a statement. Rarely is it the schoolteacher who happens to live on the cusp of the neighborhood or the school crossing guard. It is so often somebody like the crack head who just happens to be standing around uttering some cliché, or poorly structured sentence.

People like Tavis Smiley get on the media and they endeavor to give an un-jaded, unbiased perspective of a story. Do you ever wonder why you do not hear that much from him in the mainstream? It is not because he's Black; it has a lot more to do with content if his message.

The message of 'go along to get along,' is always preferred by *The Establishment*. *The Establishment* will do whatever it takes to perpetuate itself. What better way to maintain Black Cotton, than to constantly stir up civil unrest and strife between the powers-that-be and the people that are mad.

What happened to George Floyd was horrible, needless, and unconscionable. Fortunately, I have yet to find any police officer who can even conceive of justifying the manner in which that event occurred. Nevertheless, to indict all cops for this is no different than indicting all Blacks because of O.J. Simpson. Any Black person stopped or arrested by the police that is still alive, knows this to be true; why lie?

What the media needs to stop portraying is the fact that these events occurred because of racism. This White individual may have been a racist; this individual may have been many things but what this individual was not, was a comprehensive representation of their police department and the law enforcement professionals in the United States of America.

I wager money that if the offending person was a security guard, a bartender, a park ranger, or even an ice cream salesman, he would probably have exactly the same problems, he simply would not have had the authority to do anything as reprehensible.

If fired from one police enforcement agency for Behavior Unbecoming, you absolutely should not be allowed to transition to another agency. This is common sense, if you did not have what it took to be a police officer in another jurisdiction; chances are you still do not, unless you want to send them to rehab or some type of severe additional training.

Just like the unscrupulous lawyer I referred to previously, the media has a habit of telling people with sticks and rocks to fight the *established system*; that is the wrong way to go about vindicating George Floyd and all the other Black lives ever taken. The methodology most effective against *The Establishment* is to attack its Cotton Foundation©. Take a moment and read the Secession Letters. The bloodiest years in internal American history were White people fighting other White people over money.

No matter the number of unarmed Black people killed in this country, until the end of Cotton Economics© nothing will change. The main difference now is that you have all these businesses Disney, UFC, Amazon, and many multibillion-dollar industries giving support to this Black Moment. What this does is it resonates with the Cotton Foundation's base nucleus; the voters. Lots of money resonates; too few votes result in not being elected; that is how you can help affect a change for the better.

The Deep Cotton Response© is to get a lawyer or get a team of lawyers and sue for millions of dollars every single time the police do something they are not supposed to do. Sue them personally as well. Instead of taking to the streets and burning down the business of somebody who had absolutely nothing to do with this event, sue the police department, the mayor, the police chief and the officers involved. This is how you get policy changes this is how you get little changes, this is how you get to shake up a police department because if you read police department policies there are catch phrases in most policies to indemnify the department from being sued; it is a political organization. Getting pissed off does not hurt *The Establishment* as much as pulling money out of its deep, oppressive pockets.

Personally establish a Deep Cotton Response Team when there is a problem with the police department. The only way to make this work is to bankrupt *The Establishment*. The point of the police is to ensure that property owners have property and maintain the preeminence of their 'will'. If you take that 'will' from them, then the police are not doing their jobs. What it boils down to as long as at the end of the day *The Establishment* has working plantations making them money, nothing is going to change, especially a few more mad slaves. Threaten their billions; and you will get a response.

In regards to burning businesses, there is a theory that those who benefit indirectly from their White privilege also deserve to have their business destroyed. Newsflash: Unless you eat through osmosis or photosynthesize, everyone on American soil benefits from *The Establishment.*

The media had a captive audience during COVID-19 pandemic and demonizing the police was convenient. The Media used social reform as a red Herring issue to mask Covid and economic woes in the country. Black people did not just start being victims of police brutality, and of the 200+ legislative attempts to aid Black none have passed currently. The use of the media masks far graver matters that the *Establishment* concerns itself with;

- National murder rate - U.S. murder rate jumps in 2020 to highest seen since 1990s[94]
- DMV rates Domestic violence statistics are surging during the COVID-19 pandemic[95],
- School dropout rates - Experts predict a big increase in high school dropouts is on the horizon[96]
- Suicide rates - Study reveals increased suicide rates across U.S[97]
- Over dose rates - The deadliest year in the history of U.S. drug use[98]

BLM and the current Black awareness, is not a genuine outcropping it is just another social concern on a long list, next to animals, environment, and the ME Too Movement. How can White people rioting and committing acts of violence at Black protests help the Black movement, what do these insincere White people protected by their Whiteness offer Blacks?

6.2
Do Stereotypes Exist?

"Stereotypical thinking deprives us of the ability to discover the truth and justice, and it sets the stage for future conflicts[Sunday Adelaja] ."

Profiling and stereotyping are staples for *The Establishment*[11]. Why waste the information gathered over years of plantation management by not using it to maintain *The Establishment*.

Understanding their 'livestock' with great accuracy became the method to weed out and predict the fearsome Anti[nigger][c]. Once discovered, Anti-niggerism[c] was isolated and roped off like spores in a Petri-dish. It took hundreds of years for Whites to distance themselves far enough from the plantation to relax enough to fight and undo their indoctrination. Make no mistake; the same Whites that formed the walls of the Anti[nigger] Petri-dish out of fear, eventually broke down the glass walls of segregation and to this day try to live with the problems they created.

Anti-niggerism[c] can explode from anywhere. Remember the *Establishment's* methods required complete control of the environment and monitoring of the mental state of the potential Anti-nigger[c]

Adelaja points out the three most destructive aspects of stereotypes;
- Blocking the truth
- Blocking Justice

---

[11] {[LMAS4]They watched, therefore with skilled and practiced eyes, and learned to read with great accuracy, the state of mind and heart of the slave, through his sable face.

[LMAS5]Unusual sobriety, apparent abstractions, sullenness, and indifference indeed, any mood out of the common was afforded ground for suspicion and inquiry}.

- Engenders future conflict

These three aspects are why the use of Media is imperative to the *The Establishment*; it needs to block the truth, so it can skew justice. Once a people learn to see ethnicity as a threat, internment and discrimination are natural by products and become acceptable to the society.

Prior to denying justice, discriminating against or oppressing, a group experience shows that belittling and demonizing them is the first step. In order to convince moderately moral citizens that it is ok to treat people unfairly we ridicule and belittle them. This process is useful to devalue or escalate the value of a group. *The Establishment* simultaneously raises and lowers people values via the use of stereotypes.

[Fig 19] depicts four of the most influential Anti-kuntas who refuted and railed against the effects of the stereotype. Their input destabilized the *The Establishment*, but the third tier of the stereotype activated. The Anti-Kinta was an unwelcome and dangerous member of the society.

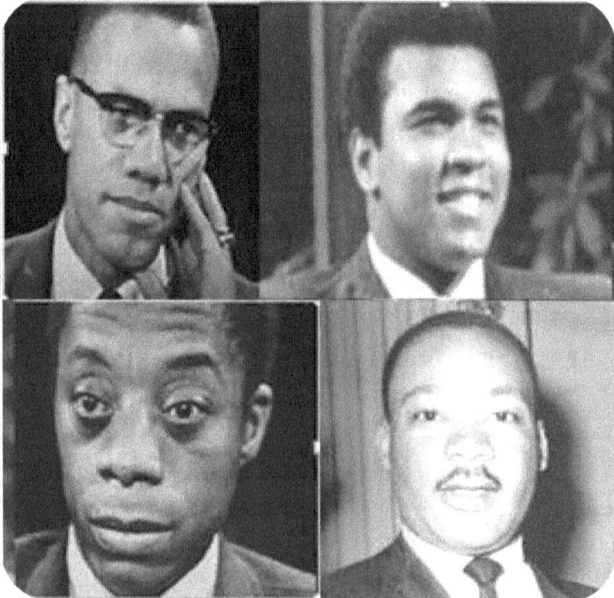

[Fig 19] 'The A^K-4'

How do you continue to convince people of ignorance, and uselessness when you have these 'uppity' African American'ts. These men made blocking the truth, and blocking justice difficult by preaching self-awareness and self-esteem. Institutionally speaking, their existence made people hear and see them for what they were. By disproving the stereotype, it became evident the other members of the targeted group, also potentially had value.

Whites had their Big 3 (Stalin, Roosevelt and Churchill) Blacks had the A^K-4. Once Blacks established value injustice became more difficult. Today we rely on cell phones to break stereotypes, unlike the 'The A^K-4'. You-tube selfies and Tik-Tok fail in comparison to the global coverage and Supreme Court decisions involving these men, by mainstream, White media outlets.

My Black Side

It is hard not to slap your tail in the water in warning after looking at the legacy of American police treatment of Black people. There is a pervasive expectation that when the police arrive, Black people should back down. However, this does not seem to be the case often when dealing with White people. Both the police and the White people respond differently. I observed many instances of the police dealing with White people, they go back and forth as equals; it is as though the Whiteness diminishes in some way, the same authority that the Black person was supposed to respond to, submissively.

I think that the times I was asked why I do not talk Black is an indication of a stereotype. President Obama was a Black man does that mean he did not talk Black because he went to Harvard and made grammatically correct sentences? If that is the case; that is a nonsensical contention. If you went to the same high school as a White student, why on earth would we not speak in the same manner? This is why separate education was required. When they asked why I did not speak Black what they really wanted to know was why and how I learned to sound like a White man when I speak.

I think if you have bias towards the manner in which I speak you probably have other perceptions about how I should think, act, and what I should believe.

As long as *The Establishment* pigeon holes individuals, Blacks will always be cast as;

- The magical negro
- The Black best friend
- The thug
- The angry Black woman
- The domestic
- The angry bastard
- Shiftless father
- Watermelon
- Mandingo (The Black Buck)
- Uncle Tom

These personas justify or exemplify *entrenched racism* and its treatment of stereotypical individuals. The AK-4s, aimed to destroy these typologies, yet Blacks decided to revive many of them. According to the Ak-4, Blackness should be a rally cry, to bettering self and the race, not just a reason to divest from the mainstream

My Blue Side

I listened to a comedian make a joke about a woman not wanting to be called a whore even though she was dressed like one. Her response was "Just because I'm dressed like a whore, I don't think you should treat me like one." To which the male comedian replies, "Well if you get robbed and I had on a uniform that looks like a police officer's uniform would you not come to me and expect me to act like a police officer because I have on the uniform?"

I think that Black people, especially young Black people have a culture. Once Whites had 'Valley' and 'Grunge' and I think Black people have a culture as well. This Black culture is antithetical to 2020 mainstream. I do not think it is just because they are Blacks; to me it is more because they are perceived as nuisances just like the hippies and the rockers. The people who listen to The Beatles and The Rolling Stones were nuisances when they emerged. *The Establishment* was not thrilled to have this new wild, free love, drug smoking tree-hugging persona spread through the streets; for fear of where it would lead. To *The Establishment* as long as Whites did not speak, eat, dance, or talk Black, hippies were still better than the darkness surrounding White America.

I think mainstream America finds stereotypical behavior refreshing especially within the Black community; it gives *The Establishment* the opportunity to continue destructive interference. However, people, even liberal people tend to notice when they research the color of the statistically predominant group violating social values they consider important. Since Whites frequently abuse drugs, they do not find Blacks affinity for Marijuana and recreational drugs offensive, but they draw the line at things like murder and armed robbery.

Leading the murder and armed robbery demographics reinforces stereotypes and fear more than skin color, but the outer shell gives the police something to target, a face and a body. The police respond by enforcing mainstream (White) American laws. This is not a racist statement, White people kill people too. And when they do the police go after them, and according to statistics shoot more Whites numerically than they shoot Black people. Calling the law White is not derogatory, the laws were not written for Blacks; White people did not allow Blacks the protection of their law until the Constitutional Amendments.

In consideration as to whether or not stereotypes exist look to Jesse Jackson, the self-proclaimed Black justice fighter. I cite two instances. One is his admission about his fear of Black males. And the second is the manner in which he spoke about President Obama, in regards to wanting to cut his nuts off. Some speculate that he used racial emphatics in the story, but I was unable to verify the same.

After years of standing in the foreground fighting for Black justice against *The Establishment*, what is it about Black males that he fears. Why would the Rev. Jesse Jackson after understanding the history of scrotal separation in the America's in regards to slaves, use such incendiary terms? If this politician and man after spending more than 40 years in the Black fight gives credence in his own belief to stereotypes, what would prevent Whites from believing as he admittedly does?

The singular thing that keeps stereotypes alive is Action. Each individual action positively empowers stereotypes. What better example of the ongoing battle between field and house slaves, or the 'Crab-mentality' than a respected politician and minister on national television condescend the Black President of the United States of America. Which racist does not relish in Jackson's remarks and say boisterously; see that is why they cannot be trusted and cannot get a head. Yes stereotypes exist, and shall as long as stereotypical behavior gives them vitality.

7.0
Training
and
Tactics

"A recent police study found that you're much more likely to get shot by a fat cop if you run{Dennis Miller}."

7.1
What Do Cops Do Anyway?

"Let me tell you how the city runs. We serve the rich and in return, they raise us above the primordial filth, and God help us if we do not keep our end of our bargain to them; you and I are nothing but dumb animals, no better than the lowlife scum we protect them from. It doesn't matter that they have soft hands or wear silk underwear, so long as they have money, we do their bidding [Chief Thomas Burns] [99] ,"

As a Black male, I fall into a variety of different high-risk categories; high-risk health issues, increasingly higher risk for suicide, high risk for violence by members of my own race, high-risk by violence of members of the White race; law enforcement in particular, or at least that is what the media would have me believe.

7.2 It is not just a job

One of the basics of any discussion is respect. I always thought it Elitist to show your braid (credentials) during debates and discussions. However, over the years my position changed. The media helped shaped a generation of people who believe if they agree with what you said it must be true. There is no such thing as personal truths. By definition a 'truth' is universal, which is why it is rare. For example, in every police related death there are at least four truths;

1. Someone is dead
2. The police were involved
3. What really happened
4. Why it really happened

For any evaluation, we may be able to discuss our opinion of these truths but we cannot to change them nor should we try. One such truth is that Law Enforcement is NOT A JOB.

A job is defined as 'a paid position of regular employment or a task for which you are paid'. If it is a job, who is the employer: because it absolutely is not the general public.

Remember the Boston Tea Party? How are cops paid? Through taxes, there are not elected officials at least not most of them. If you live in America, you have no say about how much cops are paid, when paid, their retirement, vacation, or any other employers concerns because taxpayers are not the employers.

Who then is the customer? This is a trick question because the answer is duplicitous. Yes, Law Enforcement has customers and beneficiaries, but the true customers of Law Enforcement are the criminals. Laws are only 'enforced' upon the lawbreakers therefore, lawbreakers are the customers. Society on the other hand, is the beneficiary. This is why police cars should read *to protect and serve law and order*.

What other industry other than undertaking has an entire client base of people that want not to do with or hate their service provider? Because of its uniqueness, the profession comes under scrutiny for many things.

Another vast difference, immense in Law Enforcement's importance; other then soldiers cops are the only professionals specially trained to take human lives as a routine part of their duties. The military grasped the enormity of this concept long ago. People trained to thrive and function in stressed filled violent environments, that possess specialized training and lethal skills must by default be handled differently than people without the skills.

Unlike most jobs where loss prevention undertakes investigates losses from the employer most commonly via theft, Law Enforcement internal investigations most commonly have other humans as the victim or person that takes the loss. In other words, both the beneficiary and the customer are targets of 'internal losses or damages' perpetrated by the police.

Fact is that the sole purpose the "Good Faith Exception' exists. If you analysis any law enforcement use of force under the ideation that this is just a job, (as though this person worked as Wendy's or Home Depot) you already have overlooked the truth. Therefore removing this staple taints the outcome. If you have to taint the outcome to get outcome you want then it is neither just nor true.

7.3 Police Officer Job Description (Not applicable to all agencies)

- Police officers are responsible for protecting lives and property by enforcing laws, responding to calls, issuing citations, and making arrests within a designated area
- Police officers aim to preserve law and order. Police officers oftentimes advance into roles like police supervisor or detective
- Police officers must have a high school diploma or equivalent. Usually, they must also have completed a minimum of 60 college semester hours in criminal justice or a related field
- Police officers need to complete a training academy, pass a written and physical certification exam, pass a criminal background check, have a valid driver's license, and be at least 21 years of age
- Patrol assigned locations on foot and by vehicle in order to prevent and discover crime
- Enforce traffic regulations, recognize violations, and issue citations
- Secure and investigate crime scenes, and collect and preserve evidence
- Makes arrests in accordance with proper apprehension techniques
- Complete appropriate reports, forms, logs, and citations
- Testify in court when subpoenaed
- Provide emergency aid as needed
- Maintain contact with citizens regarding potential law enforcement problems and preserve good relationships with the general public; take an active role in the areas of public education relative to crime and crime prevention

- Participate in training courses and programs
- Monitor and properly identify, interpret, act and respond to information transmitted over a mobile and base radio system;
- Book prisoners; assist in the custody, care and welfare of prisoners; transport prisoners
- Perform general police work in the protection of life and property;
- Provide the public with safety information and explain laws and ordinances
- Perform specialized duties requiring application if abilities and knowledge acquired through experience

7.4 Qualifications for Police Officer

- Successful completion of police officer training academy or State Academy
- Current CPR certification
- Valid driver's license in state of practice
- Ability to pass a criminal background check
- Ability to pass a physical agility test
- Working knowledge of local, state, and federal laws

For so long Law Enforcement has allowed the Blue wall to exist for everything. Much as every practicing Catholic does, and the truth is that this is not right. But the media again muddied the issues by mixing internal violations with criminal actions. Not all internal violations are criminal; the converse is that ALL criminal action are internal violations.

Long before I entered Law Enforcement corruption existed with the ranks of the cops. Much of the corruption in Law Enforcement comes from its evil Task Master-Politics. More than corruption, and apathy I was more surprised at the influence Politics has on Law Enforcement. It may have be naiveté, but I thought all laws existed to benefit the beneficiaries of Police protection; that is not so. Many laws are political in nature; sadly most police policies are also political in nature. The police are always a task oriented microcosm of the society; otherwise there would be no empathy.

I entered Law Enforcement believing it to be a job. My plan was to spend three years as LEO, then go to law school, work as DA office and finally end up in politics, hoping to work with my father. What I soon learned is that it gets in your blood. Policing is a gut wrenching exploration in to the human bowels. For eight hours per day, everything mom, school, and church told you about human nature is challenged. Every day, your nature is challenged. Every life you lose or suspect that evades becomes personal, not from the perspective of a victim, but as a failure in ensuring that you kept someone safe from that perpetrator. Cops do not hate to loose, because they hate to lose, if cops loose; someone else out there pays a heavier toll than they pay.

I feel more misgivings come from Blue Logic than Badge Side manner. A lot of Badge Side manner is testosterone and ego driven.

My Blue Side

My perspective on law enforcement is that it has become more of a pulley system than a system of actually enforcing the law. I believe that in the 20 plus years that I was a cop, what I saw was a paradigm change. Although the people that were cops before I joined were not overly diverse, they had more pride in the job that they performed. As diversity and inclusion came on board, the mission that the police served changed to reflect values in society.

[Fig 20]

The gun belt clarifies the job of the police officer definitively, expertly, and completely. I think everything you need to know about a Cop is right there in [Fig 20].

Police officers basic issued gear;

- Firearms and certification
- Handcuffs and certification
- Pepper spray and certification
- A Taser and certification
- Flashlight
- ASP expandable baton and certification
- Extra pistol magazines
- Radar Traffic Enforcement certification
- Radio
- Latex gloves
- First Responder certification

[Fig 20a]

What a cop is not issued is:

- An MD
- PhD in Psychology
- Geriatric certification
- DMV counselor certification
- ADA certification
- ASPC certification
- Child Psychology certification
- Social Work certification
- Crisis Intervention certification

[Fig 20b]

Here is what I mean. Look at those two lists [Fig 20a/b] whatever the officer is expected to do they must have the authority, training and equipment to accomplish. A major problem is that what society expects officers to do does not match [Fig 20a/b]. If it is possible to do all the things society expects, officers would have those certifications listed in [Fig 20a/b] but instead they have 50 bullets.

Society has options; they train officers, they pay officers, they empower officers. Look at what society has created. What society asks officers to do they cannot do. What society pays officers to do; they say they do not want officers to do. How can officers not be confused?

The police officer woefully under serves the man who needs a psychologist, because the only thing I have are my fist and my handcuffs. I do not know what to do with people who run away from home because they have Alzheimer's; all I can do is hold onto them until somebody else comes.

When the fire department arrives at a scene where there may be an active shooter or somebody with a knife or something to that effect, do you know what they do? They stage. Staging is the process whereby first responders go to a location within striking distance, park the vehicles and wait. What are they waiting for? They are waiting for the people with [Fig 20] tools because they do not have them.

The fire department has ladders, bandages, and water, they are going to use the tools that are available to them, and they have much more medical training than police. The ambulance driver does the same thing. Before the ambulance driver can come in and render Aid, the officer uses tools from [Fig 20] has to render the situation safe.

What has become the problem is that people call the police, and the police are dispatched to many scenarios that the police are powerless to fix. It's an abomination. What is the police department powerless to resolve?

- Civil disputes
- Ongoing domestic disputes
- Property issues
- Bad kid issues
- Stupid husband issues
- I had too much to drink issues

What law enforcement can do is put the suspect in jail. If police cannot arrest or shoot the suspect or try something else police have the authority to do, officers have nothing else except offer a [Fig 20] option.

When the Dollar General calls and says there is a customer in their store refusing to pay, there is nothing the police can do until that customer runs out into the parking lot and can be charged by theft. The problem is the police do not have the ability to charge that man with theft because they do not own the property. Only Dollar General can prosecute that individual. Officers can catch him, and can transport him; but if Dollar General does not want to prosecute; then officers cannot do anything with him. They get to sit there and watch him walk down the street with the property.

The Black community knows there is an internal problem with violence. Whether domestic, gun, or drug violence and they know that the only people in society that are able to handle it are the police because of what is on their belts. Sadly, there is collateral damage. In order for the police to look for Black suspects the Black community want gone, they have to enter the Black community. The complaint is that the police seem to treat all the members of the community like suspects, or at least in a disrespectful manner.

My Black Side

The African-American't is NOT A WARD of the State. The *entrenchment* did not succeed fully in making a perpetual race of dependents. The Native American has been rendered obsolete, and all but extinct. They live on land provided for them and still get beans and blankets from the Government. They are an invisible reminder of what Non-White America once looked like.

For too long, the attitude amongst cops is to treat people like they are beneath the heel of a master. Although cops are generally rude to people across the racial divide, it seems more prevalent amongst the poor and minorities, according to complaints. Maybe Whites do not complain.

It is not that cops necessarily have any more derogatory names for Blacks; they added their bias to stereotypical terms to the preexisting names. The jaded perspective of cops, due to constant dealing with the underbelly of society, creates a Blue Prejudice©.

This Blue Prejudice contains arrogance and contempt for those that are not blue. It is difficult to understand the attitude of a cop unless you are a cop. But the gunslinger, cowboy, John Wayneistic demeanor comes along with the blue uniform. Cops walk around all day in gun-belts dealing with other people's problems.

Look at the gun belt in [Fig 20], do you see mantras, incense, wind chimes, dream catchers or any other tree hugger type device? Cops do not come to take you into custody for immorally clubbing a baby seal; they came to take you into custody in the name of the King (Now *The Establishment*), the owner of the seal. Salty cops, avenge the evil while they accomplish the task of taking you into custody.

I think cops have additional problems. From my observations, their attitude towards Blacks engenders an attitude from Blacks. If some officers are going to treat Blacks with no respect, they will not only get no respect, Blacks will not cooperate nor acknowledge their illegitimate authority. Good officers need to notice and fix the problems caused by the illegitimate authority, unprofessionalism, bias, and racism. Failure to do is not just complicity; it has brought contention to the level it is currently.

7.6
What Was The Officer's Call & Last Does It Affect Their Behavior?

"How we perceive a situation and how we react to it is the basis of our stress. If you focus on the negative in any situation, you can expect high stress levels. However, if you try and see the good in the situation, your stress levels will greatly diminish{Catherine Pulsifer} ,,

My Black Side

I do not really care what the last call was; be a professional. If the doctor has a bad day prior to work, should he then botch surgery because he is angry. He should not botch the surgery but his decisions making process may be altered. When the doctor messes up he has to pay for his mistakes, as should the officer.

My Blue Side

I do not really care what the last call was; be a professional. Cops are human too. Real cops, those that are True Blue, are great because they are human. If people cannot even live in their tiny world without requiring assistance from the police, how is a police officer supposed to balance all of these issues, stressors, and macabre situations and their personal lives?

The evidence bears out that the police have trouble dealing with the effects of their job. If they did not, they would not be in the highest demographic for suicide, alcoholism, domestic violence, high blood pressure, hypertension, and heart attacks. The current call for service might be the trigger but even this is not the norm. The overwhelming majority of police officers are professional, and they deal with all of other people's problems as well as their problems during their shifts.

Of the many legitimate complaints filed every year against the police, what percentage are valid?

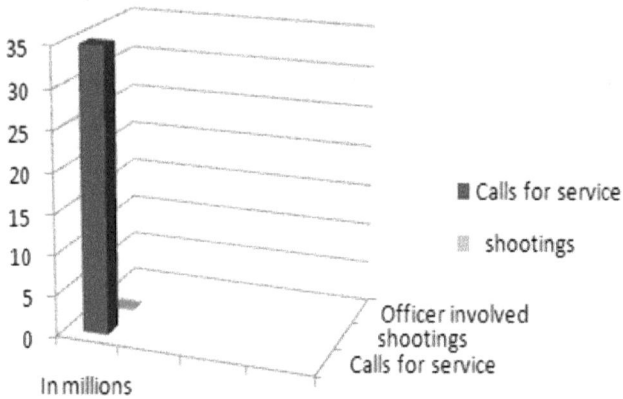

[Fig 20c]

There are 250,000 medical mistakes in the United States of America annually and even a higher number than that of pharmaceutical mistakes in the United States annually.

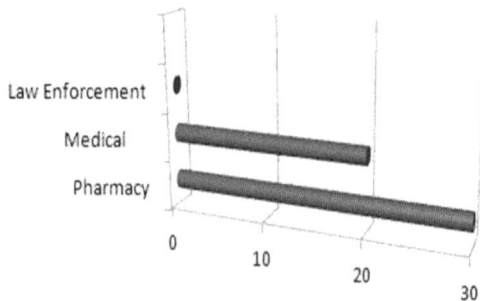

[Fig 20d]

The police are no different, but people have not stopped going to the doctor and they have not stopped taking drugs yet or defunded big pharma for all the deaths, crimes and addition directly related to Oxycodone and Oxycontin?

7.7
Do Police Get Training On How To Handle Different Cultures?

"A racist cop pulls over a Black driver for no reason other than the fact that the driver is Black and a recent robbery was committed by a couple of young Black guys in a White community. The cop quickly realizes the driver is not one of the robbery suspects. He sees a man with a wife and two small children. They are not a couple of young punks. Still, he persists. Why? "He asks to see the driver's license and registration. While locating the appropriate documents, the Black driver respectfully volunteers that he is legally carrying a handgun. The cop panics; is it the image of a Black man with a gun? He barks out conflicting orders and then shoots the man to death, in front of his family. Why? "Is it because the cop is an insensitive racist? Maybe he wasn't trained or taught any better? Perhaps he lived a completely different life in a completely different world than that of the Black man. In this cop's world, we are all Black men, potential criminals, and people to be watched, people to be feared?[Mark M. Bello}100,,

My Black Side
I think the police need to take into consideration that when you come into a neighborhood of any ethnicity, that neighborhood should be treated the same as the neighborhood that you live in. People should not be spoken down to because they came from Vietnam, because they are poor, because they do not have sidewalks, or because it happened to come from a country that has camels; that should not figure into how they are treated.

Professionalism is not in seeing the person but in seeing their problem as important. I do not care if you are Black or White or whatever you are; when people call 911 they need the police. That is why Black cell phones and White cell phones both have 911 on them. However, if you feel compelled to treat me differently because I'm Black, then you do not need to be in Law Enforcement.

No matter the ethnicity of the person dealt with, nobody wants to be arrested. If the subject of the investigation is already angry and feels like they are being treated unfairly and then you speak down to them and exacerbate the situation, how could it not be a confrontational and potentially violent encounter? Sovereign citizens are far more volatile than most Black people and more dangerous, yet still they seem to be arrested, incarcerated and have fewer violent encounters with the police than Black people.

My Blue Side

At my former department, it is called Diversity Training. I think it was useful. I think it corrected a lot of vocabulary; a lot of profanity, a lot of derogatory terms were brought to light. With the modernization of Departments and the integration of more women, minorities, gays and other inclusions that are not male White exclusively, different terms and different methodologies of interacting became necessary.

If we could not make it out of the locker room without calling each other names, then I agree that our chances and likelihood of being effective in the community and not being offensive were diminishing. In addition to cultural changes, with people from other countries, we had to get rid of as many racist and provocative terms as we could while maintaining professional candor.

Professional language does not override personal choice nor personal prejudices but it does teach you to keep them to yourselves until you get home and get your first beer.

7.10
What About Substance Abuse Amongst LEOs?

"One out of four police officers on the street
has an alcohol or drug abuse issue[101]."

My Black Side

I do not really have a Black side on this issue, as I do not feel substance Abuse has any place in Law Enforcement. Unlike the regular junkie, this junkie carries a badge and a gun. I personally think Substance Abuse amongst Law Enforcement officers is tantamount to corruption because it leads to lies and other behaviors so that the chemically dependent cop does not lose their job. What manner of officer, knowing what happens to the mental faculties (of unarmed people with no responsibilities), would undertake to walk the beat on drugs or drunk?

My Blue Side

My blue side agrees; perhaps this feeling is why I was not as popular as I would have liked to have been in my Law Enforcement career.

As a recruit, I soon fell prey to the typical Blue Lies, that everyone internally punished, was screwed and victimized by the Administration. The Blue Fog© disappeared from my eyes in one instant.

A Code 5000 went out, officer in distress. A fellow officer needed help; I went. The officer sustained several bullet wounds and gave a description of his assailants. The description was three Black guys, in all Black driving a blue Honda. They all allegedly wore masks, but were identified as Black by hands, and speech patterns.

Firstly, I went to the area. In the unmarked car, I intended to lay in wait for the cop shooters and return the favor. Then a second bolo (Be On The Lookout) went out with a different vehicle description, and number of suspects.

I went to the hospital to see my friend. I walked into his room, glad to see my friend still alive. We spoke, and then I asked him what happened. His story was safe with me, I was there to help.

He called me by my first name and began his story. He was on a particular side of town, and then these guys ran up on him and pointed guns at him. They demanded his car, and when he refused, they shot him. I delved further; I needed to know more about them, to hunt them down. Describe their clothes I asked, hoping for gang graffiti.

Then the details changed again. Three Asian or White boys was the new description. I looked at him, lying in the bed in the gown, and tubes. I asked him bluntly, because at this point his story was suspect. The likelihood of three White or Asian guys being in the location he described was unlikely. It was even less likely for them to go into this neighborhood and start trouble; it was far too dangerous.

As I pressed, he showed signs of deceit and anxiety. Whatever happened, this was not a robbery. My Black friend made me realize the dangers of blindly assuming that cops tell the truth, to other cops all the time. Here I was, like many in the department, ready to draw blood to avenge this lying fool, and the blood we were to draw was innocent.

Sometime later, my suspicions were confirmed, the entire car-jacking was a lie. I withdrew from my friend entirely. I was not about to go down that road again. I learned of the truth of my friend's drug and social problems, just before I went to his house and arrested him on other charges. It saddened me; deeply, to have to handcuff a friend. He looked lost, he looked helpless -- but he was a lying, deceitful, dangerous cop. He called down the thunder to cover his lifestyle.

Having worked in Vice for many years, I was not surprised or angry that he lied to cover his behavior, but this lie violated our trust and had the circling sharks out looking to avenge a wrong that never happened.

My issue was not with his addiction, that is a behavior problem; and frankly, I do not agree the characterization as a disease is accurate. People catch or contract diseases. Oxford defines a disease as, "*A disorder of structure or function in a human, animal, or plant, especially one that produces specific signs or symptoms or that affects a specific location and is not simply a direct result of physical injury...*" A disorder of structure implies internal flaw or dysfunction; perhaps *infection* would be a better diagnosis. Drug addicts cannot get addicted if they do not ingest drugs. Predisposition is scientific, but even crack-babies do not have a disease, it is a birth defect or complication. 20 years of training, enforcement, and teaching certification, and I never met a junkie that 'contracted' their addiction. This is an industry-imposed diagnosis, a result of The Corporate Practice of Medicine. By declaring substance abuse and addiction a disease, they can increase their financial bottom line. The FDA has rules regarding permissible treatment of diseases, and pharmaceuticals are a first tier treatment. In other words, *big pharma* gets insurance and Medicare to pay for substance abuse treatment, because if its disease designation. Incidentally, this was one to the things Obama care originally intent to remedy prior to the filibuster.

I take issue with my lying friends and all cops that undertake substance abuse; what were you thinking? When was the last time you saw someone get on TV and tell us how wonderful an addiction made their lives, there are no happy, "My life is so much better!" drug stories. So why start? If, as all cops do; you find yourself stressed, seek help. I did sought help (not for chemical dependence); no shame here. If you are not ashamed to be a junkie, you cannot have as much pride as you pretend.

Do not go through a door with me on drugs, do not stand behind me with a loaded weapon on drugs, and heaven forbid do not point your weapon at any human being under the influence of an intoxicant: especially in the name of doing police work, neither Black nor White Americans need junkie cops.

7.11
The Human Aspect From Both Sides?

"We all have inherent biases; All of us. The problem occurs when police officers or community members allow those biases to affect the choices they make as they do their job or have interactions with others[Bobby F Kimbrough]."

❦

My Black Side

There are no words to describe the duplicity of how it feels to be a Black cop sometimes having to stomach some of the ignorance and racism. A particular issue I had was when a suspect (Black in this case) called the White cop a Nigger, and the cop replied, "Look at me I am the wrong color." I got loud and indignant with the officer but the damage was done, the truth was out. To this officer, Nigger meant Black skin, which meant to him I too was a Nigger. I never went and filed formal complaints or anything like that, I invited them outside to formally discuss the implication. He declined the invitation.

I personally never witnessed any overt racism, in my 20 plus years. I saw other things. As stated previously, I spent most of my career working in small undercover teams, composed of former patrol officers. There were pockets of clichés, off-color jokes, and maybe even some laughter at inappropriate jokes; but the officers in my decorated squads never crossed the line in my presence.

I got tired of the officers saying things like, 'What did you expect?' Or 'The usual suspects' or 'Well, that is the ghetto for you'...etc when the suspects were Black. What purpose did it serve to defend the 'honor' of a criminal, just because he was Black? Perhaps I should have made more trailer park or deliverance references.

Actually, it was embarrassing to me, and I took pride in locking up suspects of any color. It made me feel good when I looked at the victims who looked like me, and was able to help remove a stain from their lives or community. My Blackness has no fraternity with offenders who brutalize, terrorize, and victimize people that look like me. Why should Blacks wait for White officers to come to the aid of Black communities?

Moreover, I tire of society seeing my face but associating me with criminal behaviors commonly ascribed to Blacks suspects. The same people that say, 'Do not lump us all together,' and 'I never owned slaves,' to then I say do not lump all Blacks together, I never robbed anyone.

I believe Black victim's lives matter; to me they matter more than the lives of any offender. I believe too many protests and public outcries stem from events unworthy of redressing. I believe too many decent Black people are accosted by Black people, to the deafening silence of no redress. How can innocent Black lives not matter? Why aren't Black people protesting other Black people when they victimize their own?

As in the case of Mr. Floyd; overt indifference and callousness by the police should be decried and disdained. However, the same vehemence against the police shown, in Mr. Floyd's wrongful and shameful death, should be shown for all the Mr. and Mrs. John Doe's murdered by Black suspects. When Black suspects murder Black victims; should Blacks not then riot, march in front of their house, and if need be burn their house to the ground? If not; if Blacks are not outraged, internally by murdered Black people; why hold White cops to the standard?

The police should protect and serve and stop being racial about it; is the current pervasive attitude amongst many Blacks, but the cops do not always bring the racism to the table.

My Blue Side

Might makes right, when in fear right takes flight is a saying I grew up with. I believe that all people, of color or not had better believe that the rage that lies within them also lies within cops.

I believe deep down in my blue heart, that if you thought what happened to Mr. George Floyd incensed you: if this one egregious incident provoked you to anger, then you understand a little of what cops feel daily, seeing all the victimization they witness.

Policing; true blue policing occurs amongst a particular personality type. Cops have more in common with soldiers that any other profession. Do you realize that most cops do not possess the medical knowledge to stave off the death of an offender they shoot; Cops are trained to shoot to kill, this is the reason they are issued dozens of bullets.

When speaking to children you use small words. Cops command respect, not because they are wonderful people, it is because it is necessary for their work. In terms of *The Establishment,* someone has to pick the cotton. In the case of cops, someone has to protect the cotton. Might makes right, when it comes time to fight, more accurately reflects cop-think.

The cop is not there to fight fair, to give a sporting chance, or in fact consider the importance of your life. That consideration is up to you. Your life should be more important to you than to anyone else. Therefore, if your life is valuable, protect it and shy away from needless encounters with people that carry 30 or more Hydro-shot bullets designed to mushroom to max diameter to prevent over penetration as they simultaneously cause lethal damage within a body; when fired.

To the officer, the law-abiding person is a person, the offender is <u>not</u>. The officer may be heard saying Sir or Ma'am, to an offending scumbag, but that is to maintain appearances to the public; it is unequivocally not a sign of respect, interest, compassion, or concern.

Under-grad is 4 years, Medical school is 4 years, and then 4 years of residency learning to save lives. Police Academy is 6th months max, learning to protect or take lives. Cops look upon the worst society does to each other and are supposed to dole out dispassionate enforcement every day; this cannot be done. Passion moves most cops to action in the first place. Training helps a great deal, but a unique experience makes the police officer a unique individual.

In his article, New Police Shooting Stats Show Law Enforcement Is Not the Enemy, Bernard Kerik writes, "So, here's the 2018 breakdown of the 995 people shot and killed by the police. Out of the total people shot by Law Enforcement Officers in 2018;

- 403 White
- 210 Black
- 148 Hispanic
- 38 classified as other
- 199 were classified as unknown (not sure what unknown people are)

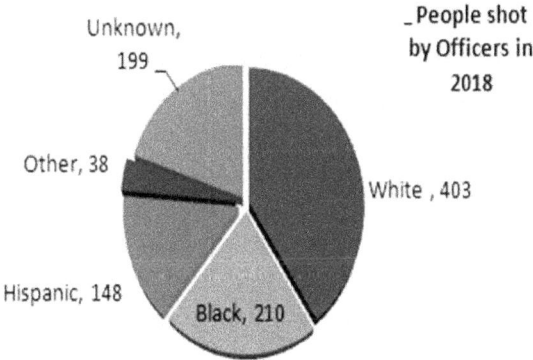

[Fig 21]

Out of that 995, 47 people were unarmed people shot by officers in 2018;

- 23 White
- 17 Black
- 5 Hispanic
- 2 were unknown[102]."

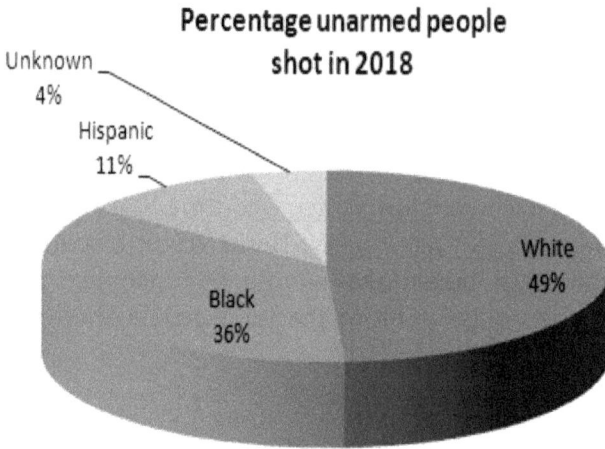

Percentage unarmed people shot in 2018

Unknown 4%

Hispanic 11%

White 49%

Black 36%

[Fig 22]

Note; numerically, more unarmed Whites were shot by the police in 2018, than any other group. Why is the media not covering this?

I asked a White officer why when White cops shoot White people it is not really a big story. He replied, "When a Black is shot by a White, the media spins it and tries to make a media-spun narrative. People argue that it was too harsh when the victim is Black. When the victim is White however, White people, he said, just look at the dead offender and ask, 'What the *uck did you think was going to happen?' I take from this wisdom, that White privilege has a cost, it is an agreed upon ecosystem: maintained at all cost indicated in the Letters of Succession.

7.12
Is there a Presumption
of Innocence?

"I don't think the law exists to arrive at the truth. If it did, we wouldn't have exclusionary rules, we wouldn't have presumptions of innocence, we wouldn't have proof beyond reasonable doubt. There's an enormous difference between the role of truth in law and the role of truth in science. In law, truth is one among many goals{Alan Dershowitz} "

My Black Side

Again, my observation is limited when it comes to racist cops; I have not had the misfortune to witness it firsthand. It is hard to call a Klansman a racist when he apprehends a bank robber. He did not make the African American suspect rob the bank. Should he then release the Black suspect, and lie in wait for a White one? This is not equality; it is a lack of common sense. I have seen White officers let Black suspects go for all manner of crimes. I have also seen them lock Blacks up for silly little issues. Ignorant? Yes, but is that racism?

It is difficult to ascribe all the police misbehavior to just racism. Quotas account for much questionable policing. The illegal quota system enacted by many departments under the code names NIBRS[103], COMPSTAT[104], and other Federal methods to lie about statistics and arrests also accounts for victimization. For example, if a guy robs a Convalescent Home, and its #25 residents, NIBRS lists that as #1 robbery to keep the numbers down. This lie helps to ensure people sleep better in their beds at night; not because they are safe, but because the Federal Government says they are safe.

You cannot have it both ways. If you want to use statistics (skewed as they are) to disprove the racism narrative, then they should be acceptable to prove it exists. The National Exoneration Registry[105] provides some damming but nebulous information, as does The Equal Justice Initiative[106].

- <u>Exonerations in 2018</u>, added 151 exonerated people last National Registry, bringing the total number nationwide since 1989 to 2373 exonerations.
- Official misconduct was the cause of the exoneration in at least 107 cases.
- Official misconduct and perjury/false accusation were the leading factors contributing to wrongful homicide convictions - 79% of which involved police and/or prosecutorial misconduct and 77% (52 cases) of which involved perjury or false accusation.

WRONGFUL CONVICTIONS

NATIONAL STATISTICS

2,471+
EXONERATIONS IN
THE U.S. SINCE 1989

21,725+
TOTAL YEARS
LOST IN PRISON

[Fig 23a[107]]

RACE OF EXONEREE

■ BLACK	49%
CAUCASIAN	37%
■ HISPANIC	12%
OTHER	2%

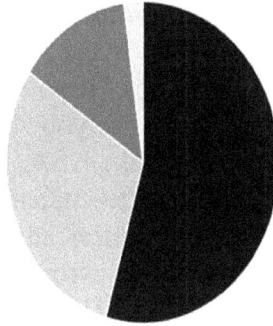

CONTRIBUTING FACTORS

MISTAKEN IDENTIFICATION	28%
FALSE CONFESSION	12%
FORENSIC SCIENCE PROBLEMS	23%
PERJURY/FALSE ACCUSATION	58%
OFFICIAL MISCONDUCT	54%

[Fig 23b]

This makes me angry; *The Establishment* has many flaws. There are so many things wrong with [Figs 23a & b], it breaks my heart as a Black cop first and then as a Black man. Yes the numbers show that only 54% of the overturned cases were caused by police corruption, but I guarantee this number is not correct; it is too low. Cops and prosecutors, who lie, also allow perjury and other types of misconduct this accounted for an additional 58%. But why do it in the first place? With all the bonafide criminals in the world, why waste time and money on lies and impropriety? There is obviously something going on for this many garbage cases to result in convictions. Regardless of whether we want to admit it or not, the statistics show that Blacks lead in the category of victimization as well.

What then is freedom for? Monkeys at the zoos do not find themselves surrounded by bars, they are surrounded by water. The water compels them to stay in the space, because they cannot swim. Is this freedom however? The lack of a noose does not equal freedom.

Another problem outcropping from the issue of police misconduct is the idiotic policy of hiring cops fired from other agencies. If you are not qualified to be a cop in one city, and they fire you should never be able to be a cop again anywhere in the USA.

According to statistics, "African Americans are only 13% of the American population but are majority of innocent defendants wrongfully convicted of crimes and later exonerated. They constitute 47% of the 1,900 exonerations listed in the National Registry of Exonerations (as of October 2016), and the great majority of more than 1,800 additional innocent defendants who were framed and convicted of crimes in 15 large-scale police scandals and later cleared in 'group exonerations[108]'."

I believe cases exonerated like these cases support the crop-numbers© theory. Bad cases exonerated like these cases occur because the Criminal Justice System ignores facts and presumes dirty cops to be innocent. I would not say this is a result of racism, but the fact is these things seem to occur less when their victims are White. Amazingly, enough of these cases spend little time in the news and there is little public outrage. These Black lives matter too. Death is not the only way to ruin lives; life sentences ruin lives and families.

My Blue Side

Yes, cops desire to arrest only the guilty, but this utopia will never exist. The main reason this utopia cannot exist is that people; victims lie. Greed, anger, racism, bias, and jealousy in my opinion are the main causes of false arrests.

The final issue of guilt determination is NOT THE PREVIEW OF THE OFFICER ON THE STREET. But the officer on the street operates both by the authority and the mandate to drag anyone into court that has been reported, observed, or in the cop's opinion, committed a crime.

The authority and the mandate to drag anyone into court are so important to *The Establishment* there exists laws against violating them. In other words, you may be innocent, but we are going to ask the judge. How you get there is up to you, but you are going. This is where the need for/use of force arises.

The presumption of innocence is a legalistic, courtroom rhetoric, not a mandate or policy for the police. The sheer fact that cops are arresting a person means the police no longer presume them to be innocent. No cop slaps cuffs on people they do not believe are guilty of some infraction; perhaps that is why many of them use the phrase, "You are under arrest for..."

Authority and Mandate are the backbone of the Criminal Justice System, not justice. Sadly, *The Establishment* abused, poisoned, and warped authority and mandates so much so that Blacks have little regard or respect for these sacred symbols of the Criminal Justice System.

The modern cop finds themselves blamed for systemic abuses they personally did not commit, yet have to face the brunt of disdain. Law Enforcement has been both myopic and slothful in its response to the problem of Excessive Force. Law Enforcement has reached a turning point; it now has to look at what both *The Establishment* and the society wants from it. The two interests are slowly divesting.

Less and less frequently, you will find officers who think it ok to deny Black children entry into the schools, but society had to change the law first. Modern police officers are more educated, more diverse, and more conscientious.

Make no mistake, cops deal with millions of people, some happy and some not so much. The police are well aware of both the danger and the resistance they face daily, #48 cops were feloniously killed in 2019[109], #46 killed in 2020 and the #50 killed in 2021[110]. No cop is going to rush to a stranger's aid, yet not defend themselves when attacked.

In a society of violence, the language spoken and understood is violence. Drawn from a violent culture, watching violent TV all day and them facing violence all night, cops become the Close Caption of the society. As resistance and hatred for cops expands so will the violence from the cops. The Mandates will be upheld; or society, broken as it is, will fall.

This is why the 60's was such a tumultuous time in America. Someone Black realized that violence was not the answer; Economic Revolution would prove to be more effective and more devastating than bullets ever could; they killed them.

In 2021, society still endures violence by Blacks, but *The Establishment* devised a way to never again let the concern from Black empowerment, and economic stability rear their ugly head.

7.13

Why Couldn't They Shoot The Gun Out Of Their Hands Or Shoot Them In The Knee?

"Nothing is impossible to kill. It's just that sometimes after You kill something you have to keep shooting it until it stops Moving [Mira Grant]111 ."

My Black Side

I believe there are no quarterback slides with the police, they do not serve the people; they serve *The Establishment*. The police are not here to give hook ups and slaps on the wrist. There MUST be a clear accounting of personal actions. The Laws are written down, there is no gray area. It is sheer foolishness to expect concession from the police. What benefit is that to society? What incentive does a cop have to let anyone slide?

The argument that they let White people slide is also stupid, why take the chance that they may let you slide. Maybe the officer lets Black people slide too, but is that a legal standard we should look for? Should we be more concerned with whether they let the White people go, or with avoiding the interaction with cops all together? Despite Media coverage, someone is putting White people in jail and shooting them?

Whether or not the police hooked up the White boy is none of your business; that was a decision based on the situation. Race may well have played a role in the decision. If we are playing the hook-up game, do not people of like races hook each other up when possible? If Black people play the hook-up game and only Black cops hook-up Black people: we are in trouble.

Black people; If the only complaint is that White people do it all the time and get away with it; that is not a complaint; it is a CLUE. If you know *The Establishment* has policies preferential to White, then avoid *The Establishment.* Nevertheless, if you just cannot keep your hands to yourself or live without weed - play at your own risk. We discussed the importance of White women to *The Establishment's* economy; even the White women are not being protected. **What does this mean for African-American'ts in America? The answer should be obvious.**

- "Judge said a teen from a 'good family' should not be tried as an adult in sexual assault[112]"
- "No prison for Colorado college student who 'raped a helpless young woman'[113]"

My Blue Side

The reason I do not address actual shooting cases is that my Black side agrees with my blue side 100 percent on this issue. **A good or bad shooting DOES NOT DEPEND ON RACE.**

Since 2015, the Washington Post reports there have been many officer-involved shootings, approximately 5000[114]. Prudence demands that all of the shootings be questioned, and many of them were questionable. We are going to tackle this issue more in-depth in the Use of Force portion but for now, let us look at the question. "Why couldn't they shoot the gun out of their hands or shoot them in the knee?" is probably the most common, less-intuitive question I answer. But; if you don't know, you don't know.

I wanted to deal with this topic in the Use of Force section, but now will do just as well. Although I have personally fired thousands of shots, and logged hundreds of hours on the gun range both in Law Enforcement and the Armed Forces; I am no expert.

Many officers can out draw me, and out shoot me. However, studies over decades prove that under stress shooters that perform well in non-stressful situations have a performance decline greater than those of average yet consistent shooters.

The explanation stems from several stress related fear response factors. According to science, as a result of fear in humans;

- Breathing rate increases (often shallow short breaths)
- Heart rate also increases
- Peripheral blood vessels constrict
- Blood vessels around vital organs receive extra blood
- Muscles receive additional blood
- Muscles constrict
- Glucose spikes
- Palms sweat
- Tunnel vision
- Adrenal activity
- Auditory exclusion
- Modification of fine motor skills

Marksmanship (shooting properly) requires practice. The shooter must do all 5 of the following for each individual round that leaves the chamber;

1. Control the weapon
2. Acquire a target (which includes cognizance of distance to target range of weapon, performance characteristics of ammunition used, terrain, and backdrop)
3. Control their breathing
4. Control their trigger pressure
5. Maintain aim

Not only must these steps occur, but they must occur in the interval between recognition of danger and the amount of reaction time available. In other words, an officer must run this checklist in their mind prior to drawing their weapon, simultaneous to the recognition and reaction of a threat.

A synthesis of this data, research, studies, SWAT School, and my personal experience indicates that the officers that function best under stress are those that handle the responses to fear the best (Control the #12 fear responses, in order to manage the #5 marksmanship issues.).

Over the thousands of felony drug arrests, and the thousands of encounters with armed or resistive suspects, I believe the reason my experiences are different is because I worked on a team and we had better training and equipment.

The odds of suspects attacking 12 armed officers are low, if existent. However, the odds of suspects attacking single officers, or female officers are exponentially greater. If you add additional situations, nighttime, interstate, hostile neighborhood etc, the numbers increase. We did far more dangerous things, more frequently than most, but that is what the training and equipment was for, to give us the edge. We did not expect cops without our tools to do our job. In addition, COPS DO NOT SHOOT TO WOUND OR INJURE, EVER. To reiterate my friend's words of White wisdom, "What the #*ck did you think was going to happen?"

Julia Jacobo[115] writes an article about the concept of shooting to wound.

- Police are trained to stop dangerous, life-threatening or murderous behavior
- Anytime a firearm is discharged, it's considered deadly force
- Shooting to injure or maim someone wouldn't stop an aggressive subject, and officers are trying to stop the threat to their life, or the life of their partner or a citizen
- If someone's life is in jeopardy, shooting to maim or injure will have little effect on the actions of the individual who is trying to kill
- If an officer aims at anything other than the torso area, the odds that he or she will miss increase greatly
- Officers are trained to shoot with the understanding that one shot may not stop an aggressive subject
- There are only two ways to shut down the human body using deadly force. The first is loss of blood, and the other is a shot to the central nervous system. Police officers are trained to shoot at center mass, in the torso area
- Even if an officer shoots [someone] with a lethal firearm, it may not stop a person
- When there is a threat to life right now, or serious bodily injury, deadly force is the appropriate response

This Black officer wants to reiterate that people of all races do not seem to understand. COPS ONLY SHOOT TO KILL; this is why we have both Lethal and Less Than Lethal Options. When cops shoot, we are saying to society that deadly force is necessary, in this situation. We will look at this decision making process in the Tactics and Training portion. For now, we discuss only the justified shootings. There are only two criteria; Shooting justified or unjustified.

Oh yeah, and warning shots are both prohibited by most departments, and ill advised; bullets come back down, although, some dimwitted suggestion to revive warning shots have resurfaced. I think the best warning shot is the one the codefendant observes pierce his partner's body. Otherwise, if shooting suspects is not ending the behavior it stands to reason the warning shot will not either.

I spoke to a Project Management Professional recently. He is always asking me questions about tactics and we discuss current events frequently. He is a Black professional, member of a Greek Letter Organization, and I have had the pleasure of training him in the use of firearms. He has put hundreds of rounds down range during our sessions, and one day he asked that fateful question about shooting in the knee or the arm. Recently he attended enhanced pistol training. I asked him what he thought of his question now. He replied that it was unrealistic to expect anyone to really do that or be able to shoot in the knee or the arm, even after seeing me and the other instructor shoot. He added, "That by the time the police shoot they are just, trying to stop the guy, you can't stop him unless you hit something vital."

He continued further to add that he thinks that the defunding the police is a bad idea; he says they are 'needed'. He continued "I ain't going out there, don't call me. It is different if they come to my house, but to go out there and deal with all the things y'all have to see and deal with day after day, I don't see how y'all do it."

He did however ask me the important question; how often I practiced shooting. I told him, and then added that most officers are only mandated to shoot once or twice annually. He was surprised. I added that the mission of the LEO professional is the preservation of life, lethal force is a tool to enable that the mission. Focusing on the shooting aspect changes the mission of the department to a more Military application. I did agree with the reply, "Well when y'all do shoot you need to do a better job. People expect officers to be better shots and to have the proper amount of training."

7.14
I am a trained officer of the Law

"When you have police officers who abuse citizens, you erode public confidence in law enforcement. That makes the job of good police officers unsafe{Mary Frances Berry}"

My Black Side

I was fortunate to live in a Metropolitan area with a Metropolitan Police Department. Not all departments have a six-month academy, six-month probationary period on boarding process. In addition, there is the annual 40hrs of additional training annually (for larger and C.A.L.E.A. Certified[116] agencies).

In all of that, some useless individuals slip through the cracks. Over my tenure, I saw criminal cops, wife beater cops, drug dealing, and using cops, pedophile cops, rapist cops, cowardly cops, ultra-liberal and conservative cops, anarchist cops, and gay cops. We all got the same training. The output of the officer is different in each case.

I was not a proponent of Diversity Training and Sensitivity Training, but it has a purpose. Mary Frances Berry reminds us that mistreatment of the citizens by the police leads to an unsafe environment; for everyone.

Police are some of the most highly trained professionals in the world, but along with pride and accomplishment comes responsibility. Only an Medical Doctor-MD can pronounce a person dead, but the PD can make one dead. The training does not make better people, but it should turn people into professionals.

My Blue Side

I believe that sensitivity has a place. I believe the place for sensitivity is in framing the law and later in extolling sentencing. In the enforcement of the law, there is no room for sensitivity. Enforcement (implementation, application, execution, administration) of the law allows for discretion, but this is not the same as sensitivity. An arrest is a means to stop a problem or resolve an issue; it does not guarantee incarceration. Cops do not have time or the latitude to ignore criminality, because the result would be dire environmental influences; the recidivism rates are already high enough in America[117].

When officers receives a call for service, they must respond. If the call is bogus, false, racially motivated, or some other fraudulent motive, the responding officer has nothing to do with the information provided. Upon arrival, if the officer meets resistance (attitude, flight, physical force, and civil unrest) the officer is GOING TO CONTROL the situation. This is the main reason for the training; to train officers to endure, face, and confront those things in society that it is not equipped to handle. What makes the police great at this can sometimes create a deficit. Compassion has to stand aside for professionalism which might mean providing security at a KKK Rally, Pridefest, PETA gathering or a Mosque event.

Everyday cops are required to become vending machines, and the public thinks that they are supposed to just ooze goodness no matter how many times their heads are banged or struck by fire extinguishers. However, a cop is just a professional human, they have limits. If they did not have limits, they truly would be robot gunslingers. Cops however are under no obligation to make the public feel good. How many crave the presence of the surgeon? yet we do not revile them as they hack away at our bodies.

Citizens need to realize that when they call the police, the same EMS dispatchers answer the phone. Why is it then that we do not see people taking over from firefighters, throwing bottles and rocks at EMS or providing First Responder services? Why is it that the police, who have more authority than Fire and EMS combined, are questioned and challenged daily? I agree with my White friend, when it comes to some interactions with the police the question should be, "What the *#ck did you think was going to happen?"

If and when officers are shown to be excessively rough, vulgar, unprofessional, and in some cases (like placing a car full of women, and a child on the ground) plainly asinine, that officer should wake up the next day, unemployed, sued, and/or on the way to jail. In their hand should be a letter on department letterhead, signed by the Mayor, the Chief and the DA. The letter need only have two phrases,

- Dear ex-officer
- "What the *#ck did you think was going to happen?"

Sometimes amidst disciples, there are Judases, but do we throw away all the good the others do because of a Judas? Bad people slip into Law Enforcement, and disciples sometimes lose their way when they get into the profession. The smell of these barbarous cowards permeates the air sometimes, but the numbers of these aberrations are not very high despite media coverage.

Since 2007, police officers fatally shoot approximately 1000 people nationwide annually[118]. In order for the amount of corruption alleged to be true, should there not be stories of more than 2.78 police involved shootings per day?

7.15
Trained Beyond Fear
And The Shouts

"Our police force was not created to serve Black
Americans; it was created to police Black Americans
and serve White Americans[Ijeoma Oluo] 119 ,"

My Black Side

Blacks were not citizens or property owners for a
long time in America; this is true. Community Policing
aimed to stem the tide of animosity between the races over
the last 20 years. While there has been vast improvement,
by and large, the tension still exists between the power
structure and the powerless. What the police forget
sometimes because most of them try to make the country
better, is that police are also pawns of *The Establishment*.

I watched an interesting documentary recently about
racism and equal pay during the 60's in America. In this
clip, many celebrities joined to say that equal pay for equal
work only made sense. Among these people we would
now brand as liberals was Charlton Heston. Heston, best
known for his roles in the films Ben-Hur and Moses, went
on later to champion the NRA and read scriptures on TBN.
Does this make him a racist? Cannot Blacks apply for gun
permits? It is not the individual that is always the problem?
The problem in this country is always deeper than James E
Ray, Byron De La Beckwith, Timothy Mcvey, David
Koresh, and Talmadge Hayer: after all there was a Lee
Harvey Oswald was there not?

I often think cops use generic stereotypical
language towards people of lesser means, many of which
happen to be Black. I do not think there is a concerted
effort by the police to belittle Black people. I do however
think that *The Establishment* never misses an opportunity to

overlook Civil Rights violations if it suits their fancy. Too often officers that cross the line blatantly receive no sanction. However, I cannot say that this is always racism, to me it seems often to be the callous, arrogant Badge-side manner© of the enforcers of the law.

My Blue Side

The police have training, which makes them able to overlook their humanity and stand in the face of fear. I think that oftentimes this seemingly dispassionate mannerism is just badge-side manner©. I once received a call at a strip joint. Upon arrival, the victim of the assault ran out to the lobby and grabbed me in a hug. Although she was a female seeking support, I was in uniform, and she in a manner of speaking was too. As nubile as she was, she instantly became annoying the moment she opened her mouth. Nothing but gibberish and slang rang forth, nothing in the way of useful facts. I asked twice more what the problem was, which excited her further, into yet another garbled spiel. I could not calm her down; I do not know if she spoke my language either. I stepped back away from her, and said calmly to another employee, "Is there an interpreter here I don't speak stupid." Her friend the interpreter stepped in and helped, she said something we both understood, she grabbed the naked girl, cupped her face and said sternly, "Calm the *#ck down he is trying to help you." It worked. For the record, I was the only Black person there with the employees.

I was not trying to be a jerk. She rendered me and my authority powerless to help her because she refused to communicate. Some guy slapped her over a lap-dance. Hardly a volatile situation, but she was upset. I was not insensitive, but she made the situation impossible.

In another example, a patron ran up to me while I was walking my beat. He informed me that in the alley a White guy was dragging a White girl into the alley by her neck. I walked around the corner, and saw the spectacle. The guy was indeed dragging the girl. I calmly told him to let her go, he said no. At this point, the game changed, my badge-side manner did not. He was not going to drag her much further; no matter what I had to do to stop him from hurting her further.

I continued to close the distance calmly. I could see his hands, but she was not out of danger yet. Again, I told him to let her go, as she writhed trying to free herself, he refused a second time. There was no third time. I was close enough. As he opened his mouth to speak, I opted to stop the kidnapping by punching him at the base of his throat, right below the tie knot. He let her go. As he gasped for air, she turned around and tried to assist him. As I pulled her to safety, she yelled at me, "Not him, that's my boyfriend, it is the other guy! He was trying to stop me from fighting the guy." She pointed down the alley.

On Monday, the news, if the media plays the event, it would report that *a cop abused a citizen*; correct? The fact that I acted on good information, and they both had three opportunities to fix the problem, and chose not to do so, does not figure into the equation: all because it all worked out. But what if it did not work out, and he was kidnapping and trying to rape her or kill her: were the actions justified then? **Training modifies behaviors, and actions; it does not dictate the situation**.

Despite all the training, it only takes a second to make a mistake, shoot the wrong person, or the right person for the wrong reason. Split-decisions are often suspicious, but it does not mean the motivation is racial. Two guys meet at a stop sign, and get into an argument over the right-of-way. The Black guy shoots first and misses, the White guy kills him. Which one of these two men was a racist? Ask the Tennessee Department that the men served, they were both officers; the White guy off-duty the Black guy undercover.

8.0

How to

Determine

Excessive

Force

"Force rules the world-not opinion; but it is opinion that makes use of force[Blaise Pascal]120 ."

8.1
Why Force is Necessary

"The job of a cop is to invest God's fear in human not to invest human's fear in God{Sir P.S. Jagadeesh Kumar} ."

⤳

Let us understand that every arrest requires the use of force. Unless a person surrenders themselves into the officer or warrants divisions; the phrase used to describe all successful arrests is *Taken into Custody*. Anyone taken into custody has encountered a modicum of force from a Law enforcement professional.

The issue before us rightly so is the Excessive use of force. Although this determination is somewhat subjective, there is a matrix and formula available to aid in the determination.

When looking at [FIG 24], I am reminded of the boilerplate language formerly used at any department on Use of Force reports turned in after a Use of Force incident. 'I used only that force necessary to affect the arrest.' This line was the only narrative provided, but there was other information on the form. Officers had to divulge, name, age, race, type of legal interaction leading to the Use of Force, the level or resistance, and the level of force used.

I deeply feel that my uses of force were all justified, and they range from profanity to the use of lethal force. I also deeply feel that TRAINING made all the difference in the world to my responses. At one such Use of Force review, the reviewers questioned why I used lethal force on a man who had threatened people with a knife and already stabbed one person in the neck, I replied, "It was necessary." When they asked was I afraid, I honestly replied, "No." Then why did you shoot, they replied? Because he was trying to stab me and the other officer, policy does not requires me to be afraid. You sent thousands of dollars training me to handle these situations; I am glad I was just there to help, and no one else got hurt.

The next two paragraphs are imperative for the reader to understand. I shot this individual while retreating, and pushing another officer out of the way as we attempted to evade the blade and travel backwards down stairs. The assailant was able to snatch my holster off my belt; I had to move to let him fall past me after the third shot. Two shots struck him in the sternum area (center mass - the region trained to aim for), the third shot randomly, but savagely struck him mid thigh shattering his thighbone; the only reason he fell to the ground. After falling, I assisted (very reluctantly) in demonstrating proper application of first aid. The attending officer was too gentle in his triage, when stopping blood via tourniquet requires firmness is necessary.

Notice I never revealed the race of the assailant; it never mattered much past making sure we had the correct suspect. Not only does race not matter, if you even cared or wondered about it people like you are the problem, if I was justified to use lethal force, race does not matter. Also unimportant is the issue of whether I hated a certain type of people, prior to the incident.

The truth be told, I have a severe disdain, for people like him. During the review, I told them I believe the Render First-Aid portion of the policy was, "If I didn't want him dead I would not have shot him," was my response. I was not shooting him, because I wanted to arrest him, I planned to stop this killer - by killing him. Would I have responded differently to the first aid, had I been alone? Probably, but not out of malice, I would have never given him the chance to get as close as he did were I alone. Lethal force was not the plan, less than lethal options were employed first to attempt to apprehend the suspect. The scene supervisor even put himself in harm's way (trusting me to make the difference) to try a very risky less than lethal option. I would have never tried less then lethal were I alone; Black-belt in Karate or not. There is a simple logic to a fight, fight to win, or not at all. I do not engage a suspect with the intention of fighting fairly, or using equally amounts of force; THE OFFICER MUST ALWAYS USE MORE, OTHERWISE A STALEMATE ENSUES.

What bothered me after the shooting was tactics. The morality of the event never baffled me, he needed to be stopped, therefore the shooting was not malicious but the textbook definite of tactical, and professional. This may seem cold, but logically is the best way to respond to a tactical event.

I was dismayed for a long time after the shooting because I am a competent shooter, but yet I fired wild (not at intended target) within 10 feet

- I ran the scenario in my mind for several days, trying to imagine where I went wrong
- I had the gunsmith check my sights (not that shooters rely on them at that distance)
- What confused me, was the shooting position 'Elbow over holster' all but ensured a level horizontal shot. Two bullets were within a quarter's diameter from each other but the third was not even on the mid section

Why did this plague me if it was not second guessing morality? because of all my training. I was in this position because the Sgt and I agreed that if there needed to be lethal response he wanted me to do it again because of my training. I assisted in the execution of hundreds of High Risk and Arrest warrants, many of which I ran point gunner on. The fact that I could miss a target at this range was unnerving. That meant, I was incapable of protecting my team.

In this scenario, we were in an apartment complex, many officers, and of course apartments. Bullets flying around haphazard were unsafe for everyone. It was not until I ran through the scenario physically that it dawned on me what happened. Part of my training involved SWAT School, and several of the team supervisors and members were SWAT members, so we took time during the shift to train more than most at department.

I wager the only people that trained in our department more than my unit was SWAT. One such series of training involved foot placement and shooting on the move. The step-push method allowed the shooter to slide the lead foot behind them along the ground to search the terrain for obstacles of other assailants, and also to make a smooth traverse over the terrain, but reconnecting the feet. In this case, my training, over rode my training and the science kicked in.

As I rear-stepped and pushed to get away from the marauding stabber, the positional change (as well as using the left hand to push my fellow office out of the way) changed the angle of my muzzle from 180 degrees to -45 degrees not because of the foot movement, but because I was locked in elbow over holster.

In this case, it was not my savvy that saved lives, it was the training. The SWAT mentality (Special Weapons and Tactics allows for saving lives) was pervasive amongst my partners. They took pride in training to save lives; they did not train to be a 'Hit-squad'. I shot that man, to save lives; not his, the people it was my job to protect.

There may be some actions I question from my career; this was not one of them. This is why when people indict the police or ask the questions about shooting things out of hands etc, I have to focus on not getting irritated. I had to use lethal force on a person, nothing to be proud of, but a necessity in his case. How then do you even ask me with sincerity in your tone about the welfare of the stabber? How about you consider, how I might feel, how the person they stabbed might feel, or the other officer he tried, to stab, or the other officers that were placed in close quarters area with a knife wielding individual, and bullets flying. I wonder what you would do if that man tried to attack you or a loved one? The people we were protecting I do not even know their names, my sgt and the other officers did not know their names. The host of this shooting was the stabber; had he dropped the knife prior to stabbing victim number 1, and when we arrived there would have been no party.

Cops voluntarily serve in a profession which by requisite makes them do and make decisions regular people do not, therefore they cannot be held to the same standards. Using force is one of the many things cops have to do that no one else does. Depriving people of their liberty is the source of the main contention between the police and the citizenry.

Requiring professionalism is one thing, expecting amiability and popularity towards those empowered to ruin people's buzz and their high is even less popular now than then the passed the Volstead Act.

8.2
The Use of Force Continuum

"Unfortunately, the media and our government officials have treated the death of an unarmed White teenager differently than they would have if this were a death of an unarmed Black teen. The hypocrisy that has been shown toward this is disconcerting. The issue should never be what the color of the victim is. The issue should be: Why was an unarmed teen gunned down in a situation where deadly force was not even justified? {Lincoln Anthony Blades}[121]"

To assert that 'cops are dirty' is to be illiterate and ignorant of the fact that from a society of laws where predators exist; cops have even more restrictive laws, which some opt to abuse and overlook. If society is not 'all bad' despite its proliferation of criminality, how can a statistically insignificant amount of police corruption indict an entire industry?

"The Patriot Post reports that DOJ's Bureau of Justice Statistics (BJS) shows" that in 2016, some 287,400 individuals were imprisoned for committing crimes while in possession of a firearm and 90% of those firearms were obtained illegally[122]." You can warn people all you want, those predisposed to abhorrent behavior eventually cross the lines. However, the only way for them to cross the lines, is that someone had to have drawn them in the first place.

The Department referenced in this chapter covers 630 square miles and hosts approximately 1300 officers. Many consider this a large department, in a progressive city. People argue that this jurisdiction is in the South and therefore biased, yet this jurisdiction integrated its lunch counters before the law required it be done[123].

I went to the internet and looked up a Use of Force Policy, with which I am familiar. These excerpts are examples of Use of Force Policies to show that every cop in this department has the same rules, training, and oversight.

This is a long technical chapter, but if media articles and citizens are going to protest, request defunding, and make unintelligent arguments against the Law Enforcement industry you should at least look at their infrastructure prior to rioting.

- **[Use of Force]** - The Department recognizes and respects the value and special integrity of each human life. When investing police employees with the lawful authority to use force to protect the public welfare, a careful balancing of all human interests is required]. We see that the department starts with two implicit disclaimers. Firstly, the authority to use force is lawful, yet at the same time, it requires intuition and balance in determining when to use force.

- [It is the policy of the Department that authorized employees shall use only force that is reasonably necessary to affect lawful objectives. Therefore, intentional misuse of the authority granted under this policy is grounds for disciplinary action up to and including those outlined in category A of established policy for Discipline and Corrective Action. Violation of this directive will only form the basis for departmental administrative sanction]. The department recognizes there will be transgressions of the policy, and the law, so it writes against these actions; warning the violator that they may face criminal, civil, and departmental sanctions.

- **[Definitions specific to Use of Force]**
  - Absolutely Necessary: All other options have been exhausted, unavailable, or are not feasible. {*Why include this unless you are trying to elucidate necessity*}
  - Active Aggression: Where the employee's attempt to gain lawful compliance has culminated in the perception of an attack, or the potential for such an

attack, on the employee or others. The employee makes the reasonable assessment that such actions by the subject would not result in serious bodily injury or death to the employee or others.

- Active Resistance: A subject whose non-compliance includes resistive movements or physical defiance.

- Aggravated Active Aggression: Where the employee's attempt to gain lawful compliance has culminated in the perception of an attack or the potential for such an attack on the employee or others. The employee makes the reasonable assessment that such actions by the subject could result in serious bodily injury or death to the employee or others.

- Authorized Weapons and Ammunition: Weapons and ammunition approved by the Chief of Police and the Training Division for which authorized employees receive departmentally approved safety and proficiency training.

- Conducted Energy Device (CED): A hand-held device that is designed to subdue persons and/or animals. The device uses a low dose electrical current to temporarily stun and immobilize.

- Deadly Force: Any use of force reasonably calculated to produce death or serious bodily injury.

- Defensive Force: Use of hands, feet, or any other defensive equipment to overcome violent resistance or to protect self or others from assault or injury.

- Excited Delirium: A state of extreme mental and physiological excitement, characterized by extreme agitation (including shouting and disruptive behavior), hyperthermia, excessive watering of the eyes, hostility, paranoia or panic, inappropriate nudity, exceptional strength and endurance without fatigue.

- Force-Continuum: Broad categories of force, in identifiable escalating/de-escalating stages of intensity, in response to a subject's action. They are commonly identified as official presence, verbal direction, soft empty-hand control, hand-held chemical spray/electronic immobilization device, hard empty-hand control, batons, and firearms. A subject's action may be defined in broad categories including full compliance to commands, verbal uncooperativeness, passive resistance, active resistance, active aggression, and aggravated active aggression (deadly force).

- Injury: Includes any physical pain, illness, or any impairment of physical condition.

- Less Lethal Devices: A device that is designed to reduce the potential of causing serious bodily injury or death.

- Lethal Weapon: Any weapon reasonably calculated to produce death or serious bodily injury.

- Non-Deadly Force: Any use of force other than that which is considered deadly force.

- Passive Resistance: A non-compliant subject who offers no sign of physical defiance or resistive movement towards an employee's efforts.

- Physical Force: The application of a technique, action, or device to compel a change in the actions of another person; usually compliance with a desired behavior, submission to authority, or to de-escalate a threatening behavior.

- Positional Asphyxia: Positional asphyxia is a position that can produce unconsciousness or death caused by a lack of oxygen or an increase of carbon dioxide in the blood.

- Reasonable Belief: The facts or circumstances the employee knows, or should know, are such as to cause an ordinary and prudent person to act or think in a similar way under similar circumstances.

- Restraining Force: Force, which is limited to holding and restraining persons, which shall include arm-lock and takedown holds, but shall not include neck restraints.

- Serious Bodily Injury: Bodily injury that creates a substantial risk of death, causes serious permanent disfigurement, or results in long-term loss or impairment of the functioning of any bodily member or organ.

   - Verbal Uncooperativeness: A compliant subject, who offers no sign of physical defiance or resistive movement towards an employee's efforts, yet verbalizes resistance to instructions.

Escalation is the intensification of defending or protecting oneself or others and determining how much force should be used in a situation that accounts for 21 components. De-Escalation is the reduction of force used to make it consistent with the amount of resistance present accounts for the remaining 21 components.

This list contains 21 components that officers have to include in a repository as well as the existing criminal, civil, and local crimes and ordinances. In fact, to say 21 only accounts for one side of the triangle, the true continuum contains 42 components.

[Fig 24] shows a visual depiction of the Use of Force Continuum used by most U.S. departments.

8.3 The Levels of Resistance[124]

- [LR1] - Psychological Intimidation - Nonverbal cues indicating a subject's attitude, appearance, and physical readiness (Karate stance, the finger, fist to palm, up your arm)
- [LR2] - Verbal Noncompliance - Verbal responses indicating unwillingness or threats ("Go to hell," "I'm not going," "I'm going to kill you")
- [LR3] - Passive Resistance - Physical actions that do not prevent officer's attempt to control (Ex: Passive demonstrator sitting on the ground)
- [LR4] - Defensive Resistance - Physical actions that attempt to prevent officer's control, but never attempt to harm the officer (Pulls away from officer, walks away from officer)

- [LR5] - Active Aggression - Physical actions of assault (punching, kicking, wrestling)
- [LR6] - Deadly Force

[Fig 25]

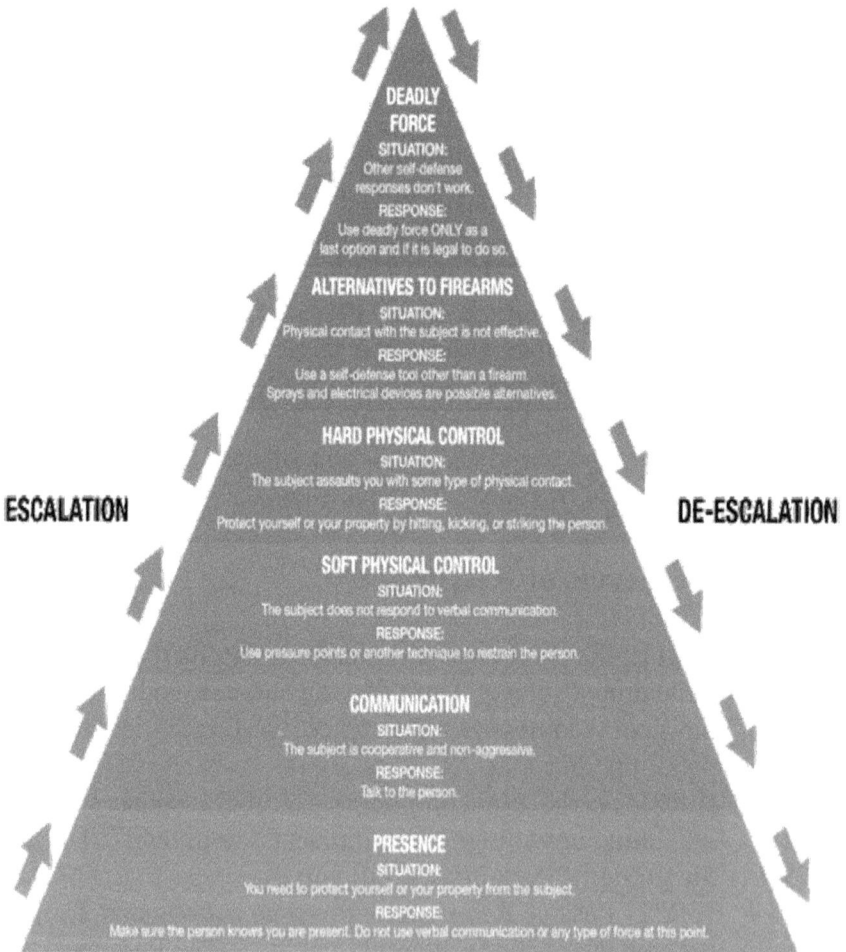

ESCALATION

DEADLY FORCE
SITUATION:
Other self-defense responses don't work.
RESPONSE:
Use deadly force ONLY as a last option and if it is legal to do so.

ALTERNATIVES TO FIREARMS
SITUATION:
Physical contact with the subject is not effective.
RESPONSE:
Use a self-defense tool other than a firearm. Sprays and electrical devices are possible alternatives.

HARD PHYSICAL CONTROL
SITUATION:
The subject assaults you with some type of physical contact.
RESPONSE:
Protect yourself or your property by hitting, kicking, or striking the person.

SOFT PHYSICAL CONTROL
SITUATION:
The subject does not respond to verbal communication.
RESPONSE:
Use pressure points or another technique to restrain the person.

COMMUNICATION
SITUATION:
The subject is cooperative and non-aggressive.
RESPONSE:
Talk to the person.

PRESENCE
SITUATION:
You need to protect yourself or your property from the subject.
RESPONSE:
Make sure the person knows you are present. Do not use verbal communication or any type of force at this point.

DE-ESCALATION

[Fig 24[125]] Use of Force Continuum

8.4 The Levels of Officer Control

- [LOC1] - Officer Presence - Identification of authority
- [LOC2] - Verbal Direction - Commands or directions
- [LOC3] - Empty Hand Control
  1. Soft Empty Hand Control - Touch pressure and joint locks
  2. Hard Empty Hand Control - Leg strikes, hand strikes, and neck restraints (**not choke holds**)
- [LOC4] - Intermediate Weapons - Intermediate weapon control includes impact weapons, chemical agents, and electronic disruption devices.
    1. The use of an intermediate weapon is justified when the officer believes that empty hand control will be insufficient, but the use of deadly force is not justified.
    2. Intermediate weapons are used only with the intent to temporarily disable the suspect and not with the intent to cause permanent injury to the suspect.
- [LOC5] - Deadly Force

[Fig 26]

8.5 [Parameters for Non-Deadly Force]

- When the use of force is needed, if feasible, authorized employees will identify themselves and determine which options in the force continuum will best de-escalate the situation in the most safe, reasonable, and prudent manner possible.
- Authorized employees are permitted to use department authorized non-deadly force techniques and equipment for resolution of incidents to:
- Protect themselves or another from bodily injury;
- Restrain or subdue a resistant person for whom there is probable cause to arrest or reasonable suspicion to stop;

- Prevent damage to property; and/or
- Bring an unlawful situation in which there is lawful authority for the employee to intervene, safely and effectively under control.
- Authorized employees may use department issued or approved hobble restraints and approved custodial restraint techniques on subjects who have been combative to reduce the likelihood of self-inflicted injury or to control further resistance while handcuffed. Employees are not permitted to use hobble restraints, leg shackles, plastic ties, or any other device to place any subject in a manner, which is likely to produce positional asphyxia.
- Any use of force on subjects who are handcuffed or otherwise in custody is prohibited unless physical resistance must be overcome. Such uses of force must be specifically articulated-with an emphasis on why a particular level of force used was necessary to obtain compliance.
- Authorized employees are permitted to use only that force which is reasonable and necessary under the particular circumstances to protect themselves or others from bodily injury, and only after other reasonable alternatives have been exhausted or it is determined that such alternative action(s) would be ineffective under the circumstances.
- Flight alone shall not justify the use of any level of force beyond official presence or verbal direction on a suspect. An officer must have reasonable suspicion or probable cause to believe that the suspect has committed or is about to commit a criminal offense before utilizing force greater than verbal direction].

• [Use of Chemical Spray] - When discharging chemical spray on an individual or animal that is within the parameters for the use of non-deadly force, the authorized employee shall:

- Give the verbal warning of "clear" to alert other personnel that the spray is about to be used so they can create a safe distance between themselves and the target of the spray; and
- Use a short burst and only the number of bursts necessary to achieve the desired effect of temporarily immobilizing the individual being sprayed; and
- Use at a maximum distance of fifteen (15) feet, and a minimum distance of three (3) feet from the target person;]

• [Use of Conducted Energy Device Taser® - Taser / CED Training & Certification, Taser Deployment]
- A. Deployment - The Taser may be deployed consistent with established policy and procedure governing the force continuum. The Taser is considered an "intermediate" level of force between soft empty-hand control techniques and hard empty-hand control techniques and may be deployed as appropriate.
- Fleeing Suspect: All other provisions of this order notwithstanding, must be probable cause to justify the arrest of a fleeing suspect for a criminal offense prior to utilizing the Taser to effect the arrest.
- When deploying the Taser, probes, or stun, at or upon an individual or animal that is within the parameters for the use of non-deadly force, the authorized employee shall:
- Whenever possible, give the verbal warning of "Taser!" to alert other personnel that the Taser is about to be used so they can create a safe distance between themselves and the target;
- Deploy the Taser consistent with department-approved training. Use only the minimum number of bursts and the minimum duration reasonably necessary to achieve the desired effect of temporarily immobilizing the individual or animal;
- When possible, one authorized employee should deploy the Taser while a cover employee is prepared with a standard weapon;
- Employees should take the suspect into custody as soon as possible after deploying the Taser thereby minimizing the

number and duration of bursts necessary while realizing that the suspect may not be able to respond to commands during or immediately following a burst;

- Follow all other techniques and/or instructions taught or disseminated by Department Training Division personnel; and

- Employees shall be aware that first responders from the Fire Department have developed specific protocols when responding to calls where the Taser has been utilized. To ensure the safety of suspects where a Taser has been deployed, officers shall:

- Where feasible, notify the Fire Department prior to deploying the Taser on a subject exhibiting behavior characteristic of, or similar to, Excited Delirium; or

- When prior notification is not possible on a subject that is exhibiting behavior similar to Excited Delirium, notify the Fire Department immediately after the Taser has been utilized.

- None of the above provisions shall preclude an employee from notifying the Fire Department and request assistance in any other circumstance wherein the presence of medical personnel may be appropriate.

- Prior to using the Taser on an individual driving or in physical control of a vehicle, the employee(s) shall immobilize the individual's vehicle to prohibit it from moving during the incident, or ensure the vehicle would not pose an unreasonable risk to persons or property should the Taser be deployed. All incidents of use will be consistent with established departmentally approved training.

- The Taser shall not be used on persons known to have been exposed to flammable liquids or sprayed with a chemical spray containing a flammable propellant, or in a location near flammable liquids or where flammable gasses are known to be present.

- The Taser should not be used on persons who are visibly pregnant or are at the extremes of age or physically disabled UNLESS there are compelling reasons to do so which can be clearly articulated.

- The normal reaction of a person exposed to the discharge of a Taser is the loss of some voluntary muscle control resulting in the subject falling to the ground or 'freezing' on the spot. For this reason, there is clearly a possibility of some secondary injury to the 'Tasered' subject, caused by falling and striking a hard surface. Particular attention should therefore be paid to the immediate environment and to assessing any additional risk factors (i.e. age, physical condition of the subject, objects being held by the subject etc.).

- Taser shall not be used in cases of passive resistance, unless a lesser means of force:

- Has been attempted and failed;
- Is not an option due to exigent circumstances; or
- If attempted, could result in a significant possibility of injury to the employee or suspect.
- Where feasible, supervisory approval should be obtained before a Taser is used to effect the arrest of a subject who is passively resisting.

- Any use of the Taser not consistent with established departmental policy or training is expressly prohibited, and may result in corrective or disciplinary action.

- Violation of policies or training governing the use of the Taser by an employee may result in remedial training, corrective or disciplinary action].

- [Use of Less Lethal Devices] - The department may issue or make available less lethal devices (i.e., bean bags, etc.) to authorized employees who have successfully completed specialized training and/or qualification in the operation and use of these devices.

- [Use of Deadly Force in Self Defense] - Authorized employees may use deadly force when they have a reasonable belief that the action is immediately necessary to prevent imminent death or serious bodily injury of a human being, including the employee].

- [Use of Deadly Force to Effect an Arrest] - Authorized employees may use deadly force to effect the arrest of a fleeing felon only when:
- The employee has probable cause to believe the individual to be arrested has committed a felony involving the infliction or threatened infliction of serious bodily injury; and
- The employee has probable cause to believe that the individual to be arrested poses a threat of death or serious bodily injury, either to the employee or to others unless immediately apprehended; and
- Where feasible, the employee has identified himself/herself as a police employee and given warning such as, "STOP--POLICE--I'LL SHOOT," that deadly force is about to be used unless flight ceases;
- If all other means of apprehension available to the employee under the attendant circumstances have been exhausted].

- [Administration of First-Aid] - Officers are required to render to aid, to persons they use force against.

- [General Provisions] - A. In addition to the Use of Force provisions stated in this order, an authorized employee may also discharge a firearm under the following circumstances:
- Warning shots are prohibited;
- When effecting an arrest, no form of deadly force shall be used which would pose a substantial risk to innocent bystanders; and
- When the use of deadly force is necessary to defend the employee or another from death or serious bodily harm, every effort will be made to minimize the risk of harm to innocent persons.

- Employees shall not discharge their firearm at or from a moving vehicle unless absolutely necessary to protect the life of the employee or others.
- Employees shall not knowingly place themselves in a position where they would be in jeopardy of being struck by a suspect vehicle or knowingly stand and/or step into the path of a vehicle, creating circumstances where the use of deadly force may be necessary. However, under exigent circumstances, other equipment may be used as a defensive impact device when the use of the baton is not feasible. If such non-lethal equipment is used as a defensive impact device within the guidelines of this policy, the guidelines applicable to the use of a baton shall apply.
- If lethal equipment (firearm, vehicle, etc.) is used as a defensive impact device within the guidelines of this policy, the guidelines applicable to the use of a deadly force shall apply.
- When such equipment is used as a defensive impact device, the member should disengage as soon as the situation permits and transition to an approved device.

• [Use of Force Training] - All employees will be provided with a copy of the current use of force at a minimum, on an annual basis.

• [Reporting Use of Force] - Officer must report all uses of force

• [Force Review Board] - The Strategic Development Division will annually provide the Chief of Police and members of the Departmental Force Review Board with a use of force analysis to assist in identifying any potential patterns and/or systemic].

Here in writing, is proof that departments endeavor to effect legitimate uses of force, and non-abusive, discourteous behavior. Through studying the reported uses of force, this particular department even tries to determine trends, identify policy failures and properly train its officers in the use of reasonable amounts of force. [Fig 24] indicates policy attempts to monitor and curtail violations of policies[126].

Remember; however, as stated in the policy samples, Policy Violations do not carry the weight of law. Persons inclined to violate the law, surly will not balk at violating departmental policy.

I asked several questions of Melvin Brown M.S., a Use of Force Subject Matter Expert, to which he gave these responses;

1. Media perceptions sway opinion on the use of force
2. The result of the action does not have to be positive for the use of force to be appropriate
3. Everything is a matter of semantics and definitions; the law sometimes has unique terms
   3a. A means to de-escalate situations is called a 'control option.' Talking to someone (verbal control), as a control option is a legal use of force term, not an actual entity
   3b. The application or threat of physical force constitutes a Use of Force
4. Use of Force continuum is not to control the officer; it is to control the suspect. Self-control and training are for the officer but they are not a part of the continuum. However, the officer's demeanor is definitely a considered part of the response
5. The definition of 'control' is; by some means you cause someone to comply with lawful direction
6. The response of the suspect should not determine the attitude, just the response. The 'OODA Loop' as a situational awareness platform that came about by Col. John Boyd
7. Orientation filters actions. The input into your orientation can affect the "D" of the loop. Training helps modify the filtering process. You do not learn to live free of anger for example, but you can learn to control how you react to personal fear and anger

8. The officer's ability and its impact on the use of forces, these are called 'officer-subject factors'. These factors (age, size, relative strength, skill level, injuries sustained, level of exhaustion or fatigue, the number of officers available vs. subjects) matter as to who has the advantage

9. Officer-subject factors to consider in the assessment of the appropriateness of action are;
   - Injuries
   - Numbers
   - Mental faculty
   - Whether the suspect is armed or unarmed

10. The Use of Force Special Circumstances consists of all those conditions detailed and articulated in [Fig 24] and in the sample Use of Force Policy

11. The Use of Force Assessment Equation used to determine the validity of a use of force incident, therefore is; Use of Force special circumstances + officer-subject factors' = Totality of Circumstances

12. The Use of Force Assessment Equation© (UOFAE) is necessary in all assessments, because the assessment of appropriateness is often subjective not objective

"According to the FBI's Expanded Homicide data from 2018, the most recent report of this kind Reuters was able to find, 80.7% of the murders of White people were committed by White offenders (2,677 of a total of 3,315) while 15.5% of the murders of White people were committed by Black offenders (514). The FBI's data, 8% of the reported murders of Black people were committed by White offenders (234 of a total of 2,925) and 88.9% by Black offenders (2,600)[127]."

According to a survey of more than 7000 officers, Black and White officers agreed that there is a problem larger than police racism responsible for many of the recent deadly encounters with Blacks[128].

According to the FBI numbers cited by Pew Research, White have more to fear from other White people than they do from African American'ts.

8.5
Why Are So Many Unarmed Black Men Shot?

"There is nothing more painful to me at this stage in my life than to walk down the street and hear footsteps and start thinking about robbery then look around and see somebody White and feel relieved{Rev. Jessie Jackson} ."

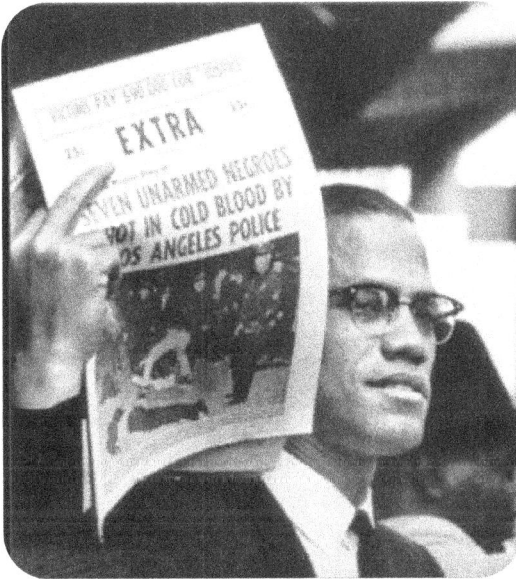

[Fig 25]

Undeniably unarmed people are shot in the U.S. annually. Inexplicably many of the persons shot are African-American'ts. The determination to shot is far more complicated than the evaluation of the shooting after the fact. This is no way excuses unjustified shootings; then again all shootings of unarmed persons are unjustified.

My Black Side

I responded to a question from a 16 year old, and asked him why he thought that so many unarmed Black people get shot and he said because people always doing stupid things. Stupid things like pretending to pull a gun. Although he was playing, he did make a threatening gesture. I believe his idea is right although the example may not be.

During the Police Academy, I do not remember an abundance of Black assailants, or target dummies in videos. One of the things that they were working on, especially in shoot-do-not-shoot drills was reconditioning the way you think about a 'Target'. By changing the color of the people all together, to colors like yellow and green so there was no indication that it was a Black person and you focused more on the weapon and the threat.

How does the academy rectify bias if you show up at the police academy already afraid of a group of people? It stands to reason, that no matter what you learn in the Academy, tactics will not replace your emotions, they usually quell or support your emotions. In other words, the redneck that comes to the police academy learns to be a better shot. The Black Panther who comes to the police academy stands against 'Whitey' with a gun. The coward learns to shoot at everybody or hide in a group because he is afraid. Sadly, all law enforcement agencies around the country find themselves plagued with unprofessional people. One of the greatest law enforcement weaknesses manifests in the huge amount of cowardice, apathy, and subjectivity shown by administrations.

Administrations that believe they must act because society is mad that the police shot somebody are doing both the officers and the city a disservice. Removal from active duty to administrative leave is a good practical first move in order to further a proper investigation. However, no comment should be made to the media or anybody during the investigation because the investigation is incomplete.

Departments and the Court System, <u>not the media</u> need to determine whether a shooting was good or bad. Death is not the focus; death is the natural by-product of gunshot wounds. The reason for the shooting needs to be the investigative focus. It is a simple but important distinction. If the officer was justified to release the bullets from the barrel of the gun, the ammunition manufacturer is responsible for the ballistics of the ammo. If the officer was not justified in firing, then two undesirable consequences resulted.

Traditionally both Black people and White people show irritation when you shoot their family members. It does not really matter why you shot them. I cannot say that it is not alarming and disgusting when innocent people are shot. Moreover, would I be racist if I said it is even more alarming when they look like me? Have I ever been afraid of being gunned down by a White officer in my 20-plus years as a cop? I can honestly say no, but I have been more fortunate that some, plus I would shoot back.

When asked if I had the opportunity to shoot people and did not shoot the answer would be yes. Because of the nature of my job, I had the ability to shoot dozens of people and chose not to shoot. That is not because many of them were Black; it was because I was not afraid of them, therefore the shooting unnecessary. This does not mean that they did not pose a threat or that this would not be a justifiable shooting. What this means is that at the time, I had either the time or opportunity, or additional support to make an alternative decision: those factors are huge.

There have been times, when officers spoke to me in an uncomplimentary manor, not knowing that I was a police officer, in which case I simply asked them to speak to a supervisor and when he arrived we hashed it out. Part of the hashing out process was pointing out that the officer was an ignoramus. The reason I called the supervisor was for the safety of both officers. The supervisor usually adds two components to the stalemate, objectivity and a witness. I did not do this out of fear; I did this out of respect for the badge and to the professionals out there. If the White ignoramus spoke to me in an unprofessional manner because I was Black, he was stupid. If as the Black officer, I was angry and beat the hell out of a White officer, I would also be equally unprofessional. There is a better way to handle anything. Moreover, I was not going to let that fool cause me to act in an unethical manner, justifying his unethical behavior and bias.

Cops do not admit it because they are cops, but many of cops are afraid. Every day when cops leave the police station many of them are afraid of what they may encounter. I do not mean cautious or reserved I mean afraid. I heard officers say they would never shoot anybody. I heard officers say they would make traffic stop a car by themselves. I have heard officers give a list of things they would never do that are 100% a part of their police officer duties. These are the kind of officers that over react and injure people killing them before their training manifests because of a fear response.

Somebody said that in all these high school shootings, the reason the majority of White suspects survive is because they surrender to the police; and that many Black people are shot because they were resisting. I do not necessarily agree with that because several Black people have been gunned down in surrender positions, or filmed being gunned down, shot in the back with a gun planted on him by the officer.

I faced the additional difficulty as an officer, of Blacks being perceived as more threatening than persons of other colors. This threat does not necessarily, only stem from fear of the Black person; there also maybe a subliminal belief that this Black person hates you because you are White. The seething hostility that Whites perceive exists from Blacks, causes Whites to be vigilant and they often respond preemptively to a threat of their own making.

My Blue Side

To that 16 year old I say it is for the same reasons; cops also shoot unarmed White people. While having viewed hundreds of videos of police shootings, I can actually say I have no logical reason for why so many unarmed Black men are shot. I can say that in many of the instances, I saw bad tactics by the police or aggressive behavior by the suspect, cause or evoke a response that cops did not anticipate. The thing people do not seem to realize is that the primary concept of self-defense is defense of oneself. Therefore, to a police officer, the definition of self-defense is subjective and completely different than yours; but that does not make them a coward.

If I am afraid of you, every action you take is going to be threatening to me. Because I am leery that you might hurt me and I do not think I can defend myself effectively against you that I preemptively strike. It is also because the inept administrations of many departments have decided to make hard empty hand control somewhat of an abomination.

The only purpose for less than lethal weapons is to manage combative and resistive subjects in less than lethal methods. The most readily accessible less than lethal options are hands and feet. In a feat of poor judgment, many departmental policies make the distance between Strong Empty Hand Control and Chemical Weapons too far a leap.

This dilemma in my opinion creates the necessity for officers to try convincing a person to voluntarily go to jail. If they decline, and simply stand still what is an officer to do under today's ridiculous media imposed standards? Prohibiting, or sanctioning Hard Empty Hand Control caused an upsurge in other police responses.

The Media does not care about people, they tell stories. The more unrest created, the more stories they have to capitalize on. I checked; there is currently no law that allows a citizen to refuse an arrest. Since most people and most officers do not fight on a regular basis, the resulting physical confrontation is a hodge-podge of emotion. The offender has already proved to you they have no respect or do not recognize police authority. Therefore, when the fight ensues, an officer is just another person to them. Officers are trained not to lose. This eventually results in the officer's frustration and exhaustion, resulting in a heightened interaction.

8.6 Anecdotal Evidence vs Empirical Evidence

Anecdotal evidence is collected in a casual or informal manner and relies mostly on witness statements.

Empirical evidence is the information received by means of the senses, particularly by observation and documentation of patterns and behavior through experimentation.

When discussing this project work with a Subject Matter Expert, he reminded me of the two concepts above. Part of the argument against the BLM movement is not its invalidity as a whole, but that so many of the factors they promulgate are anecdotal and not empirical. More than 1,000 unarmed people died as a result of police harm between 2013 and 2019, according to data from Mapping Police Violence[129]. It is only anecdotal that the police target unarmed Black men.

Whether or not we want to admit it, this is an alarming number of unarmed people shot; ethnicity should make no difference. When the police shot at an unarmed Amadou Diallo in New York 41 times, the Rev. Al Sharpton is quoted as saying, "I am not saying 41 times is too many times to shoot at a Black guy, I am saying 41 times is too many times to shoot at anybody." He is right, especially an armed person.

[Fig 26], agrees with Sharpton, there are too many unarmed people shot and killed. But we cannot look at the numbers and attribute it all to racism. Mental illness, substance abuse, and poor physical condition coupled with poor training accounts for a great deal of this alarming trend. Less than lethal training is the answer to much of this. Nothing will remove the necessity for the use of force during arrests, the best e can hope for is better practice of forcible control measures.

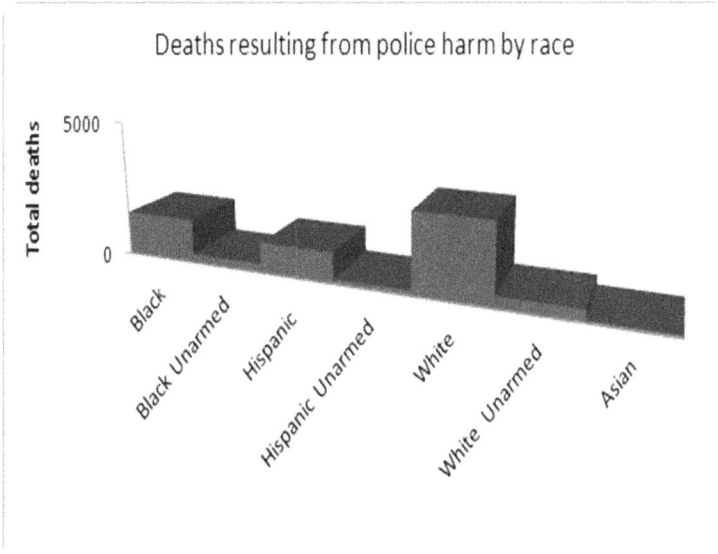

Deaths resulting from police harm by race

[Fig 26[130]]

You must have the necessary skills to force a person into capitulation. Without these perishable skills, less than lethal options slip from the grasp of officers leading to needless escalation and fatal encounters. I currently hold a 4th degree Black Belt in Wado Ryu Karate. I have also taken part in more than 10,000 felony arrests of resistive subjects. My training (which included Martial arts, physical fitness, escalation, and de-escalation training, contact avoidance {not getting hit}) helped me not have to shoot people.

Here is a pictorial depiction of an annual training cycle at my former department. It is not that the smaller categories are less important, but In-service is only 40 hours. Other classes like Diversity/Sensitivity Training, 1st responder training and other types of required courses also have to fit within the allotted timeframe. This department requires In-service training annually, across the country, many small departments lack the budget and staffing to a lot training of this kind.

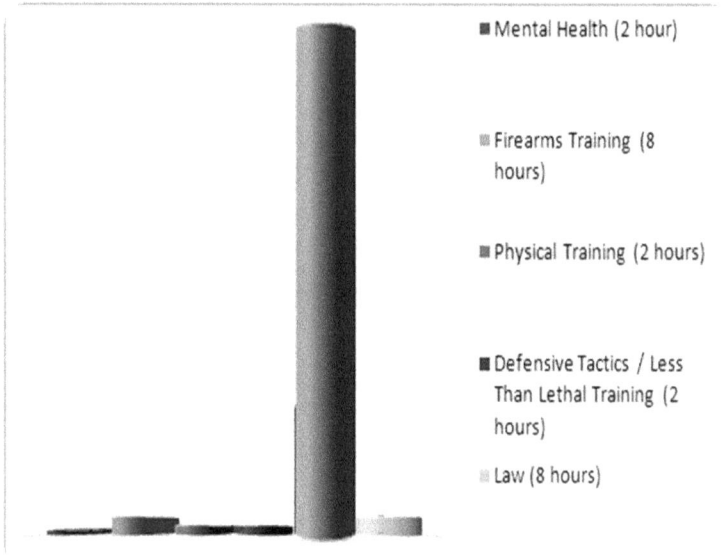

- Mental Health (2 hour)
- Firearms Training (8 hours)
- Physical Training (2 hours)
- Defensive Tactics / Less Than Lethal Training (2 hours)
- Law (8 hours)

[Fig 27]

I have used hard empty hand control on 85% of my arrests, because I had to. In one such arrest, I made a traffic stop. The stop was for an expired tag, the driver an Asian male. He had no driver's license. When I asked him out of the car, when I told him he was under arrest, he ran. I caught him. I started to handcuff him, at which point he grabbed my hands and flipped me over in the parking lot. The entire fight took two minutes and 30 seconds according to the video.

Humiliated, I stood up to face him. He wrapped the cuffs around his fists like brass knuckles. I got into fighting stances and we fought a cinematic karate duel in the parking lot. After he realized he was losing, he picked himself up off the ground and dragged his bloody face towards a gas station. I chased him and wrestled him into custody in the doorway of the gas station. Whites, Blacks, and Middle Easterners walked past and around us, and nobody helped. Backup could not find us, because I gave the wrong location for the traffic stop because he moved past the address I gave. I never relied on them anyway. The guy was APG (Asian Pride Gang) and trained in jail and at gang meetings how to resist arrest. The reason he fought was not the driver's license, it was the 15 guns in his car, and the outstanding warrant for aggravated assault.

What's my point? I did not resist shooting him because he was not Black; it was because I had enough other training to offset the need to shoot. Had I needed to shoot him, I was both capable and prepared mentally. Fortunately, for him, however he is still alive because I am capable, with or without a gun.

U.S. Police Shootings: Blacks Disproportionately Affected

Number of people killed in police shootings in the U.S. since January 1, 2015

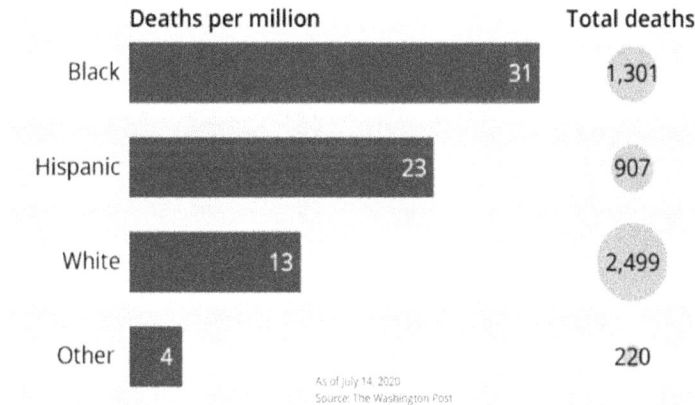

	Deaths per million	Total deaths
Black	31	1,301
Hispanic	23	907
White	13	2,499
Other	4	220

As of July 14, 2020
Source: The Washington Post

[Fig 27a]

Empirically, something needs to be done about the number of unarmed persons shot, someone needs to study the tactics used to determine the causal failure resulting in the deaths. Bear in mind however, I am in the category of people that would qualify to be shot even if unarmed because of those officer subject factors discussed in the Use of Force chapter due to my skill-set not my skin tone.

However; I can neither give nor find and intelligent explanation for these Washington Post statistics, other than systemic disparate treatment. Proudly I can state, I was not a contributor to these statistics, but they do cast a stain on the purported objectivity of the U.S. Law Enforcement profession, if not why are Blacks and Hispanics shot 2 and 3 times as often as Whites and others - per capita?

8.7
Why Do The Police
Seem So Violent?

"In keeping people straight, no principle is not as powerful as a policeman{Abel Hermant131}."

[Fig 28] and [Fig 29] depict information gathered from a report by the Prison Policy Initiative, so is the following quote, "There is no question that the number of police killings of civilians in the U.S. - who are disproportionately Black and other people of color - are the result of policies and practices that enable and even encourage police violence. Compared to police in other wealthy democracies, American police kill civilians at incredibly high rates[132]."

U.S. POLICE KILL CIVILIANS AT A MUCH HIGHER RATE
THAN POLICE IN OTHER WEALTHY COUNTRIES

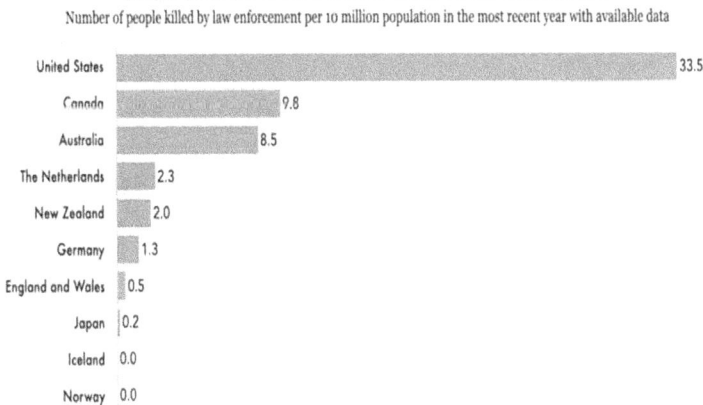

Number of people killed by law enforcement per 10 million population in the most recent year with available data

United States	33.5
Canada	9.8
Australia	8.5
The Netherlands	2.3
New Zealand	2.0
Germany	1.3
England and Wales	0.5
Japan	0.2
Iceland	0.0
Norway	0.0

[Fig 28]

I think that the statistics show that between 2013 and 2017 of the 5,400 people killed by Law Enforcement; 2,353 (42.83%) of those killed were White and 1,487 (27.07%) were Black. The numbers also show that the police shoot an average of 1100 people per year (over the last five years), and that risk of violence against Blacks by police, was highest in predominantly White neighborhoods[133]. There is not just a problem in the country with police violence; I believe the information is inversely anecdotal in that the violence shown by U.S. Law Enforcement is merely a microcosm of the violent U.S. macrocosm.

U.S. POLICE KILL FAR MORE CIVILIANS ANNUALLY THAN ANY OTHER WEALTHY COUNTRY

Total number of people killed by law enforcement in the most recent year with available data

United States	1,099
Canada	36
Australia	21
Germany	11
The Netherlands	4
England and Wales	3
Japan	2
New Zealand	1
Iceland	0
Norway	0

[Fig 29]

My Black Side

I default to maintaining the stability of *The Establishment* as the reason. White Americans throughout their history have proven themselves willing to use violence to further their aims. The Civil War sticks out as a testament to the will of those in power not to return to any state they think disdainful. I think White privilege creates intolerance, systemic disparate treatment and oppression.

My Blue Side

I think people misunderstand police Use of Force. A study of Use of Force data suggests, the introduction of force introduces emotions into the fray. The offender is now not only angry; fear begins to set in; when blended often turns to rage. Now the officer, who intended to use the least amount of force necessary, has to escalate to control the enraged person.

In other circumstances, it is my opinion that the police engage too late in the interaction. Once the officer establishes that an arrest is in order, they need to make it happen. Standing around arguing and discussing the arrest changes the dynamics of the encounter and places the offender in control. If action is faster than reaction, the offender has the upper hand. The longer the encounter lasts prior to handcuffing, the more likely a physical encounter is to ensue. Authority = No Discussion. Either society gave cops legitimate authority, or we are security guards.

The Use of Force is calculated to cause damage when necessary; pain compliance is always better than injury. However if the offender opts to resist, officers are trained to subdue combatants and force them into capitulation. In other words, officers have to strike, spray, tase, or shoot an individual until they willingly comply. Citizens do not have to agree with the arrest, or like the officer, but when people resist in any manner, police use of force becomes necessary. Now there are additional charges, and aches and pains to go with the arrest.

Remember, police officers exist to exert force into a situation where regular civic institutions fail to maintain compliance. In other words, the only reason a person interacts with the police is that they broke a law. Lawbreakers, by definition, are people that need to be coerced into compliance - ergo Force.

8.8 Pack Mentality

Part of the reason for police brutality is the same reason there is so much violence within society; pack mentality. Pack mentality is a phenomenon in which people make decisions based upon the actions of others, sometimes without even realizing it. It stems from the animalistic drive to want to fit in," according to the Empathy Bulletin[134]. Cops want to fit in and gain social acceptance within their pack of coworkers, and there is ample evidence of cops making decisions based upon the actions of others.

I think cops have split personalities when it comes to pack mentality. I think they have a Blue Pack mentality wherein they want to fit in within the cop environment, and I think they have an Anti-blue Pack mentality wherein the pack protects itself from outsiders, no matter the cause of the interaction.

There is no morality amongst animals. If wolf pack A goes to the borough of pack B and eats a cub, there is no remorse. There is no makeup, or apology for the attack and the benefactors of the stolen meal, will defend it with their lives. This metaphor is only scary because its validity reflects a pervasive police mentality, Us vs Them. This xenophobic behavior is endemic of America because of *The Establishment's* imbalance. America has a warlike (gunboat diplomacy) tradition and rich history of violence as an internal conflict resolution strategy.

Ironically, however, to show that this behavior is not unique to law enforcement, I have included the link to a video you must watch. The title of the video is, Group of Black Men Save Police Officer's Life When the Man He's Trying to Arrest Breaks Free and Attacks Him[135].

I think many who say defund the police because of racism will have a hard time explaining why these young, Black men came to the aid of the White police officer? Even though the guys in the video stereotypically look like the prime persons described as often targeted by law enforcement.

[Fig 30]

I think this is an excellent example of many things discussed in the book.

- Pack mentality
- The need for training
- How quickly things go wrong
- An officer failing to escalate at the correct time, in the correct manner
- What White cops fear most in when making arrests in the Black community
- An illustration of the perceived violence prevalent amongst Black males (Despite the fact that the Black males are assisting the White officer)
- Many Black people still believe in supporting Law Enforcement
- Many young Black males are victimized by Media hype versus racism

I think failing to watch this video is a mistake and allows continued anecdotal responses to police interactions from both perspectives. I also believe that failing to acknowledge every stereotype, perception, and belief from both sides of the fence; you will not understand why the resolution to these problems has not been forthcoming.

8.9
Why Do The Police Seem More Violent Towards Black Women than White Women?

"The negro has suffered far more from the commission of this crime against the women of his race by White men, than the White race has ever suffered through his crimes[Ida Wells]."

My Black Side

The Black woman exists between the worlds of desire and utility. The Black female finds that *The Establishment's* effect makes her less desirable to the Black spouse as a mate and desirable to the White males as a plaything. The Black female is not taken seriously; she is often considered the lowest educated female in the community. The lack of respect given to the Black female carries over from the workplace and the manner in which she is treated by Law Enforcement.

Dr. Condoleezza Rice is the; First woman to serve as National Security Advisor, Former U.S. Secretary of State and National Security Adviser, Ph D, Master's Degree, Bachelor's Degree, University professor. Why was Dr. Rice constantly referred to (by her less educated colleagues and the President) as *Condy*, instead of Dr Rice, a title which she earned?

The Black mother also finds an enemy in Law Enforcement because her contribution to the community: male children; are considered a blight. The Black female is seen as the criminal-baby factory. Black females are considered by many cops to have an antagonistic view of the police (because of its unjust incarceration of Black males). Because of this antagonism between Law Enforcement and the Black family, the interactions between

Law Enforcement are best described as a clash. The officer is prepared to drag them both to jail, and they are quite willing to go. The repressed rage of forced silence and indifference generates within the Black female both rage and desperation.

Officer involved shooting deaths of women; especially unarmed women experience a different type of scrutiny. Since 2015, 250 women had been fatally shot by U.S. law enforcement. #48 of the women fatally shot were Black, and seven of those were unarmed.

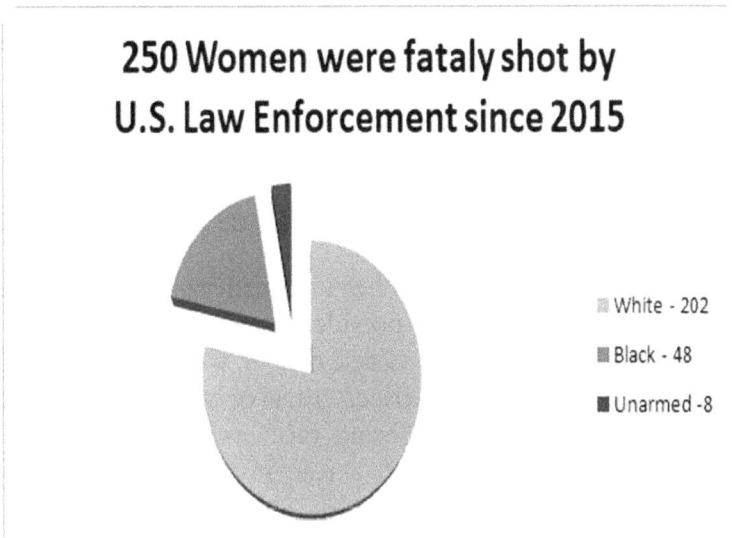

250 Women were fataly shot by U.S. Law Enforcement since 2015

White - 202

Black - 48

Unarmed -8

[Fig 31[144]]

An article in the Washington Post indicates that this type of shooting receives less media coverage than White on Black shootings of any kind.

In contrast, the officer involved shooting death of Justine Damond, an interracial police shooting of a unarmed woman garnered a peculiar set of responses.

Black women are fatally shot at rates higher than women of other races

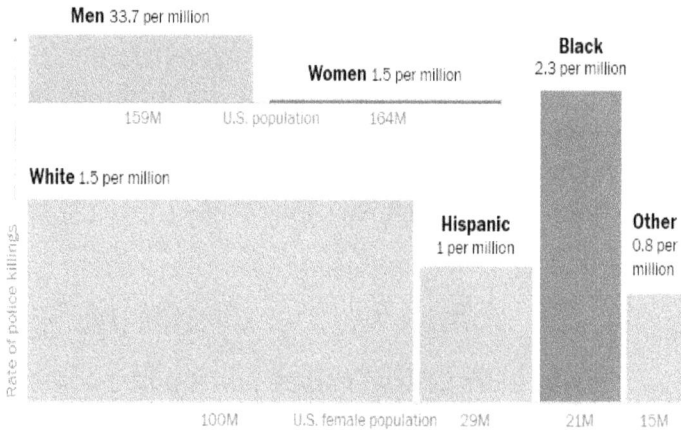

[Fig 32[136]]

1. Response #1 by Nekima Levy Armstrong, a civil rights attorney and former president of the Minneapolis NAACP cited that the Black officer was not given the same latitude White officers receive when they shoot unarmed people of differing race and gender. "Race and affluence has played a role in terms of how this case is being handled."

2. Response #2, another response from Shaun King, a Black Lives Matter activist and writer focused on the manner in which the victim was portrayed by the media, "We want Black and Latino and native victims of police violence to be treated like her. You can have the sweetest person ever killed, but if they are Black, poor, and in a particular zip code, the portrayal is nothing like the portrayal that she received in this case. I felt like from day one she was treated the way every victim of police violence should be treated."

3. Response #3 King went on to say that he feel relatively confident that Officer Noor would be convicted, "It is hard for a jury to identify with an immigrant, Muslim,

Black man. He said the defense of fearing for one's life can work for White officers, but he has a hard time believing it will work for Noor[137].

In response to Armstrong's assertion in Response #1, the old adage, 'two wrongs do not make a right' should suffice, however it does not. I find it appalling to look at minutia in light of the gravity of this situation. The facts of this case; Two officers respond to a 911 call, regarding screams heard in the alley from a female. Harrity testified that he was startled by a noise in the alley, pulled out his gun and pointed it down, then saw a figure out of the corner of his eye when Noor fired. Noor claims he fired his gun that night while sitting on the squad car's passenger side because he feared for his and Harrity's lives after hearing a thump and seeing a figure by the squad car shortly afterward raising an arm.

'When asked why he didn't shoot if he was startled, Harrity said because he didn't get a chance to "analyze the threat" and couldn't shoot at a shadowy figure before seeing the actual target and the person's hands. Harrity went on to testify that he thought of the victim as a threat until the shot was fired, then he saw her hands and saw the victim wasn't a threat.

As the opinion given in Response #1 does not come from a cop, I think there are important considerations ignored.

- Two armed officers in a car
- Mobility of the car
- Unarmed barefoot female
- Nature of the call (female screaming in the alley)
- Officers were partners
- Noor claims he fired to save Harrity's life

Partners do not turn on each other especially in a situation where one was covering for the other's life unless they feel they have to. Race has something to do with this, in this case the Black officer gave in to the same foolish Blue belief that it is better to be judged by 12 than to be carried by 6; and fired without justification.

Harrity testified that the sound in the alley alarmed him, and that he believes in considering all persons to be a threat. Had Ms. Damond been Black perhaps he would have fired first; but the fact remains he did not, and there is nothing to suggest that he would. I have no basis to assume the officer is biased or racist in that the victim's Whiteness made her less threatening. Harrity stands behind his training in this case, as most officers do and states he waited until he had a target, and could see their hands - a tactical consideration, too many officers seem to rely upon judging by the numbers if unarmed women shot in the U.S. However, Response #1 seems to make the argument that Noor should be exonerated like White officers that shoot unarmed women. How is that just, and who does that benefit?

Response #2 and Response #3 come from the same source and come from interesting perspectives. Response #2 is an extremely valid point, *The Entrenched racism Media Support Story*©, aims to garner support for White officers in questionable shootings by demonizing the suspect. I would be the first to admit a healthy dislike for criminals, but each interaction is unique. A conviction for a previous crime is indicia, and a warning, <u>not proof</u>. Just because the person is a convicted rapist or pedophile does not mean that they deserved to be gunned down on the way home from Wal-Mart. Because trial by media is a popularity contest, negative characterization of the victim allows people to ignore facts (This is why the Armed Forces belittle and dehumanizes the enemy intending to make lethal engagements easier).

Response #3 is somewhat an end-run, where King reminds readers of the disparity between the manners in which officers are treated. In an opinion that mirrors Response #1, King implies had this been a White officer, the conviction may not have occurred. Simultaneously King's subtle Emmit Till like situational reference, that Noor's race and religion though giving him the right to be afraid, did not empower him to defend himself, or take lethal action against a White woman.

My Blue Side

I will say that a person in the heat of battle sometimes is too emotional to think clearly. In addition, when fighting and being pulled off the opponent by someone, the first response is usually defensive.

That being said, why the male officer was not mud stomped for beating up his partner is beyond me. Not to mention, what does it say about a system of justice and a Department that punishes an officer for trying to stop police

[Fig 33[138]]

brutality? By the way, Civil Rights Violations are charged Under Color of Law, which means she could have gone to jail as well as him[139] had she not intervened.

That being said, why the male officer did not face retribution from other male officers for beating up his partner-in-blue is beyond me. Not to mention, what does it say about a system of justice and a Department that punishes an officer for trying to stop police brutality?

Two witnesses against one, and the male White won. How can any Law Enforcement Agency agree that choking (considered a lethal police tactic unilaterally) a handcuffed suspect is not against policy? It appears that the only person who came to defend Horne's actions was Mr. Mack the suspect, who is reported as saying, "He was choking me. I was handcuffed."

This was not just racism; this was *The Establishment* at work all the way up this department's chain of command. I am unsure of this department's policy, but surely striking a fellow officer is a violation of policy and proof that the male officer was out of control thereby violating any existing policies in the U.S. regarding discipline and deportment.

Horne was finally vindicated A judge ruled her department pension be reinstated despite termination more than a decade ago.

8.10
Female Officers and
the Use Force

"A good society is characterized not just by liberty but by mutual respect and responsibility. When this breaks down it takes a lot more than police officers to put things right[David Lammy]".

Admittedly I had a jaded view of female officers when I joined The Force. I did not have a purely feminist view, but my bias formed from encounters with female soldiers and other females in leadership positions that performed subpar. It turns out that this was not because they were female; it rested more on their personal ethics than physical ability.

All humans have different abilities, and females are no different. It makes no sense to offer handicapped parking, yet contend that all people are equal, there must be differences. The differences are not negative, just as being Black is not a negative, but there are differing characteristics between races and genders.

One of the best things that happened to me was to have a female training officer as my first partner. She was not as fast, aggressive or strong as I was, but she never left me hanging. This was important for two reasons.

- It changed my opinion of female officers forever
- It taught me never to get an any situation I could not get myself out of

Rosa Brooks, a law professor makes a nonsensical point regarding the numbers of police females, "Women make up just 12.6 percent of all police officers. Much of the debate about police violence and misconduct has focused on race while skipping past this stunning statistic. No honest observer can deny that too many American policing practices reflect and contribute to racial injustice, but the focus on racial injustice should not make us lose sight of the gender disparities that also distort American policing. One simple way to achieve a less violent and more equitable form of law enforcement is to push agencies to hire more women." Not only is this contention baseless, it implies that the primary source of the problem is because of male. That seems a bit inconsistent in an argument against gender disparities. In no decade in American history has the female officer outnumbered the male officer. This is not due to hiring improprieties no longer (since the 70's and 80s), it due more to the same reason there are not as many minorities, policing is not the most glamorous job in the world.

Prison Policy[134] cites statistics, which I believe more accurately reflect the inequity in the number of females. The issue has to do with the value of the White woman. The White woman carries the White seed, and therefore continues their progenies. Why should White society push their treasured daughters into the dangerous, thankless world of policing?

Brooks[140] goes on to say they decades of research show female officers can handle hostile and violent suspects as well as their male counterparts. A 2017 Pew survey found only 11 percent of female officers reported they had ever fired their weapon while on duty, compared with 30 percent of male officers. Female officers were also less likely to believe aggression is more useful than courtesy, less likely to agree with some people, "Can only be brought to reason the hard, physical way" and less likely to report their jobs had made them callous." This is another lop-sided reference, it does not account for the input from the suspect.

In a male oriented society, where chivalry still partially exists, men still regularly rush to the aid of females in trouble in public. To say that this social paradigm does not carry over into the interaction between police and criminals would be reckless. The only way to validate this study would be to place both genders in identical training scenarios requiring use of force determination; then take the poll.

Geoffrey P. Alpert criminology professor at the University of South Carolina provides a more logical explanation than too many men with badges in that he postulates, "Even when they have a confrontation with a police officer, they're less likely to have a weapon, they're less likely to have the same threat level as a man." This practicality explains much, it's not so much that police women mind shooting, women typically do not posture themselves in as threatening a posture as male suspects. Despite the validity of the belief, most men feel less threatened by female opponents, assuming them to be less capable of severely injuring them.

Routinely, I witnessed Confrontation Training at my department, and assisted in some of the training. In the decades I served as an officer, I noticed a trend. In confrontations where de-escalation was the better pathway, males deescalated to a greater degree. I did not use the term more because the comparison is not equal. Men react to men differently, as a matter of course. Females that I observed deescalated less because they rarely escalated, opting to maintain distance and waited hoping for back up or a surrender. I do not know if this is a good thing or a bad thing, it is what I observed.

What I also observed was that when the situated required force, the women responded slower, and with less force, and often performed less successfully as males. This information, I believe, accounts for why female officers take different tactics. Female officers use distance and discourse more than men; I would tend to agree, when the situation allows for it. However, when an arrest is required, I observed what I think Parks misinterprets.

A Chicago police department case study indicates that minority officers stop arrest and use force against civilians less often than White.

Black officers	**Hispanic officers**
29% reduction in stops	6% reduction in stops
21% reduction in arrests	5% reduction in arrests

32% reduction in use of force   12% reduction in use of force

Female officers[141]
5% reduction in arrests
28% reduction in use of force
[Fig 34]

Researchers studied 2.9 million officer shifts and 1.6 million enforcement activities performed by nearly 7,000 officers their numbers indicated, "Black officers made 15.16 fewer stops, 1.93 fewer arrests and used force 0.1 fewer times than their White counterparts."

Being smart enough to try to avoid a confrontation that you will most probably lose, is not a gender effect; it is common sense, and it relies completely on the actions and response of the suspect.

Women's share of all police-initiated contacts is even higher than their share of arrests

Percentage, by sex, of 2015 arrests and police-initiated contacts, by type of contact

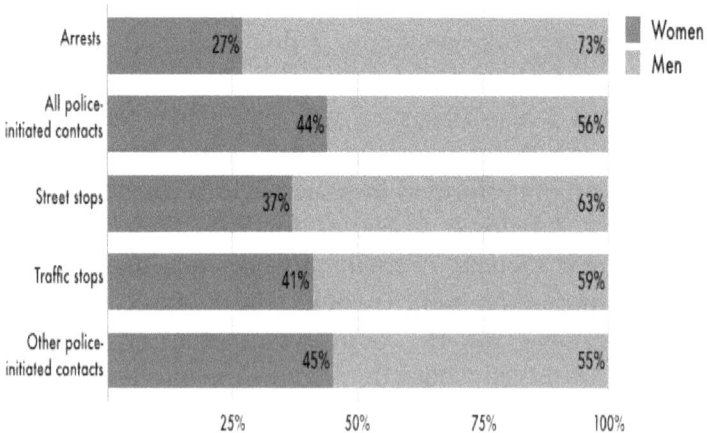

	Women	Men
Arrests	27%	73%
All police-initiated contacts	44%	56%
Street stops	37%	63%
Traffic stops	41%	59%
Other police-initiated contacts	45%	55%

[Fig 32]

Women experiencing police use of force rose dramatically between 1999 and 2015

Percent increase from 1999 to 2015 from the estimated
number of people that experienced use of force in 1999

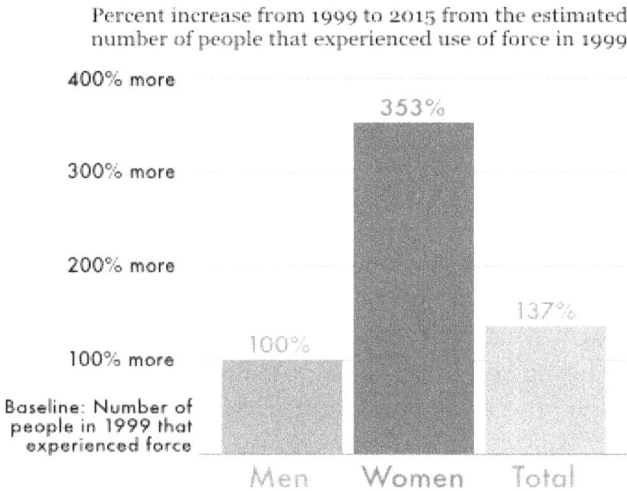

[Fig 33]

My Black Side

[Fig 33] data may be the perfect example of anecdotal evidence. The statistics bear out the problem which is the subject of this book. Racist, discrimination, and bias do not always manifest in term of negative behaviors. The victim may always see behavior as negative, but that too may be subjective.

The evidence suggests a reverse application of what White officers are accused of doing. Fewer minority stops by minority officers, might imply favoritism, not professionalism.

Not stopping me on a traffic stop because I am Black is just as bad as stopping because I am Black. You cannot enforce the law based on skin color nor should exclude potential criminality based on skin color.

How silly it is alleged that White officers profile Blacks in an insidious manor, yet say it is a good idea to ignore violations because the violator is Black. While law enforcement officers are busy playing racial trick-or-treat, who is locking up the 2.5 million burglars, prostitutes, murders, and drug addicts?

My Blue Side

"Society questions the police and their methods, and the police say, do you want the criminals off the street or not[Kurt Russell]."

Cops are <u>Law</u> enforcement professionals. A lack of dispassionate objectivity is antithetical to police duties. Because of the nature of my job, I arrested majority Black suspects during my Vice career. I charted empirical data showing the progression of my duties by assignment.

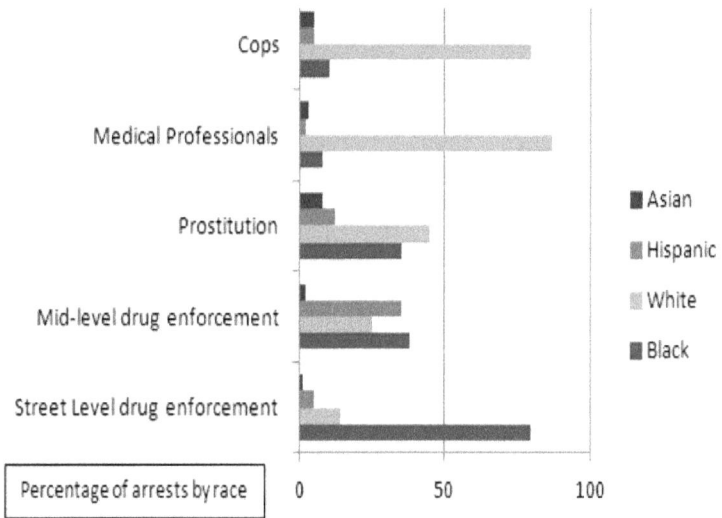

[Fig 34]

The striations in the numbers can be accounted for, but they do not explain everything.
- The targets of the investigations were selected by complaints or danger posed to society, not my unit
- The location for the drug sales and trafficking were set by the drug dealers (street corners, school-yard, alleys, parking lots etc.)

- Prostitutes and hookers market themselves in areas of town convenient to their work needs
- Medical professional ply their trades at medical facilities and pharmacies
- Cops exist in the workplace

The question becomes however, do you want the cops to do their job or not? I arrested those responsible for the problem. If my arrests seem jaded, there are; they are jaded because of the choices made by the criminals, victims, and those that support the criminals.

Street level drugs move on the street; unfortunately, the areas of town wherein the streets are savory sadly happened to frequently be in the Black community. The numbers are less skewed when you look at the user data in [Fig 38]. Notice the predominance of White users.

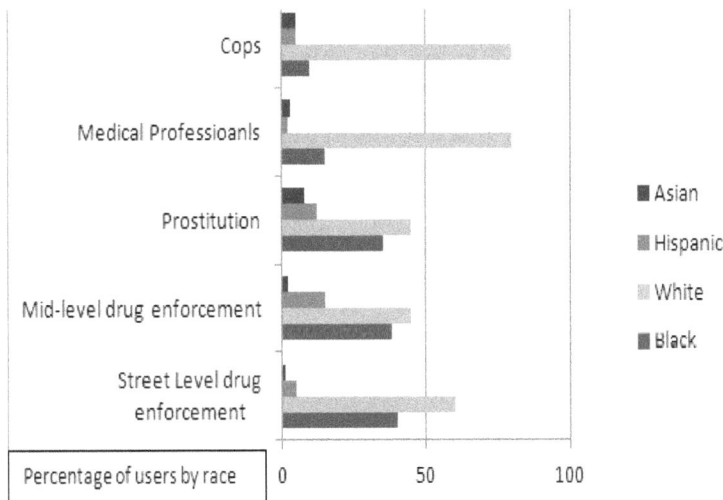

[Fig 35]

What people do not realize is that *The Establishment* is responsible for these striations as well. Why is the seller the primary target when the dual prongs in economics are supply and demand? *The Establishment* modifies its cannibalistic tendencies, and looks more towards Black Cotton.

According to the Department of Justice, there are 2.5 million burglaries and approximately 75,000 prostitution arrests annually. These figures show *The Establishment* at work. *The Establishment* allows these useless eaters to exist as fodder for the New Cotton Economic system. While Blacks are the primary cash crop, White drug users act as fertilizer.

Kurt Russell is correct, at some point society needs to decide if it wants the police to remove the barnacles from society or not. According to statistics, within 5 years[142] of conviction 70% criminals (not race dependant) will either be arrested again, or convicted again for the same type of crime. No matter their color, criminals have a distinctly unpalatable place in society. The criminal either engages in behavior society disdains, or stands convicted for behavior society disdains.

The police are by no means perfect, however the consequences to removing the only people willing to stand in the gap, and even try to keep the society, including your family safe - is not just foolhardy, and will have disastrous consequences.

8.11
Why Does Society Not Punish Excessive Force More Often?

"Our democracy is controlled by wealthy elite; politicians who work for the wealthy need the police to protect them from the people. And so the whole chain of command protects the killer cop. The ruling class give carte blanche to law enforcement, who in turn press down on those most stranded by the neoliberal state, the poor--and more so, the Black poor[143]."

My Black Side

Why punish a dog for biting. The police receive calls for service the majority of the time because someone is disturbing the peace or disturbing the smooth operation of Society. There are signs posted everywhere in America, that remind us to abide by the laws as posted. When people opt to walk outside the line, society sends in their Ambassadors of Order and Compliance.

My Blue Side

Emotions have no place in the determination of the Use of Force. For too long police actions have been judged by people sitting in a boardroom. The process of determination of Police Action, by default, must differ from the evaluation of all other physical interactions. Only the Police have the authority to take Police Action; therefore, there are a unique set of circumstances.

- Was there a Legal reason for the interaction?
- Was a violation committed?
- Was the officer clear in instructions and explained that the person is under arrest?
- Did the officer escalate within policy?
- Did the officer de-escalate within policy?

The final result of an interaction IS NOT THE DETERMINING FACTOR. There exists an expectation of injury or death when Force is used, that is why we have a Use of Force designation for the actions. No arrest requires force, except one which cannot be made without it. I have arrested murderers with no resistance, and chased people all over the city over a suspended driver's license.

The Use of Force should be a dispassionate reaction to resistance; too often however it looks personal. Sometimes it is personal; more often than not it occurs because departments do not teach Gender Specific Tactics. This means women and children receive the same levels and components of force, as males.

If you wonder why officers are rough, and sometimes brutal; look at the tools they are given to work with, their tool belt [Fig 20]. There is no kid's menu, on the gunbelt. Many officers simply default to training, often in lieu of thinking. Training is a faster, more objective response to a situation, but it often lacks empathy. The experienced officer, given time, can incorporate both: Given time, but there is often no time preceding the use of force.

When standing around a hostile group, or with a resistive subject, it is hard to stay focused on the task and remain objective. It is hard to be dispassionate, when the situation keeps escalating. Studies show that the longer the suspect is allowed to resist, the more force is required to end the conflict. My guess would be their adrenaline is pumping more and more, driving their aggression or resistance level higher, and reducing their susceptibility to pain.

8.12
Why Do The Police Seem to Point Guns At Black People More Often Than They Do At White People?

"Most middle-class White have no idea what it feels like to be subjected to police who are routinely suspicious, rude, belligerent, and brutal[144/145]."

The University of Colorado conducted a study, on racial bias and the decision to shoot. This decade-long study concluded that there were increased error rates, decreased lethal force response times. The conclusion was, "These findings suggest that Black crime enhanced the tendency to respond as if a threat were present, implying an association between Blacks and threat."

The University of Colorado further concluded, based on criterion to Shoot, "A lower, more lenient criterion suggests that participants will open fire frequently, whereas a higher, more stringent criterion suggests that participants will only fire at extremely threatening targets."

My Black Side

A study is a study. Facts are facts. If we dispute only the studies we find offensive, then we are not interested in the truth. The truth of findings spanning 10 years indicates a significantly lower threshold for Lethal Force concerning Black subjects. Thusly the interpretation of this data suggests that White cops in this study fired upon Black subjects sooner and with less justification than White suspects.

The perception of the threat is real. All the posturing, joking, and cursing during the clashes, causes an unseen reaction. The study provides insight into part of the problem. I believe there is a disparity in the interpretation of resistance. I believe in many cases while Black subjects express their rage, and disdain, which in truth, places the subject at the level of [Psychological Intimidation], I believe many White officers' perception is that the subject is at the level of [Passive Resistance].

1. [Psychological Intimidation] - Nonverbal cues indicating a subject's attitude, appearance, and physical readiness. (Karate stance, the finger, fist to palm, up your arm)
2. [Verbal Noncompliance] - Verbal responses indicating unwillingness or threats. ("Go to hell" , "I'm not going" , "I'm going to kill you")
3. [Passive Resistance] - Physical actions that do not prevent an officer's attempt to control. (Ex: Passive demonstrator sitting on the ground)

This disparity causes the officer to react to a situation that has not yet arisen. The officer appears enraged, brutal and out of control, when in fact there is a deficiency in training. When deficiencies in training meet animosity, unfortunate circumstances are often the result.

My Blue Side

I default to the statistics. There seems to be something going on, I do not know which it has to do more with, but in my opinion, this is more a functional result of subliminal fear, and bias than racism. Perhaps in time, it becomes the case that fear and bias give rise to racism as a protective measure. Those in fear can hide within the safety of White privilege.

9.0

Police

Corruption

and Reform

"The sex abuse crisis in the Catholic Church is the result of what police call 'Noble Cause Corruption," the belief that because you are dedicated to doing good, you can do no wrong[Alex Gibney]."

9.1
Police Corruption

"Police are inevitably corrupted...Police always observe that criminals prosper. It takes a pretty dull policeman to miss the fact that the position of authority is the most prosperous criminal position available{Frank Herbert}."

Police corruption is neither new nor surprising. What is surprising is that society and the media has overlooked police corruption for decades, and now in the light of a few cell phone videos the concept has become a rally cry. Use of force and excessive force are seemingly Black and White areas, but they are not. Having to decide exactly what to do to control another human is not easy trying to gauge exactly how much force to use is difficult. Oftentimes the true amount of force needed to affect the arrest cannot be measured accurately until after the arrest. Sometimes the persons physiological response to the amount of force is extreme, and unexpected, in these cases intellect must prevail, not mob mentality.

In a seven year of the study, researchers compiled 6,724[146] cases, 674 officers were arrested on multiple occasions during the study. Although approximately 60 percent of the crimes happened off-duty the study indicated many of the crimes involved police related elements;

- Off-duty officers flash a badge
- Use of an official weapon
- Abuse their power, relationships with DA's office or the Blue line of silence to authority to commit crime

The same study found that more than 81 percent of the crimes were committed by patrol or detective-level officers and that nearly 85 percent were reported in metropolitan as opposed to rural agencies.

Excessive force has been a chief complaint from the Black community since the 1960's, when the Law forced Whites to accept integration and civil rights. The same people that fought prohibition, fought integration, and there is still a resistance to equality prevalent according to complaints filed.

Yes; something should be done to preserve the integrity of the Law Enforcement profession the problem is deciding how best to effectuate the modifications.

From 2005 to 2011, there were a total of 6,724 police arrest cases.

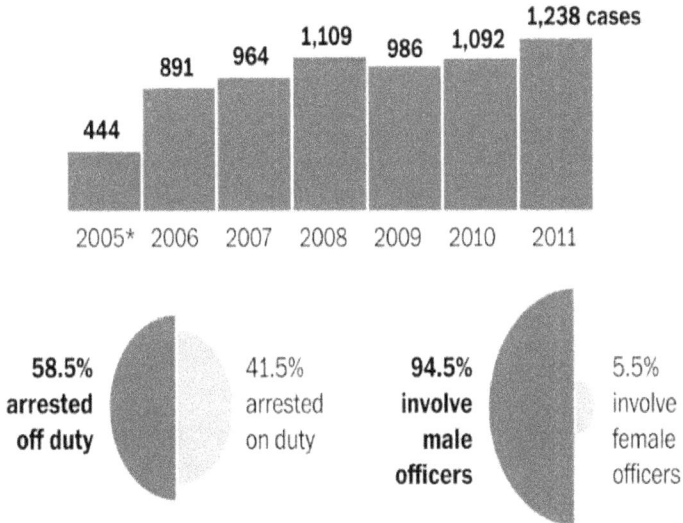

						1,238 cases
444	891	964	1,109	986	1,092	
2005*	2006	2007	2008	2009	2010	2011

| 58.5% arrested off duty | 41.5% arrested on duty | 94.5% involve male officers | 5.5% involve female officers |

[Fig 36]

Police corruption is but a tiny portion of the problem, the problems also lie in the judiciary, politics and societal influence. Statistically only 54 percent of the arrested officers were fired, and 37.5 percent of the officers arrested for domestic violence lost their jobs.

I firmly believe most of the categories of crime, with the exception of sexually oriented issues stem from work related stress and Excessive Force Subjectivity[c].

Victims of police crimes

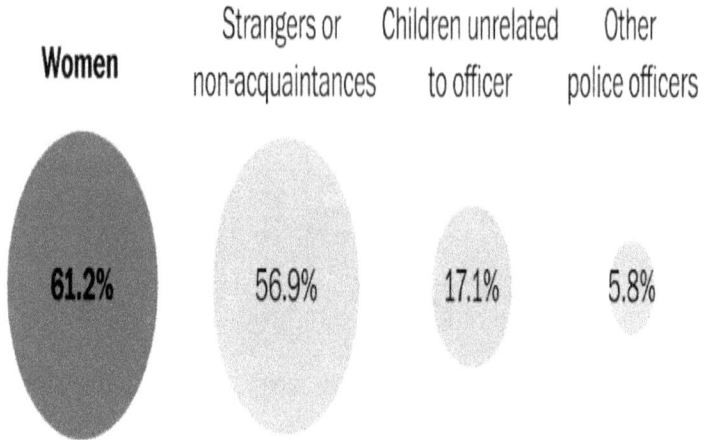

	Women	Strangers or non-acquaintances	Children unrelated to officer	Other police officers
	61.2%	56.9%	17.1%	5.8%

[Fig 37]

I do not believe excessive force is necessarily the same as corruption, but as a pattern it rises to official oppression thereby becoming corruption. John Kelly and Mark Nichols in USA Today[147] cite statistics that over a ten year period 85,000 officers were investigated for excessive force, and more than 30,000 officers that were decertified by 44 state oversight agencies. They additionally cite;

- Results include 22,924 investigations of excessive force
- 3,145 allegations of rape, child molestation, or sexual misconduct
- 2,307 cases of domestic violence by officers
- 2,227 instances of perjury, tampering with evidence or witnesses or falsifying reports
- 418 reports of officers obstructing investigations
- 2,500 have been investigated on 10 or more charges
- 20 faced 100 or more allegations yet kept their badge for years

85, 000 Cases over 10 years

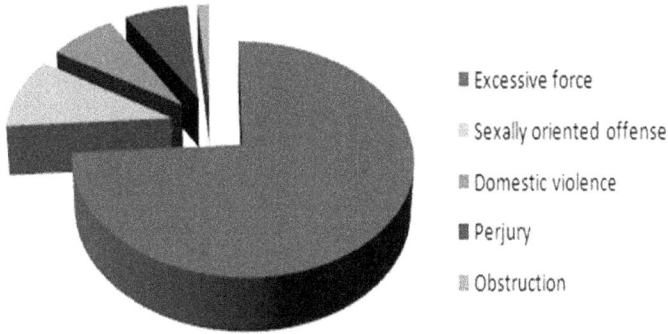

- Excessive force
- Sexally oriented offense
- Domestic violence
- Perjury
- Obstruction

[Fig 38]

There is an alarming number of excessive force complaints, and the research highlighted what events most of the officers prohibited from returning to police work were censured.

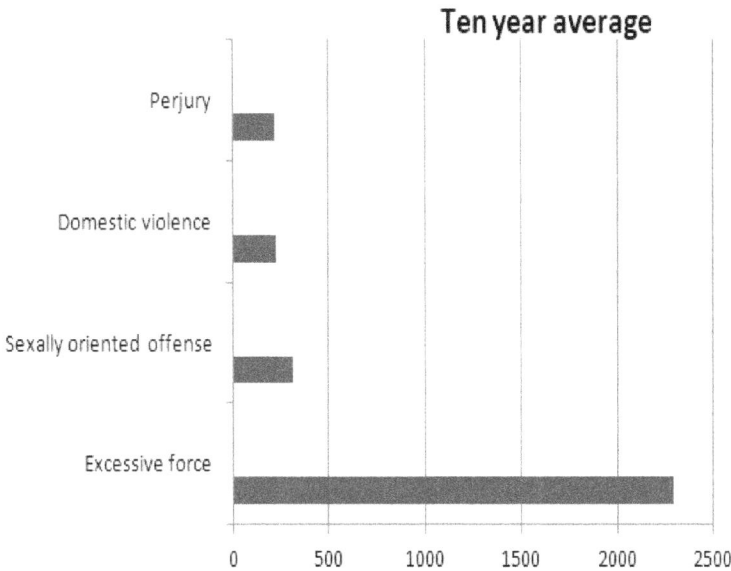

[Fig 39]

What most cops get banned for

In 44 states, USA TODAY obtained records of more than 30,000 law enforcement officers who lost their certification. In about one-third of the cases, states would not provide specific reasons. Here's the breakdown of reasons in the documented cases:

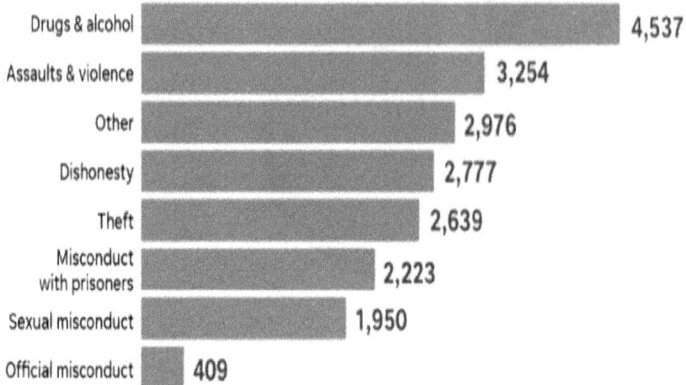

Drugs & alcohol	4,537
Assaults & violence	3,254
Other	2,976
Dishonesty	2,777
Theft	2,639
Misconduct with prisoners	2,223
Sexual misconduct	1,950
Official misconduct	409

SOURCE State police licensure records and USA TODAY research

[Fig 40]

Excessive Force Subjectivity is when an action deemed appropriate by the officer and that falls within policy is subject to political and media conjecture, and ruled Excessive or out of policy. As an example; during a drug deal, the dealer initially drives over one officer and then attempts to strike another with his car. A SWAT officer fires three rounds into the car. The officer was charged with 'Firing rounds' out of policy, because someone used a slide ruler and decided that the officer's last round was towards the rear of the fleeing vehicle violating policy. The reason this is inordinately stupid is simple, the car was moving and the officer was defending other officers trying to stop the threat. Ironically the policy read DO NOT SHOOT AT OR FROM A MOVING VEHICLE, which by strict interpretation made all three rounds violations.

The ruling was not based in logic, or due to a sense of corrective actions, it was a social-political decision. By ruling that there was an out of policy, the Agency indemnified itself against the potential lawsuit.

While there are neither excuses, nor condoning of crimes of violence committed by officers, to pretend that job related stressors do no effect this behavior is folly, and part of the reason there is so much violence. Father Leo Booth writes a book, Father Leo Booth wrote a book, "When God Becomes a Drug[148]". I believe violence is a coping mechanism for many officers, and then there are just plain bullies.

I believe Herbert is correct in pointing out that authority is the most prosperous position. However, I disagree that cops seek to become criminal's, I believe they become criminals in more than 50% of the incidents trying to assert, accumulate or retain power.

Do not be deceived cops wield a kind of power you will never understand. The power to save lives and do good is intoxicating. But the lower tier sinister power is the ability to wield power to make one feel good. The abusive coercive persona is the more dangerous of the two.

My Blue Side/My Black Side

Another item upon which both of my sides is that there is corruption amongst the rank and file of the U/S Law Enforcement community. That however is the only area upon which both sides agree. The media pretends that profanity, and poor judgment equals corruption; it does not.

I think corruption is dangerous for both the same and a far more grievous reason. The corrupt cop in my opinion is the most dangerous member of community. There is no other member of the community bearing both the responsibility and authority than the Law Enforcement professional.

Over the years I have worked with, for and around corrupt cops. I look upon police corruption as the danger it is. The cop can lie to judges and district attorney's get search and arrest warrants under false pretenses, alter, or disappear evidence, plant evidence, fabricate charges and last but certainly not least - use lethal force.

While I maintain that I have investigated and arrested more cops than most officers in internal affairs, I feel that great care is required to make determinations of excessive force, and corruption. False charges, arrests, and cases, and bonafide excessive force should not be tolerated.

In the same manner however, the Blue Witch Hunt© should not be allowed. Indicting criminally and morally app officers is a ridicules concept, and frankly insulting. There are so many things wrong in American society, there is no pure facet. Unlike the criminal, selfish, addicts, abusers, molesters, corrupt politicians and any other blight on morality; cops try to make the country a better place for everyone to live - even those protesting and spitting at them.

Unlike societal erosion, police corruption is an easy fix; prosecute cops more effectively for the crimes they commit, and keep media and politics out of the courtroom.

9.2
Police Officer Angry Aggression
Theory© (POAAT)
vs
Nobel Cause Corruption

"Therefore, it's not enough for an officer of the law to have combat training and legal knowledge, it is also imperative that you learn about biases, that you learn about the fears, insecurities and instinctual tendencies of the human mind. An officer of the law without an understanding of biases is like a ten year old with a knife - they may feel that they have power, but they have no clue as to the real life implications of that power. Remember my friend, power that doesn't help the people, is not power but pandemic.

Your combat training doesn't make you a police officer, for when enraged even an ordinary civilian can take down ten police officers - your knowledge of law doesn't make you an officer of the law, for when pushed even a mediocre college student can defeat an army of elite legal minds - what makes you a police officer is your absolute acceptance of your role in society - the role of selfless servants. Once you accept the role of selfless servants wholeheartedly, people are bound to trust you.

My brave, conscientious officers of the law, if you want people to trust you, don't use the phrase "police are your friends", for it only makes you sound authoritarian, egotistical and condescending - instead, remind them "police are humans too" - acknowledge your mistakes and work towards correcting them, so that you can truly become the Caretaker of People, which is the very definition of COP[Abhijit Naskar]."

Noble Cause Corruption is corruption theorized to be caused by an adherence to a teleological ethical system, resulting in unethical or illegal means to benefit the greater good. In terms of Law enforcement the same paradigm manifests in the philosophy or drive to make the world a safer place.

The other side of the pendulum is POAAT (Police Officer Angry Aggression Theory). This theory Suggests that the chronic stress of police work along, with the inability to respond to the actual sources of that stress increase both the perception of threats and the aggressiveness of responses to perceived threat[149].

I think there is a third perspective, for the purpose of the book let us call it the Blue Halo Complex[©]. The Blue Halo Complex is a progressive degeneration from morality to utility.

[Fig. 41 - The Blue Halo]

Once you enter Blue HALO, (this does not have to be a permanent state), perceptions and deportment change;

- Development of perceptions of threats to 'The greater good'
- Hyper vigilance, marred by a sever disdain for all that is criminal

Us vs Them is almost a mantra for a holy war, in many officers, and more so than racism, PERCEIVED THREAT, abounds often manifested by short temperedness, quick responsiveness, and a zeal to use force of some kind.

The reason so many officers do not perceive the Blue HALO as corruption is that the intention on many of these seemingly malevolent actions, are Blue HALO reactions - limited in scope and reason, fueled by fundamentalism. Cops just want t maintain the peace and keep people safe, those who wish to harm others find an vigilant defender of people; Black and White. Too often, Blue HALOs (HALO officers [Fig. 41]) respond to the personalities of the people rather than the incident. When arrest is necessary, the officer MUST determine the most expeditious manner in which to proceed. Violence is undesirable but it is expeditious. All that needs to ignite the Blue HALO is the resistive belligerent criminal. Although no officer should standby and be cursed at and yelled at, Blue HALOs cannot abide the perceived threat and reactively either to a nonexistent threat or over reacts according to the USE of Force Continuum.

I never relished arresting cops, unlike Internal Affairs I never had to nit-pick officers, when I got their case, there were always criminal accusations. It was my pleasure to remove them from the ranks of the honorable. A hand-strike against a resisting prisoner was not a case I had to investigate, someone else made that decision. I think my job was better; a crime leaves very little room for subjectivity. You either stole or beat your wife, or you did not. Whether or not four punches was too many, is not a course of decisions I would have been interested in making.

There is no real way to reenact an event, even duplicating the facts cannot account for adrenaline, and other emotions readily on the scene. Two individuals, neither willing to lose, there is going to be a clash; Mike

Tyson bit off an ear in frustration, and in his defense he offered the because, that 'It was a fight.' Cops have emotions too. My point is that reform; though needed, is not always cut and dry, even professionals when they fight safely in the ring, lose their temper.

9.3
Legitimate Suggestions to Reform Policing vs Defunding

"Social reform is not to be secured by noise and shouting; by complaints and denunciation; by the formation of parties, or the making of revolutions; but by the awakening of thought and the progress of ideas. Until there be correct thought, there cannot be right action; and when there is correct thought, right action will follow{Henry George150}.

[Fig. 42]

Making history is not always a good thing, and St Louis's crime rate since 2017 places them in the top three most dangerous U.S. cities. Unless the police in St Louis contribute heavily to the crime rate, hampering their efforts is counterintuitive.

Having served in Law Enforcement and required to prosecute other LEOs, I do not support, nor agree with the spectacularly ridiculous concept of *Defunding the police*. This would leave the society in a worse predicament that it already endures. There is already ample evidence that fear of retribution, prosecution, incarceration or lethal encounters with the police have minimal dissuasive effect on those intent upon violence.

Some of the cities proposing Defunding already show that the numbers of violent crimes rose. In addition to the potential or unfettered violence to rise, there is the distinct problem that Police agencies will face personnel shortages causing lower disciplinary action, and hiring of less qualified applicants

[Fig. 43[151]]

I have found one of the difficulties in prosecuting cops is that there is a lack of applicable law. The police officer is the most unique individual in the society in my opinion. As discussed previously, there is no one in society with the knowledge, skills, ability, versatility, and responsibility of a police officer. This being the case, I suggest the following approaches to resolve a great deal of police impropriety.

• **The oath sworn by all badged Law Enforcement Professionals should be federally overseen**. How can this be established and not violate State's rights? Grants-in-Aid. Few departments do not rely on federal funding for training, or equipment. This is not accomplished by Law by via Grants-in-aid. Almost every Agency in America uses grant monies. This also aligns with the Constitutional protection of life.

• **All sworn personnel take FBI established certification training annually** in Use of Force, biased based policing, civil rights violations, and official corruption, creating a national LEO response to sworn responsibilities.

- **All fatal shootings should trigger an FBI/DOJ inquiry** as depriving a person of life is a Constitutional issue as well.
- **Each State must systemize a different set of crimes for Law enforcement officers.** The language is crucial, because it allows the prosecution of cops who hide behind legal doctrines, and good faith exceptions. Prosecutors no longer would find themselves trying to force cop-crimes into civilian laws: most of which do not adequately cover crimes *Under Color of Law*[12].
- **Murders committed by LEOS on or off duty should be punished under federal statutes** and sentencing guidelines and the return to the usage of corresponding civil rights violation penalties.
- **Use terms like maliciously, malevolently, with criminal irresponsibly, these terms clearly differentiate crimes from civil torts.** Intentionally, consciously, or recklessly are meters used to measure actions for arrest purposes. This places ALL officers at a disadvantage since all force falls in this category. There is a reason society has a wrongful death civil statute.
- **The sentence for cop-crimes should be at 85% versus the standard 30% requirement to serve.**
- **No longer allow the misuse of "suspect similitude" as a ruse to reasonable suspicion or probable cause.**
- **Require all citizen complaints be in writing and submitted via sworn affidavit.** Prosecute fallacious reports.
- **No longer allow the abuse of pretextual stops.** The pretext must support the stop.
- **Better train officers in mental health issues**. In 20 years of policing I have had a total of about 23 hours of mental health and crisis intervention training.

---

[12] The phrase Under Color of Law, is when a Law enforcement officer; using granted authority, willfully deprives or conspires to deprive a person of a right protected by the Constitution.

- **Each Sector needs to have a two-officer Crisis car**, with specially trained officers with more than 20 hours of training. If possible the Crisis car responds to all potential MH calls for service, and if the officers have to make an arrest or commit the patient, the other Crisis Officer can get in with another zone car and remain in service.
- **Give EMT's limited police powers and arm them with Tasers and handcuffs.** While they cannot enforce law, they can defend themselves and people in the area surrounding the patient. Since EMTs have the training and the medication to handle non-lethal mental health issues, dispatch them first. The police only need to respond to cases where EMTs lack the ability to control the situation.
- **Truth in sentencing is a necessity in Law Enforcement long overdue, and it should extend by default to convicted LEOs.**

By way of example to change:

[Criminal Homicide - First degree murder by a Law Enforcement Officer] is:

- A premeditated and intentional killing of another by a Law Enforcement Officer
  - A killing of another, committed in the perpetration of or attempt to perpetrate any first degree murder, act of terrorism, arson, robbery, burglary, theft, kidnapping, unjustified lethal force; causal positional asphyxiation, chokehold
  - A killing of another, committed as the result of the unlawful throwing, placing, or discharging of a destructive device, the result of a warrant secured or executed by subterfuge.
  - No culpable mental state is required for conviction except the intent to commit the enumerated offenses or acts in those subdivisions.

❖ A Law Enforcement Officer convicted of first-degree murder shall be punished by:
  - Death;
  - Imprisonment for life without possibility of parole; or
  - Imprisonment for life.

❖ "Premeditation" is an act done after the exercise of reflection and judgment. "Premeditation" means that the intent to kill must have been formed prior to the act itself. It is not necessary that the purpose to kill pre-exist in the mind of the accused for any definite period of time. The mental state of the accused at the time the accused allegedly decided to kill must be carefully considered in order to determine whether the accused was sufficiently free from excitement and passion to be capable of premeditation. Legal doctrine under which the Law Enforcement Officer interacted with the victim.]

- **Second Degree, Murder, Felony Murder, Voluntary Manslaughter, Involuntary Manslaughter**]

- **[Agg Assault by Law Enforcement Officer]** A Law Enforcement Officer commits aggravated assault who: Intentionally or knowingly commits an assault and: Causes serious bodily injury to another; or uses or displays a deadly weapon; or recklessly commits an assault, and: Causes serious bodily injury to another; or coercively uses or displays a deadly weapon. Threatens physical or oppressive reprisal against a citizen in retaliation of a complaint, or refusal to submit to random questioning.
    - **[Assault by A Law Enforcement Officer**]
    - **[Vandalism by an Officer]**
    - **[Harassment]**

You cannot cure racism, and you cannot successfully cull the criminal minded; however, the evildoer, and weak-minded followers can be encouraged to stay with the bounds or fear jail, for behavior previously acceptable.

I agree with Aberjhani but I think this is a systemic societal civic failure. People need to take the opportunity to avoid violent confrontations with officers...they more often than not will result in lethal results.

9.4
Citizen Oversight Committee

"I sometimes wish that people would put a little more emphasis upon the observance of the law than they do upon its enforcement [Calvin Coolidge]."

∽

I pulled this off FB, and I know the author, a career LEO. The comment was in regards to the idiotic suggestion to stop funding the only thing currently, that's helps keep violence in a holding pattern. I think this could never be more applicable than regarding the qualifications for the Citizen's Oversight Committee.

"I've kept pretty quiet on defunding police, mostly because officers are asked to do a hell of a lot of stuff that has NOTHING to do with public safety...but here are my questions for you 'Defund the police' fans.

- Have you ever one time asked an officer what a day working is like?
- Have you ever done a ride along?
- Have you ever been an officer?
- Have you attended a citizen's police academy?
- If you can't answer yes to at least one of these...then you need to keep your opinion to yourself, because you have NO CLUE about the expectations put on these officers every day. Not just from the citizens they serve, but from the officials they work for
- If you have never ridden in a car running emergency through rush hour traffic, where no one will get out of the way...only to arrive on the scene of an accident where someone's loved one has died...you don't get to voice an opinion
- If you've never seen a woman who is bloody and beaten by the man who says he loves her... you have no opinion

- If you've never held the hand of a young boy who wrecked his motorcycle on the interstate while he begs you to help him...please don't talk to me about defunding the police
- If you've never spent hours trying to help someone who believes the government is watching him through his TV, I really don't want to hear what you have to say
- If you have not gone home from work in tears over something that happened on a shift. You are in no position to judge
- If you've never held a baby while medical staff is working on his mother because their car went off the side of the interstate, I don't think anything you say matters to me
- If you have never had nightmares about being shot, or having to shoot someone, or a bad call you responded to...please do not offer your opinion

Being a Police Officer is one of the hardest jobs in the world. Could it use some reform? probably. Is the best way to cause reform, to defund it? No it's not. If you think things need to change, I'm ok with that...but please have some clue as to what an officer does before you run your mouth about defunding.

If you had any knowledge about the job you would insist on better training, more resources, more officers, less pressure, better benefits to bring in the best candidates for the job, better working conditions, and better overall pay; Just my opinion!"

Why do I think these experiences are vital considerations? because this is not a jury system. Citizen Oversight is not 12 average citizens deciding whether or not a person committed a crime. When cops are charged criminally, they leave the Law Enforcement community in my opinion and should be judged along the same criterion as criminals.

My experience prosecuting does not make me an expert, but it does give me more insight than most people do on an Oversight Committee. I think the minimum requirement to sit on this arbitration board should be that you have to attend a Citizens Police Academy and do 40 hours of Police ride-alongs, which include time spent at the department Emergency Communications Center.

My Black Side

Cops make a lot of decisions every day, more than most people, with the possible exception of soldiers. There is no one else whose job ranges from giving stickers to kids, to taking lives. Even judges cannot execute people; they can only order it done, after due process. I think cops are held to a standard that does not equate to their tasks. Empowering citizens with no understanding of the requirements of the average patrol officer, is a disservice to everyone.

My Blue Side

There have been a total of 1,962 nationwide exonerations since 1989[152]. These are just DNA exonerations alone, not racism, corrupt cops, or jury tampering. This number makes medical errors are the third leading cause of death of 251,000[153] annually in the United States[154]. Medication errors harm an estimated 1.5[155] million people every year, costing at least $3.5 billion annually[156].

In Millions

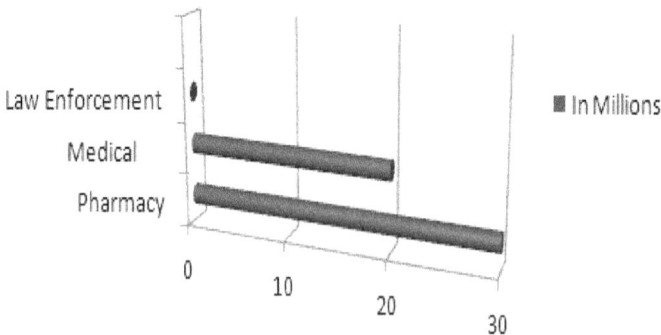

[Fig 44]

With all these errors and deaths every year, why is the populous convinced that the archenemy of all Black people and decency everywhere, is Law Enforcement? In my opinion, the architect of this lie is the media. Why is there no media frenzy over the other tragedies to citizens listed in [Fig 44]. Every year medical malfeasance results in the death or injury of more Americans than Law Enforcement intentionally kills annually.

The Establishment is flawed, and yes, there is much improvement needed in the actions of many law enforcement officers across the country. However, giving the powerless the power to judge those we trained and empowered is nonsensical.

Running out and putting a useless patch on a problem is not a solution; it is the beginning of another problem. Why is there no Citizen's Oversight Committee for the Supreme Court? There is the Criminal Justice System; as is with cops. When they break the law, we drag them out of their tall tower, take the guns and bullets, and make them sit in the same seat with every person they ever sent to prison.

I interviewed a former colleague who has managerial, investigative, use of force and oversight experience in Law Enforcement. He indicated to me that he believes much of the problem in the LEO community, is a workplace culture issue. He states that the old bitter officer motif has been passed along to through the generations, and the younger officers get swept up into the toxicity. He cites an Administrative failure to ensure the necessary generational shifts within the cadre.

As part of my Executive Consulting duties I prepared a multigenerational C-Level Workshop, to address the generational shift. The current workplace hosts;
- Baby Boomers - born 1946 to 1964
- Generation X - born 1965 to 1980
- Millennials - born 1981 to 2000
- And soon, Generation Z - born 2001 to 2020

failing to address the differences in values, work ethic, and social morays is a major industry failure, it is not unique to Law Enforcement. However in Law Enforcement, the results can be lethal. Furthermore, he asserts that the Law Enforcement community failed to change as rapidly as the society, making the Blue-Belief System archaic and potentially Machiavellian.

Part of that toxicity he points out manifests in bias. "If you believe you are war with a particular group of people, you might respond aggressively towards them." His point of view also draws upon experience in the armed forces. The perspective of 'being at war' I find of particular interest, as it brings to mind my military training in regards to the way we think of the 'enemy'. This bias often leads to fear in officers. Fear of dastardly outcomes, fueled by perceptions and bias, again lends itself to hyper vigilance and over reaction.

Interestingly enough he said he disagrees with defunding; he thinks the better transition is to lessen the non-police related tasks officers currently have to address. Having to constantly deal with situation beyond the scope of their authority and training places both the officers and the community in harm's way.

I believe The U.S. has a Citizen's Oversight Committee; it is the Criminal Justice System. Overhaul the Criminal Justice System and the trickle-down effect will resonate into the Law Enforcement community.

My Blue Side

Oversight is necessary, but the participants, should be trained, objective people of all walks of life; including former cops like myself, familiar and comfortable with prosecuting official corruption.

9.5
Social Worker Injustice

"Send Social Workers Instead Of Cops!" Ends Tragically As First Social Worker Killed By A Violent Client In Seattle

Someone tried to convince me that social workers should respond to calls as a part of the defunding the police strategy. This tragic headline[157] is a caption that covers more than 40 years of failed Mental Health Services by the Government, in the service of mentally ill people. This is absurd. In a hospital environment, the individual has been rendered weaponless prior to engaging with the social worker, and is housed in a facility preventing collateral defame potential.

By way of example, I received a Code 3 call to a Mental Facility. The text of the call read, "Mental Health Patient, has locked himself in a bathroom and is biting himself." There were so many things wrong with this call for service.

- Firstly I did not run code three this was NOT an emergency
- This individual was already in a facility, and then became uncontrollable
- This person was self-harming (not an arrestable offense)
- In responding to this call, I would have apprehended the person and taken them to the facility, they were already housed within
- The society already dispensed its responsibility to this patient by housing them in a treatment facility
- No crime was being committed, not trespassing, nor assault of another person, and despite suicide being against the law the police had no authority over this individual under the current law.

The Potential to harm oneself or others' is the catch all phrase these type cases fall into. Since Departmental policy allows for arrest in these instances (which allow police to take drunks, homeless, Alzheimer's, demented, person in for service and protection) there was nothing to be done. Which is what I told the staff as I pulled up to the building. Call me when he commits a crime.

I did not shirk my responsibility; Law Enforcement had none in this case. What did the facility really want? They wanted me to transport their patient elsewhere and not have to foot the bill for the process. They would have to restrain (chemically or physically) the patient, and then provide secure transport (at least on guard and one medical personnel if chemically restrained). Effectively, then intended to throw the patient into my trunk and be done with them.

In the 1960's, "deinstitutionalization[158]" freed mentally ill men and women from the bleak mental hospitals began. *The Establishment* of community-based mental health services envisioned by the architects of deinstitutionalization never materialized.

According to statistics, approximately 15% of the U.S. jail population is mentally ill, 'suffering from schizophrenia, bipolar disorder, and major depression, among other illnesses'. This sad statistics exemplifies the *Intuitional* response to things contrary to Non-Cotton Economics. This means the police answer an unconscionable 4.5 million calls for service involving the mentally ill.

Mentally ill people are a burden to the budget in the eyes of the *Establishment*. Non-Cotton Economics has a use for Crop-Niggers, illegal's, even Native Americans, however, since deinstitutionalization, Mental Ill people are only a cash crop for one segment of the Economy - The carrion known as Pharmaceutical Companies.

Despite the outlawed Corporate Practice of Medicine the Pharmacy industry found a loophole; they turned mentally ill (including geriatrics) into a cash crop. Since they are no longer housed they need to be medicated, in order to function. The resultant Pharmaceutical fleecing of the tax-payer came into being. The mentally ill, most often fall to the budgets of States and Medicare. This blank check allows for another level of humans as a crop fleecing.

I learned a lot during my years in drug enforcement. In one such case, I assisted the FDA in dismantling and counterfeit drug operation (housed less than 1.5 mile from a police precinct). I was astounded to find that n controlled substances were being counterfeited. This facility only counterfeited 'maintenance drugs'. It was explained to me that Controlled substances are not as lucrative due to pain management laws. I might get #270 Oxycodone, but that ends my 90-day allowance. Maintenance drugs (blood pressure, cholesterol, COPD etc.), are a year round necessity. "Older Americans are particularly vulnerable to medication overload. Today, 42 percent of adults over the age of 65 take five or more medications - a red flag for harm. The rapid increase in the number of medications older people are taking has led to a sharp rise in serious side effects, known clinically as adverse drug events. We estimate that 1 in 5 older Americans - that's 10 million people - experienced an adverse drug event in 2018. More than one-quarter of a million were hospitalized because of a reaction to medication. If nothing is done, adverse drug events over the next decade can be expected to cause 4.6 million hospitalizations of older Americans, 74 million outpatient visits, and nearly 150,000 premature deaths[159].

What my point is that the police are indirectly 'gunslingers' for big pharma as well. The old adage that there is more money in treatment than cure holds true for big pharma. The infirmed are a cash crop. When a 'crazy' gets out of hand, The Establishment calls upon the police simply put them down. It is not that there is not a better solution to dealing with the mentally ill, it just costs more.

The scenario I most often hear suggested is to dispatch social workers on calls where the suspect is mentally ill. Problem; no one knows what the mental status of the person walking down the street is; drunks do all manner of stupid things.

What people do not consider when they complain about police response is more often than not they have no firsthand knowledge of police response. The police have to go because they are the only service other than animal control that has the devices specially designed to restrain and control humans. Dispatch informs the officer that is a possible mental health issue, prior to arrival. Some believe that this information makes the officer feel more at ease, but the converse is the case. An unstable person is dangerous mentally ill or not.

The ideal and prescribed response is that EMS is on standby and the police assess the situation. If given the time, and the ability, the responding officer will contain and control the subject. If the person can be restrained, they are transported to a medical facility, and remain in police custody until the facility determines the treatment regime.

Too often officers are called to transport mentally ill persons with the appropriate paperwork to another facility. Why are the police used to save money? It is not that the police do not care, this is a job, they should not be tasked with. IF THE POLICE CANNOT MAKE MEDICAL DETERMINATIONS, they should not be tasked with medical missions.

Big business and societal indifference is why so many mentally ill people find themselves facing the barrel of an officer's weapon. The people are mentally ill, if we need to medicate them to make them functional - what part of their illness affords them the ability to self-care?

Undeniably, this incident would have resulted in another police shooting. According to the article one of the detectives is quoted as saying, *"The murder of Ms. Benson was horrifying, an unarmed victim, trapped in her own office, unable to escape or fight back against the defendant's rage and blade. Equally terrifying was the defendant's willingness to violently attack others who came to Ms. Benson's assistance."* There was going to be a lethal event with this individual, had the police interacted with him first, then he would not have been able to harm the victim.

In the detectives quote the suspect is called defendant, this means he survived. Ask the question, now what do we do with him? You do not want mentally in jail, and you do not want them shot. How many social workers do we plan to retrain each year to replace the ones we leave in harm's way.

Many drunks and homeless are mentally ill persons over or under-medicated would fare better inside a facility. Many that call the police barbarians and in the same breath say they do not have the budget to pay for facilities and privatize the care of the mentally ill.

10.0

Legal

Issues

"Strength used for oppression is violence; strength used for defending the weak is justice{Abhijit Naskar}160 ."

10.1
Biased Based Policing
And Deportment Policies

"Because implicit bias feeds into systems like incarceration, housing, and healthcare, these systems continue to flourish while racial disparities grow. As racial disparities grow, so does implicit bias and stereotypes against BIPOC[161], creating a harmful cycle. For example, when using a similar resume, job seekers with Black-sounding names received 50 percent fewer callbacks than job seekers with White-sounding names. Here we can see that implicit bias clearly affects the hiring process. When Black people are given fewer opportunities, it makes it that much harder for them to succeed[162]."

We now have more words in our arsenal to explain the injustices and the shortcomings of the Criminal Justice System. One of the words, which ties into the schemata or decision-making is bias. This concept is not insignificant, yet it is rarely mentioned in the media as casual. The problem with not understanding or using this term accounts for much of what we mistakenly term racism.

I will not hyperbolize about each of the 13 listed components in this sample policy, other than to articulate that many departments set out such guidelines in an attempt to ensure professionalism. CALEA (Communications Assistance for Law Enforcement Act) and other professional police standardization organizations require departments to implement similar policies prior to receiving their seal of approval. For decades, departments have laid these rules out as requirements to wear the badge, and receive bullets. Yet year after year, officers transgress the regulations. Officers do not blatantly violate police policies just because they are racist or biased since most policies regarding excessive force and racially motivated behavior also break the law.

1. [Biased Based Policing] - is the selection of individuals for enforcement intervention based solely on a common trait of a group, such as race, ethnic origin, gender, socioeconomic status, sexual orientation, or age. This however does not preclude consideration of race or ethnicity when it is part of a suspect's description or is otherwise validly related to an officer's investigation of criminal activity] simply put, race and ethnic demographics cannot be the sole or primary basis for police engagement.

2. [Reasonable Suspicion] - It is a conclusion based on a set of expressible facts and circumstances that would warrant a person of reasonable caution to believe that an infraction of the law has been committed, is about to be committed, or is in the process of being committed, by the person or persons under suspicion. This can be based on the observations of a police officer combined with his or her training and experience, and/or reliable information received from credible sources. No individual, once cited or warned, shall be detained beyond the point where there exists no reasonable suspicion of further criminal activity, and no person, vehicle, or dwelling shall be searched in the absence of a warrant, a legally recognized exception to the warrant requirement, or the person's voluntary consent. NOTE: It is strongly recommended that consent searches only be conducted with written consent, using the proper departmental form. If the individual indicates that they will consent to a search but are refusing to sign the form, fill out the form anyway and indicate "consent" to search but refuse to sign," inserting initials and the signature of any witness in the signature block. In the absence of a specific, credible report containing a physical description, a person's race, ethnic origin, gender, socioeconomic status, sexual orientation, or age, or any combination of these, shall not be a factor in determining probable cause for an arrest or reasonable suspicion for a stop.

On an annual basis, the Office of Professional Accountability will compile an administrative review of all profiling complaints for the year, including the findings as to whether they were [Sustained], [Not-sustained], or [Unfounded] including a review of agency practices including citizen concerns. This report will be made public through the Office of the Chief of Police. Members will not collect intelligence data on any individual merely on the basis of that person's religious and/or political affiliations, race, sex, nationality, sexual orientation, ethnic background, or the basis of that person's support of unpopular cause. The deliberate recording of any misleading information related to the actual or perceived race, ethnic origin, gender, socioeconomic status, sexual orientation, or age of a person stopped for investigative or enforcement purposes is prohibited and a cause for disciplinary action]. This departmental and legal requirement sets about delineation between legitimate and illegal police action. Either officers have reasonable suspicion, or they must fabricate it. Those that fabricate the information are more insidious than racists are; they are criminal.

3. [Traffic enforcement/Vehicle Stops Forms] - will be accompanied by consistent, ongoing supervisory control to ensure that officers do not go beyond the boundary of reasonableness in conducting such activities. Supervisors will monitor traffic activities of assigned employees to ensure that biased enforcement of traffic violators does not occur. Supervisors shall review reports filed on stops by officers, and respond at random to back up officers on vehicle stops, and shall take appropriate action whenever it appears that this policy is being violated, being particularly alert to any pattern or practice of possible discriminatory treatment by individual officers or components] in order to discourage bias based policing, departmental mandates the recording of the demographics of the citizen in questions. This is another measure departmentally derived to aid in identifying and bias within the department.

4. [Training Measures] - Officers will receive initial and ongoing training in proactive enforcement tactics, including training in officer safety, courtesy, cultural diversity, laws, governing search and seizure, and interpersonal communications skills. Training programs will emphasize

the need to respect the rights of all citizens to be free from unreasonable government intrusion or police action based on a common trait of a group, such as race, ethnic origin, gender, socioeconomic status, sexual orientation, or age.

5. [Property Seizure and Forfeiture] - All seizures of property shall be subject to the same standards set forth in the above order in that the decision to seize property shall not be based solely on a common trait of a group, such as race, ethnic origin, gender, socioeconomic status, sexual orientation, or age.

6. [Profanity] - Employees shall not use abusive, indecent, or profane language or gestures in the workplace, in the performance of their duties or in the presence of a member of the public.

7. [Obstruction of Rights] - Employees shall not knowingly deprive any person of any right to which they are entitled by law or the rules and regulations of the Government.

8. [Discrimination] - All employees shall perform their duties in a manner that is fair, impartial, and without prejudice toward any person or group.

9. [Intimidation] - Employees shall not by verbal threats, physical means, or color of office, inhibit or discourage any person from engaging in lawful activities.

10. [Abusive Treatment] - Employees shall not treat any person or animal cruelly by the use of excessive force or failing to act in a humane manner when circumstances justify such action.

11. [Self-Control] - Employees shall not argue unnecessarily with any person or otherwise show a lack of self-control.

12. Derogatory Notices - Employees shall not post or circulate notices of a derogatory nature.

13. [Acting Impartially] - Employees shall not use their authority as an employee of the Police Department to take any action in a matter in which they are an interested or involved party. This shall include, but not be limited to, intervening in or making arrests, issuing arrest or traffic citations, etc., in controversies arising between their family members or household members, arrests stemming from

their own quarrels, or between themselves and their family members or household members, friends, and/or neighbors Employees shall be allowed to act to prevent injury to another, imminent or ongoing property damage, or when a felony has been committed. In the event such circumstances arise, the involved employee shall notify the appropriate supervisory authority. This provision shall not preclude the lawful detention of any offender until the arrival and/or intervention of the appropriate supervisory authority. The supervisory authority shall ensure appropriate investigation and/or reports are completed, and under no circumstances shall any supervisor assign those duties or tasks to the involved employee.

My Blue Side

Despite media witch hunts, the media, nor the departmental policy control officer's behavior; self control is still paramount: otherwise the incidents of corruption would be more common.

10.2
Do people Have A Right To Know Why They Have Been Stopped?

Knowing your rights is not as important as understanding the terms under which they were granted.

The 4th Amendment protects against Unreasonable Search and Seizure. In order to facilitate this, the Courts upheld that a traffic stop, where a ticket is issued is an arrest because it has a court date and the person was seized. Therefore, legally you do have a right to be informed of the reason for the stop at some point during the stop. This in no way grants the right to argue the infraction but you have a right to know what you are being cited for.

Even if no ticket is issued; I could not find case law, but most departmental policies require the reason for the stop be provided prior to requesting a driver's license and insurance from the vehicle operator.

Failure of an officer to tell you why they stopped you does not mean they are lying, or corrupt. Often times, the more polite you are to the officer the less likely you are to receive a citation. In most cases, the officer has full discretion over issuance of a citation.

Do not respond angrily to the stop, especially if you committed any infraction. Snide comments do not help, nor does sarcasm. In many cases, departmental quotas are the reason for the stop in the first place. Officers do not want to make the stops either; they are required to make a certain number of stops per shift. Humiliated by the departmental mandate on traffic stops, officers do not respond well to the awkward position they find themselves in. This discomfort often translates into the traffic stop as rudeness towards the driver.

My Black Side

As the traffic stop is considered an 'arrest' in the truest sense of the word (because there is a court date), citizen's obviously have the right to know why they have been stopped. This right to have the information however, DOES NOT determine the following;

1. When the officer tells you
2. Guilt or innocence
3. What will happen of you refuse to sign and accept the ticket
4. What your punishment will be
5. Whether the officer is a racist, biased, unprofessional, stupid or a law enforcement professional
6. The validity of the stop

In my opinion, from a cop's perspective, failing to inform the person of why they were stopped prior to issuance of a ticket should be considered a technicality, resulting in dismissal of the citation. A person does not have to plead guilty, but they absolutely have the right to know, prior to being required to agree to a summons to appear for a crime, what they are accused of doing.

Be diplomatic about it, do not try to talk the officer down, or berate them because you caused yourself to endure a traffic stop. When he gets to a pause or break, simply ask him for the basis for the stop, if he refuses to tell you then ask to speak to a supervisor.

My Blue Side

Traffic stops have long been understood as one of the most dangerous duties an officer performs. The officer is usually alone, and far from backup, criminals know this.

Far too many drivers want to argue and have court on the side of the street with officers. This is not safe for the officer; therefore, they may come across as curt or irritated. Oftentimes, they are, but in all cases, they want to end the traffic stop as quickly as possible.

When officers issue a citation, the officer's name and badge number are on the ticket, so there is no need to ask for them or argue about them; especially on the side of the interstate, it is not safe even for you. Studies show that distracted drivers are dangerous, and the color blue many departments use for emergency equipment has a captivating effect on drivers with certain medical or chemically induced conditions.

10.3
Is Profiling Legal?

"The best way to protect young Black, brown, men of color, women of color, is to actually stop profiling, stop the prejudice, and stop the judgment first{Hill Harper},"

⁓

Definitively, profiling (of any race) is illegal. With that said, profiling behavior is perfectly legal. For example, stopping a White guy during business hours for slowly driving slowly through a neighborhood is not legal. Stopping a male White, during business hours, whose age or socio economic makeup does not fit and who is wearing dark clothes or a hoodie is not illegal. Why? because this demographically fits the profile of more than 75% of burglary suspects. So in this case the suspicion behavior is based on nationally recognized demographic strata, not race.

On the other hand, a Black guy pulls into a gas station, and is wearing a hoodie; so you investigate him as a robbery suspect. This is not be legal, there were not enough criteria met to justify this stop. Although the demographics indicate that more than 70% of armed robbery suspects are male Blacks, that is all you had to go on. Even if this stop was not racially motivated it would be characterized as such because race was the only criterion utilized.

My Black Side

Stopping any person based on one set of criteria is not good police work. If the man who shot the president was Asian, you cannot legally justify stopping every Asian in the country. But if you add criteria, like they were speeding away in the immediate area, you would at least have reasonable suspicion to stop the person. The stop would also be legal, because the suspect was speeding.

Another common practice among officers is to make a sketchy stop and use the, 'You matched the description of a robbery suspect'. Although you have no reason to doubt the officer, you certainly can file a complaint and ask that the description of the suspect be provided for verification. Nevertheless, do not argue with the officer and escalate the situation.

There is a fine line between profiling and racial profiling, cops tread upon this tightrope daily. Oftentimes the officers cross the line, it may not be intentional always, but it happens too readily. Breaking the law, to enforce the law is not the best policy.

Obviously, there is some malfeasance, but I do not personally believe that racial profiling is as rampant as reported by the media. There is evil afoot, and I personally believe that a lot of the profiling and the bleeding over is a result of genuine Law Enforcement efforts to quell the amount of violence in the country. Sadly, many perpetrators of the violence are young Black males.

I agree with podcaster Leonydus Johnson when he asks why BLM is not worried about children murdered by Black suspects. Malcolm said it first, "Having once been a criminal is no shame; the shame is in remaining a criminal".

Anger has no place in a Conscientious Movement. We need to separate legitimate issues from Media Glory Stories. Enough non-criminal people interact with the police or privileged America and find it to be a lethal interaction. It is to these innocent people that BLM and Black people in general should direct attention.

As we stand in the eve of indiscriminate shootings against officers, do you think joining the criminal underworld helps anyone? One more thing to think about, BLM argues against White privilege: Do you think the White people walking around inciting unrest in the name of BLM will face the same consequences the Black members will?

If you have been profiled and can prove it based on facts or language by the officer, utilize the Deep Cotton Response, do not get into a pissing contest, or riot.

My Blue Side

I can honestly say that too many of the incidents involving police shootings are reported without important details like what the suspect did to cause the interaction, or what they did to exacerbate the incident. If the suspect is wrong, and a criminal I do not care. However, if the suspect is merely selling cigarettes, and ends up dead: That is a problem.

We cannot rely on things like whether or not the non-combative suspect has drugs in their system, nor had a criminal history. If you are stopped by the police, and end up dead there must be an investigation. If you are asked to produce your wallet and end up dead, Officers should join the ranks of incarcerates. There should be a charge in all states of criminally negligent homicide by cop. Wherein if willful blindness is proven, or malice, it should be charged.

There needs to be a set of charges automatically charged with officer involved murders; Official misconduct, intimidation of a state witness, and murder under color of law. In charging crimes involving cops properly, a distinction will form between those that tarnish the badge and those who make errors.

10.4
Pre-Textual And
Investigative Stops

"I sometimes wish that people would put a little more emphasis upon the observance of the law than they do upon its enforcement[Calvin Coolidge]."

In 2018 there were #686,665[163] active Law Enforcement Officers employed in the USA. BLM movers need to stop recklessly asserting that Law Enforcement Officers share any commonality other than being sworn Law Enforcement. Just because I am Black does not make me guilty. If this is true; it is just as foolish and ignorant to indict another group of people (Law Enforcement Officers) as guilty for the criminal behavior of individuals. Law Enforcement occupations do not justify criminal behavior; neither does slavery; people are responsible.

My Black Side / My Blue Side

FBI and the Bureau of Justice Statistics indicate more than 10 million arrests in the nation annually. That is 14.5 arrests per officer, to get the total arrests. How do officers self-initiate arrests, or use investigative techniques to make arrests from traffic stops? Pretextual (false reasons that hide true intentions for legal actions) and Investigative stops.

Why do BLM proponents want Black violators exonerated anyway; because they are Black? Is not racially motivated behavior the impetus for the movement in the first place? Racially motivated behavior of any kind is not a good policy.

In addition to the tools on their belts cops have legal doctrines that aid in their investigations here is a list of a few.

- Terry Stops
- Carroll Doctrine
- Plain Feel/smell
- Constructive possession
- Furtive movement

- Preservation of evidence
- Citizen information
- Veracity of details
- Reasonable suspicion
- Probable cause
- Good faith Doctrine

It is reasonable to assume that many police interactions do not lead to arrest for various reasons, innocence and discretion (mercy) being among them. 4th Amendment protection does not make you innocent; it just means that the officers have to work harder to make the country a better place.

The 'pretext' means that the police want to arrest you for another reason, but this pretext' was a means to get there. 56 mph in a 55 is illegal. Is it a nuisance? But it is the law. If you do not agree with the conditions of your driver's license, vote differently or turn it in. Until then, slow down or drive right.

Why is there no rebuke from the public of a Criminal Justice System that releases rapists and murderers because of technicalities during the arrest? These same technicalities exist when the suspects are cops. Loopholes in *The Establishment* exist and the public stands for it every year.

Pretextual stops are not loopholes; they are legal tricks. When you get your driver's license issued, you sign and make an agreement with the State that you will brandish it upon request of Law Enforcement if driving a motor vehicle upon a non-private road. Additionally, you agree to abide by every traffic law in the jurisdiction of your license.

Pretextual stops (nickel and dime) are invaluable as long as criminals drive to and from crimes. The best thing about pretextual stops is that they cannot be challenged successfully because you made the agreement with the State as a condition of the privilege of driving. In order to get to that 14.5 number per officer, the police use trial and error. Although this may be inconvenient, this is their function in society to try eradicating criminality and victimization. If you are found to be in violation of others laws during this legal but annoying, stop...par for the course.

In the Federal Case Whren vs. United States, 517 U.S. 806 (1996) the Supreme Court unanimously sanctioned 'pretextual stops'. Many less reasonable condemners of the decision argue that this caused racial profiling. They say ignorance is bliss, but it is not when it has a pen, a voice, and a public forum.

The Criminal Justice System does not decide who sells dope. In all the years of drug enforcement, Law enforcement has uncovered few tools as valuable as Confidential Informants and pretextual stops based on criminality not race.

One definition that explains Target-Based Policing is that, "Selective enforcement occurs when government officials such as police officers, prosecutors, or regulators exercise enforcement discretion." This practice comes into play when there are chronic issues as determined by calls for service and quality of life complaints. In other words, when enough complaints come through a department, city council, or mayor's office, the police response is basically what Project managers call a Root-Cause analysis.

Once the cause is determined, a strategy to combat the issue is developed and implemented. This is most commonly encountered within neighborhoods regarding speeding. The response is often new signage, speed bumps or heightened traffic enforcement. If the results of this dragnet approach yield ambiguous racial results, that is empirical data, not racism.

"The major source countries for Heroin are Afghanistan, Pakistan, Lebanon; Myanmar (formerly Burm a), Thailand, Iran, Laos, Mexico, Guatemala, and Colombia. Heroin production rose dramatically in South America in the 1990s. Colombian and Mexican heroin have supplanted Southeast and Southwest Asian heroin in much of the United States. Major source countries for Cocaine are Bolivia, Colombia, Peru, and Ecuador.

However, in the 1990s, the governments of Bolivia and Peru substantially reduced those countries' cultivation of coca plants. Despite these efforts, drug traffickers shifted their production to Colombia, which by 2000 had become the dominant producer of cocaine. Major source countries for marijuana are Mexico, Belize, Colombia, and Jamaica[164]."

If we agree that pretextual stops are racially motivated, what then, can Black Americans base the fact that the targeted DTO (Drug Trafficking Organizations) and traffickers on the largest scale into the country, and cities (before the drugs hit the street) are not Black?

10.5
Does Not The Suspect Bear Any Responsibility?

"When you choose an action, you choose the consequences of that action. When you desire a consequence you had damned well better take the action that would create it[Lois Bujold],"

⁖

My Black/Blue Side

Indignation is normal in the face of abuse, or perceived abuse. There was a YouTube posting which highlighted an example of the absolute wrong behavior by the police[165]. The man in the video showed great restraint, but he must have felt both despair and rage during the incident. The officers could have ended this ordeal, by admitting their error. The officer's inability to provide salient data about the identification of the suspect showed extreme unprofessionalism and bias, not necessarily racism.

Whatever information the officers used to ascertain that there was a warrant, was flawed and the officers did not have enough information to interact with the man. Not because the warrant was invalid, but because the only thing they were investigating was based on a male Black with dreadlocks. If this had been the suspect, they apparently could have done nothing about it, because they did not have useful information. At least it appears that they did not use it before approaching the guy.

Just as we expect officers to be held responsible for their action, shouldn't any person over the age of 13 be held to a standard? What idiocy provides that a Black thief should be allowed to flee because at some point a White thief was once? The police have discretion to make decisions, and they do. If we find their discretion lacking integrity or diversity, I agree this is unprofessional. I would, however, request they raise the White side of the scale rather than lower the Black side. No community should want criminals released back into it's ranks.

Look at the statistics in [Fig 47-50]. Black males lead the country in arrests for murder and robbery. Since officer's rarely catch these suspects in the act, their description had to come from victims and or witnesses. I personally want these Black people off the streets. I do not want the White ones on my street either, but there is currently no rioting and looting for a WLM Movement.

James Comey says "When I worked as a prosecutor in Richmond, Virginia in the 1990s, that city, like so much of America, was experiencing horrific levels of violent crime. But to describe it that way obscures an important truth: for the most part, White people weren't dying; Black people were dying. Most White people could drive around the problem." Dr. Michael Eric Dyson says, "White-on-White crime is devastation in America like so-called Black-on-Black crime. It is not Black or White-on-White crime. It's proximity murder." They are killing whoever is closest.

Recently a City board delivered the opinion that criminals may not be responsible for their behavior. Then who in the hell is responsible for their behavior? 300 million+ in America, most do not commit crimes even though many of them live in less than desirable circumstances or negative environmental nurturing. I dare say if the criminals are not responsible, then how can cops that commit crimes be culpable: are they not simply criminals? Stupidity is a slippery slope.

The Establishment created nightmares and monsters this is undeniable, but we must not fight to defend them or retain the monsters. On the contrary, we should spend our efforts on reverse engineering Black youth, undoing the damage.

10.6

Does A Criminal Record Hurt Your Life And How Do You Remove Something From Your Record?

"Black men with criminal records are the most severely disadvantaged group in the labor market[Michelle Alexander]."

Yes, a criminal record hurts employment chances, as does dropping out of high school, and a dishonorable discharge. According to studies, thousands of inmates exit the prison system each year, mostly young men with less than a college education, about two-thirds of ex-prisoners remain out of work a year after prison release, and 60% are rearrested within three years. Those that find work are less likely to return to prison and are better-equipped to assume the mainstream social roles of spouse and parent[166]."

If you add race, and bad credit ratings to the criminal history and educational issues, you guarantee zero or undesirable employment with the established norms. Entrepreneurship is an option, but it requires many of the same components such as business acumen, a residence, and some sort of start-up capital. Even in jail, education is the one thing that cannot be stolen once obtained.

Here are some terms you might find useful.

- Expungement - Expunging a criminal record alters your record, removing certain offenses. An expunged conviction remains on your criminal record for Law Enforcement and Governmental purposes only. Sex offender registration and immigration violation are not usually expungable. Expungements usually only apply to the following conditions;

- First offense for certain crimes

- Misdemeanor conviction
- Juvenile status

- Sealed Records - Expunged criminal records are different from "sealed" records. When a court record is sealed, the public cannot see them. Both sealing and expunging records enable you to not have a conviction.

- Pardon - Individuals convicted of a crime may apply for a pardon. If granted, a pardon restores certain rights such as jury duty as well as the right to bear arms but seal or expunge records.

- Certificate of Innocence - A certificate of actual innocence goes further than a regular expungement. It proves that you were innocent, and that the conviction or arrest never should have happened.

- Certificate of Rehabilitation - Some states offer this court order attesting to your rehabilitated.

- Trial/preliminary hearing/Bound over - A trial is a proceeding that leads to a conviction with or without a jury. A common mistake is to believe that the preliminary hearing and binding over of a case to the Grand Jury is an acquittal or a dismissal. The preliminary hearing is the gateway to even more serious levels within the criminal justice system not a doorway to freedom.

- Arrest/citation - When asked if arrested; if you received a misdemeanor citation the answer is yes. The arrest is not an arrest because you went to jail; it is a seizure by officers culminating in a court date and adjudication.

- Consecutive/concurrent sentences - Consecutive sentences following continuously (stacked) and concurrent all be served at the same time.

10.7
Ride or Die

"The concept of *ride or die* originates in 1990's hip-hop as a modern, urban take on the legendary outlaw couple Bonnie and Clyde[167]"

⁓

According to the urban dictionary, a "Ride or Die" chick is, a chick that is down for a man and is not afraid of doing anything and everything for him. A woman who is not afraid to stand by her man and is willing to stand side by side with him and most importantly, not afraid to let the world know that she is his; now and forever[168].

My Black Side

A lifetime of disenfranchisement and targeted isolation does not foster in any person a trust for their environment. A single parent home and a glass ceiling with your picture painted on it also does not encourage furthering education, or professional development.

I know how important belonging to something is for people, especially teenagers. Attaching yourself to a lifestyle guaranteeing that you encounter the injustices in the Criminal Justice System is not *street*, it is a fatalistic decision. Why subject your wife, children, and your future to discrimination, subjugation and eventually death or incarceration? Why do you have the power to draw people into the darkness, but never try to bring them into the light?

My Blue Side

Ride or die, just gives cops more people to arrest. You want to ride? Be prepared to go to jail or die. Frankly, there is little mercy for those who choose to revel in crime. The first offender or teen giving in to peer pressure finds themselves in a much more forgiving atmosphere than the gang-banger or career violent offender.

10.8
Whose Gun Or Dope
Is It Anyway?

"Marijuana causes paranoia and psychosis. That fact is now beyond dispute. Even scientists who are not sure if marijuana can cause permanent psychosis agree that it can cause temporary paranoia and psychotic episodes. The risk is so obvious that marijuana dispensaries advertise certain strains as less likely to cause paranoia. Paranoia and psychosis cause violence. Overwhelming evidence links psychotic disorders and violence, especially murder. Studies have confirmed the connection, across cultures, nations, races, and eras{Alex Berenson}169 ,,

Marijuana Laws By State

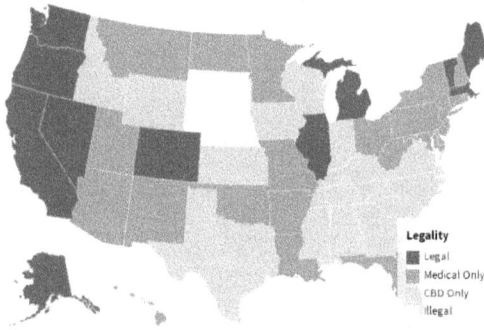

Legality
Legal
Medical Only
CBD Only
Illegal

[Fig 44]

My Black/Blue Side

This is an appeal to common sense, If you do not live in the states where Weed is legalized [170], the smell of Marijuana is probable cause to the police.

Unlike stupidity, which appears to be an airborne contagion, the only way to smell like weed, is to be in its smoke, or physical contact. I believe the police call this a 'Free Stop'. So when the cops mess with you for reeking of weed, enjoy the attention you have earned.

According to Black's Law Dictionary[171], possession is, "The fact of having or holding property in one's power. That power means having physical dominion and control over the property." A legal definition of constructive possession is a situation in which an individual has the ability to exercise actual control over real property without actually having physical control. Under the law, constructive possession is the same as possession.

The answer therefore to whose weed is it, is therefore: everyone in the car. In a house or apartment, the rules are different due to their size. The fact that you do not own the car does not matter. If you and your friends do not mind riding around wearing pot-head's favorite cologne, suffer the consequences. You cannot honestly say you did not know it was in the car.

Here is how cops use free stops to their advantage. You go into a gas station, Wal-Mart, Starbucks, etc smelling of weed. They have reason to stop and talk to you, and ask to search you. Of course, you will decline, so they just wait for you to get back into the car and then they get you, the car, and your friends. I hope this targeted enforcement is not what you consider racism, because I have done this hundreds of times. Those who like being crash test dummies should wear helmets. Go home and smoke, no one is looking for you there. However, police have a charge to investigate all illicit drug related infractions. DUI is one of those infractions.

Yup; White people love weed too! I will wait for someone highly educated to explain to me what difference that makes? If you make the mistake of playing favorites, you might be disappointed when your team loses. If you leave it up to White cops to choose whom to let go, demographically they will probably 'hook-up' just as many of their own as other types of cops. While this is favoritism, it is not racism, unless I was racists when I hooked up my Black the brothers and sisters.

For the record, I never smoked marijuana; never saw the need to destroy my long-term memory or lungs. But please enjoy yourself. Like alcohol we can always find some selfish lie to justify dead bodies directly attributed to hallucinogens, and intoxicants.

The Idiocy of legalizing drugs in Idaho, and 42 other states is beyond dialogue. According to the Bureau of Justice Statistics[172], "Almost 40% of people locked up for property crimes and 14% of those incarcerated for violent crimes reported that they had committed their most serious offense for drug-related reasons."

The concept of removing criminal consequences for drug use as a prison overcrowding method is deceptive at best. If the Bureau of Justice statistics is correct. At least 54% of crimes accounted for during the survey are directly related to drugs. 14% of these crimes are violent. There is absolutely no reason to believe that if you stop cocaine from being illegal that these people who commit violent crimes will stop being violent. After all, if drugs were illegal and they knew there was going to be a consequence and they committed a violent crime what logical reason is there to believe that these people will not commit violent crimes when there are no consequences?

All that decriminalizing drugs does is increase the incidents of the drug related violent and property crimes. **All not making the arrest, does not lessen the crime; it just stops victims from having a voice.**

Decriminalization creates another problem for the Black community. According to statistics, many of these violent crimes will occur in the Black community, perpetrated by Black offenders. Lt. Col. Cooper makes a good point when he says, "If violent crime is to be curbed, it is only the intended victim who can do it; the felon does not fear the police and he fears neither judge nor jury therefore, what he must be taught to fear is his victim." Increased vigilantism is bad for everyone, as citizens do not train in the indiscriminate use of force, nor understand the collateral responsibilities to the general public.

Africa-American'ts should not mesh valid issues like police brutality, biased based arrests and incarcerations, and racial profiling with selfish drug use desires:

Why dilute the validity of the BLM movement. Rather than asking the Police not to enforce the Law, or Legislators to change the Law; perhaps we should be less concerned with rolling up and smoking our potential away, as we complain that White people play too rough.

11.0

Racism

&

Economics

"White men have always controlled their wives' wages. Colored men were not able to do so until they themselves became free. Then they owned both their wives and their wages [Susan B. Anthony] „

11.1
How Does Racism Affect Economics

Economics are the method, the object is to change the soul{Margaret Thatcher} „ .

Ironically, *The Establishment's* ideation disdained the practice of whipping slaves, but not for the reason humans should[13]. *The Establishment* contends that lynching is both mismanagement, and wasting basic resources.

---

[13] {[WL7]You are not only losing valuable stock by hangings, you are having uprisings, slaves are running away, your crops are sometimes left in the fields too long for maximum profit, you suffer occasional fires, your animals are killed.

[BPAW1]Take the female and run a series of tests on her to see if she will submit to your desires willingly·

[BPAW2]Test her in every way, because she is the most important factor for good economics.

[BPAW3]If she shows any sign of resistance in submitting completely to your will, do not hesitate to use the bull whip on her to extract that last bit of resistance out of her. Take care not to kill her, for in doing so, you spoil good economic.

[BPAW4]When in complete submission, she will train her offspring in the early years to submit to labor when they become of age.

[BPAW5]Understanding is the best thing. Therefore, we shall go deeper into this area of the subject matter concerning what we have produced here in this breaking process of the female nigger. We have reversed the relationship in her natural uncivilized state she would have a strong dependency on the uncivilized nigger male, and she would have a limited protective tendency toward her independent male offspring and would raise male off springs to be dependent like her.

[BPAW6]Nature had provided for this type of balance. We reversed nature by burning and pulling a civilized nigger apart and bull whipping the other to the point of death, all in her presence}.

This is where *The Establishment* matures and slavery changes from simple economics, to the development of an underclass crafted for the sole purpose of carrying the upper class. This is not a novel concept; Europe maintained a zealous history of barbarism and discrimination. Those who fought for American independence reinvigorated archaic methods in the New World as the Old World separated themselves from them.

The Establishment teaches that proper Slave Management;

- Saves valuable livestock
- Dissuades, or offsets uprisings
- Dissuades, or offsets slaves running away (property loss)
- Minimizes crop loss
- Dissuades, or offsets 'accidental' fires
- Dissuades, or offsets livestock preying upon or destroying each other

It is not by accident that the Pledge of Allegiance uses the term 'Republic', elitism and its tenets are alive and well in the Americas.

The Establishment promised to develop a perpetual system in America, by embedding ideology in the minds of both White and Blacks. *The Establishment* created a system where Blacks would never be free to enjoy all the War of Independence and the Bill of Rights promised; someone has to pick the cotton.

Lynch's Pendulum© relied heavily on Return On Investment (ROI) and the Principle of voluntary returns. Historically, the Black woman had to endure humiliation just to survive the daily exploitation of the plantation. In the story 12 years a Slave, one of the women is whipped because she slid away to get some soap, because she grew tired of 'smelling herself'. Imagine the indignity of people watching your rape, or seeing your nakedness sprawled across the yard for all to see. Imagine bearing and nursing the children of the men who raped you. Imagine waking up with breasts, and a womb and knowing that the only difference between you and the cow or pig is that you have two legs. I dare say these are some of the tests *The Establishment* included horrors involving pregnancy, and children.

A study done in 2016 found men found guilty of raping Black women receive shorter sentences than men found guilty of raping White women[173]. Imagine a man who keeps you safe at night and is kind to you, he is a good slave but no one can know you love each other, and he also has to watch you pleasure the plantation staff. If you could avoid this life, wouldn't you? If you were given the choice to lie with a White rapist or a White man that treated you decently, who among us would not get up out of the barn and go inside to the bedroom. Who among us, would not rather have the ability to wash up after sex, and sit in front of a fire place than be bent over a bail of cotton in the middle of the fields, then ordered to carry the bales back to the barn?

"Nearly one in four Black people lynched from 1877 to 1945 were accused of improper contact with a White woman[174]." White males were allowed to indiscriminately sexually assault Black women. Since the Black woman had no control over her body, it behooved her to use her body to positively affect her future, by pleasuring White men.

Children added to the equation, the Black woman's choice diminished even further. The child would grow up hating the behavior; but they would grow up. Many Black kids moms had to exchange a good (White) life for staying alive. Rather than hate mom, the child soon learns to hate the man lying with mom. The child also has to escape from mom, or risk being smothered by mom into submission.

The free woman, the free White woman could lay with whom she wanted and marry when she wanted in most instances. Her gallivanting was called dating and courtship. The Black woman doing the same thing was a slut and a whore.

I believe it was Chairman Mao who said, "Women hold up half the sky." Foucault had his pendulum and so did Lynch. Lynch's Pendulum© consisted of truly balancing the scales. The happy female keeps the barn doors open. When the woman controls the barn, she nests. The ultimate drive for women is safety; the barn gives them the illusion of self-determination. The empowered broodmare now has choices of food, clothes, and entertainment. Rather than enduring constant beating, the Black female gained favor and privilege because of her sweet relationship with *The Establishment*. The buttermilk bath for the county fair does not stop the pig from becoming bacon, yet the pig revels in the event. *The Establishment* understands that small victories in the life of the broodmare made her more receptive, and pliable - the factory makes more babies. We call this arrangement, assembly line- process Welfare.

The less stressed mare/female bore healthier children, spent less time on maternity leave, rushed to work every day and gave her all. Just for the promise of controlling the barn. Since it was her barn, she had a place to tell her children was their home. She also had a reason to spend less time romping in the barn with field hands. Her children started coming, and there were fewer drawbacks like annoying fathers hanging around. She would just cut them off, and they would go away. Why spend time with a woman you could not touch and who would not share her barn.

Unwittingly, the Black female placed herself as the pivot for *The Establishment*. She also made herself a victim - forever. When does a mother stop being a mother? Only after her death. Therefore, it stands to reason why Mother's Day out retails everything except Christmas and Valentine's Day. Christmas is for the kids (she bears) and valentines for her.

The colt (the young Black male) is forever at the mercy of *The Establishment*, ingratiating the mother as well. As long as there are single Black mother's there will be the effect that *The Establishment* wanted; they will always be hostages of discrimination.

Physical violence evokes fear in women, but requires less healing time than personal violations. Victims describe a distinct difference between the blistering heat of the sun on a barn, and the heat caused from a fire within. Although the weather torn structure appears battered, beaten, and worn it still is fully capable of continuing its function. However, the destruction to the infrastructure caused by internal damage weakens the ability to both stand and persevere. Eventually the mother can no longer function as designed, it ceases to be a place of shelter, and nurture for the young, and become a pile of rubble and ash - suitable for nothing.

The harsh reality is that eventually the subjugation of women involves sexuality. In an article about war-time rape (for which racially motivated rape between tribes qualifies) asserts that rape has a distinct function; demoralization. "According to feminist analyses of sexual violence, rape has roots in the societal male-female power imbalance. The cultural backdrop to rape becomes the expression of domination, oppression, and inequality towards women. Gender socialization of male entitlement over women's bodies perpetuates the cycle of objectification and violence against women[175]." The article continues, "Rape is not a random sexual act carried out by individual soldiers, but rather a deliberate military tool to tear apart individuals, families, and communities." The article also cites five characteristics of war rape (a) scale, (b) public occurrence, (c) brutality, (d) slavery, (e) ethnic-cleansing, and genocidal rape.

Referring to Planned Parenthood, they might not be rapists, but from her own mouth, the founder espoused ethnic cleansing, making Planned Parenthood a full-fledged agent of the Lynch Method. As *The Establishment* stated many components must occur to create the new paradigm, one in which the mother cares less about her child than herself. Look at the 'Well-fare kids' of today. Not the kids themselves; we refer to the trend over the last 25 years to have kids to increase the number of government subsidies. These crop-number benefactors are not race specific, and include foster kids as well. These methods helped change generations of proud Black mothers into Baby Factories.

Baby factories generate fodder for *The Establishment*. Mal-adjusted males pour into *The Establishment* every year generating billions of dollars in Black Cotton© (revenue). The Criminal Justice System, the war on drugs, the effect of drugs in the Black community, gangs and gang violence, abandoned children, prostitution and sex trafficking are just New Cotton©; but Blacks are still the ones picking the cotton.

Stephanie Lahart implores Black parents to take a look inwards and see that their behavior is as devastating to the community as the *Establishment*. Although written to women, the inference is clear; do not choose the problems. To men, the natural result is also clear; STOP BEING PART OF THE PROBLEM.

"Dear Black Women...I encourage you to be VERY mindful of who you choose to have your children with. Too many of our Black children are growing up without their fathers. Why would you have sex with a man that you know isn't any good? Why give up your love to a man that has kids with this woman and that woman? Why have kids with a man that stays in and out of jail/prison? Why have kids with a man that does not work? Why have kids with a man that is clearly NOT father material? Think before you have unprotected sex...You can't afford NOT to. Our kids deserve better...Choose wisely!"

White Flight[14] was not just about segregation. Segregation had less to do with racism than fear. Whites were not afraid of Blacks per se, they were afraid of the Black Cloud©. No mother wants to see their daughter hook up with the unhealthy[18] the Negro. The second greatest expression of the feared Black Cloud as the 44th President of the United States of America.

Integration brought the Black Cloud with it. Now the darkness of the wellspring and hatred planted by racism

---

[14]The trend of White people moving out of urban areas, with minority populations, and into predominantly White suburban areas.

and discrimination pours over and out into the White side of the tracks. It was not just the Black skin that Whites did not want to be around; it was the fact that social contagion is a verifiable thing, and they feared the effect the Black cloud would have on their Whiteness.

11.2 Baby Factories

Medgar Evers and many others died[176,177], because the ultimate treasure in America is the White woman. If the Black woman is the key to Green Cotton© Economic Wealth[15], the White counterpart must occupy the same importance in the Non-Cotton System of Wealth©.

---

[15]{[BPAW7]By her being left alone, unprotected, with the male image destroyed, the ordeal caused her to move from her psychological dependent state to a frozen independent state. In this frozen psychological state of independence, she will raise her male and female offspring in reversed roles.

[BPAW8]For fear of the young males life she will psychologically train him to be mentally weak and dependent, but physically strong. Because she has become psychologically independent, she will train her female offsprings to be psychologically independent.

[BPAW9]What have you got? You've got the nigger women out front and the nigger man behind and scared. This is a perfect situation of sound sleep and economic. Before the breaking process, we had to be alertly on guard at all times. Now we can sleep soundly, for out of frozen fear his woman stands guard for us. He cannot get past her early slave molding process. He is a good tool, now ready to be tied to the horse at a tender age. By the time a nigger boy reaches the age of sixteen, he is soundly broken in and ready for a long life of sound and efficient work and the reproduction of a unit of good labor force.

[BPAW10]Continually through the breaking of uncivilized savage nigger, by throwing the nigger female savage into a frozen psychological state of independence, by killing of the protective male image, and by creating a submissive dependent mind of the nigger male slave, we have created an orbiting cycle that

The White man's zeal to protect his woman should have clued Black men to the importance of women. Sadly, however, Black men did not understand the message, for we do not yet fully speak the language of Freedom.

Alone, unprotected, and with the male image (present and future) destroyed; the Black woman moved into a frozen independent state. The new state, the (Strong Black Woman) SBW phase is a psychological shift along Lynches' Pendulum axis in the wrong direction. With the maternal purpose skewed and or destroyed, a vast portion of the woman's self-worth diminished[16].

With the prospect of no male counterpart, raising a daughter conceived in shame, or the worthlessness of rearing a son to resent her and abandon her, what did the transitioning Black mother have to look forward to? Not until Suffrage, emancipation, liberation, and then some, did

---

turns on its own axis forever, unless a phenomenon occurs and re-shifts the position of the male and female slaves.

[WL18]You must use the female vs. the male and the male vs. the female.

[CPNM1]For fear that our future Generations may not understand the principles of breaking both of the beasts together, the nigger and the horse. We understand that short range planning economics results in periodic economic chaos; so that to avoid turmoil in the economy, it requires us to have breadth and depth in long range comprehensive planning, articulating both skill sharp perceptions.

[CPNM2]We lay down the following principles for long range comprehensive economic planning. Both horse and niggers is no good to the economy in the wild or natural state.

[CPNM3]Both must be broken and tied together for orderly production.

[CPNM4]For an orderly future, special and particular attention must be paid to the female and the youngest offspring. Both must be crossbred to produce a variety and division of labor}.

[16] Ever wonder why so many Black females refer to themselves and other Black females as bitches and hoes?

the Black woman even have self-actualization to look towards.

Through careful planning of economic systems purported to assist Black families and single Black mothers, a system that did everything but help the recipients succeed came online. This system provided lodging and money for women who have children and no mate. In an insidiously charitable gesture, *The Establishment* increased its financial dividend as more children entered into this poor economic predicament.

The Establishment experimented; it did not posture and theorize; it dissected the marriage with the full intention of never letting it rise again in the Black community. However, the Nigger that *The Establishment* speaks about is a construct of brutality; it has nothing to do with skin color. The decayed Black marriage, an effect of *The Establishment's* Method, only lasts as long as their nigger exists. Once free-d from niggerism, the Black marriage will retain vigor,

The Media, as pointed out before, is one of the chief methods of negotiating through and to the female offspring. Since 1712, the independent and negotiable female Black was not meant to be a benefit to the Black community, just a part of the Black Cotton Gin.

Maybe we really should fear for their lives, we trained them. Stop pushing young Black men to play sports, and blast music, and take them to a library. One of the first steps we need to undertake is stop training our young men to react without thinking. Hyper emotionality is not a masculine trait; it is a byproduct of desperation, and the overwhelming female influence. The Black male emulates the personage in the community exposed and to which he finds himself accustom. Flying off the handle is a learned response to the stressful condition and environment within the Black household. This is another part of the cycle necessarily broken by *The Establishment* for the Black community to thrive. Remember the words of Sister Stephanie Lahart, as long as we are a problem to each other there will be a problem for each other.

By controlling the Black woman, and encouraging her to sit home and produce children that she does not care for, she produces merchandise in one form or another. Whether by criminality, delinquency, juvenile parenting, poor financial methods, or abandoning their own children in early ages these young offspring provide economic sustenance for *The Establishment*.

Incorrectly, we continue to assert that the Black male is the target; he is not; he is the product; the female is the target because she produces the offspring.

11.3 The Black Mask

"Blacks have emerged from an atypical environment. The emergent coping styles have been essential to Black survival in an environment of servitude and ghettoization. Impression Management - the ability to be flexible in presentation of self, to role-play according to the expectations of an audience that has superior reward powers, to decipher meanings of the dominant group made the difference between those who survived and those who did not[178]."

The Frozen state developed because the Black woman's nature was at conflict with her environment. Breast and hips developed a longing to be caressed; yet, deserted, abused or untouched by caring hands. Her eyes and ears longed to see and hear the sweet nothings of her lover; yet, overwrought with the sight and sounds of despair. Lips purposefully large and kissable, forced to form lies of affection for a master, or swollen from not smiling long enough. Beaten and exploited by White and Black men; isolation became unavoidable. Going to a place inside her head became the only escape, the only sanity left. Self; became all. Back women learned to not need men, because *The Establishment* surrounded her with so many shiftless bastards gave up she just walked away from the scene.

The reversal of gender roles morphed into the new paradigm. The strong Black woman survived the ordeal in a better posture than the Black men - this too by design. The controlling female became more commonplace. The perception became one of positivity. The reality was that the Black woman is not the lead; because no one followed. The Black family became a series of people in an extended relationship more like animals clinging to tails than a family. *The Establishment* reformatted the new Black family;

- The family was kidnapped
- The family was separated before leaving the coast
- Mutually dependent Black people formed a new society or tribe
- Newly abused, strangers, formed unions
- Unions were destroyed as soon as they solidified
- The male perpetually removed from the family unit
- Workers have VIP access to all bedrooms
- Children removed from the family unit and relocated at will

Now there is only a remnant of the family unit within the Black community. Single mothers oversee more than half of Black families in the U.S.A. and according to Pew Research Center, the U.S.A. leads the world in single-parent families.

Due to role reversal, parenting roles also reversed. The mother runs the house; the guy is simply a visitor. After hundreds of years as a solo operator, the Black woman no longer conceives of existing in the traditional family role. The 'traditional family' no longer exists in the Black community.

The Pendulum reached the other side, finally. Now, the mother raises mules for market, no longer looking to spend quality time with their sons or raise them to respect, admire and protect mom. The young Black man now learns the language of Green Cotton©.

Black on Black crime is a direct and perpetual offshoot of indoctrination. BLACK LEADERS HEAR ME; THE FOREFATHERS OF DEATH GAVE U.S. THE KEY TO UNDOING THEIR SYSTEM FOREVER. **RE-**

CULTIVATE THE ORIGINAL ROLES OF MALE AND FEMALES IN THE BLACK COMMUNITY.

A publication by The National Center on Violence Against women in the Black Community[179] cites three unfortunate statistics;

- "Black women ages 25-29 are 11 times more likely than White women in that age group to be murdered while pregnant or in the first year after childbirth.
- Firearms were used in about 54% of all female homicides. Compared to all other racial groups, Black women are most commonly killed by firearms.
- According to the CDC, Black and Native Indian/Alaska Native women experienced the highest rates of homicide (4.4 and 4.3 per 100,000 population) and over half of all homicides (55%) were related to IPV (intimate partner violence).

The Establishment plans to resist morality and common decency feared to overturn the Slave-centric economic base. I believe Oscar Wilde once described patriotism as the 'virtue of the vicious'. How can oppressive behavior, and race hatred be a virtue; other than being the basis for every elitist society?

I served in the Armed Forces long enough to meet many true patriots; men and women who worked side by side with people from all walks of life. In the Armed Forces, reliance on others, equals survival. This does not mean there are no bigots in the Armed Forces. Just as 'Don't' ask don't tell' did not eliminate homosexuals; the service strives to keep 'Isms' in check; for the good of the service.

Since WWII, America pays a large portion of the bill for Japan's military expenses. Consequently, Japan has resources to reallocate to research and development. America has wealth, but it has to squander a great deal of its wealth to maintain its top-heavy lifestyle.

According to facts compiled by the Bureau of Justice Statistics, America spends approximately $182 Billion annually on incarcerates; a disproportionate number of whom are Black and Latino[180]. According to the Drug Policy Alliance, the amount spent annually by the U.S. on the war on drugs is $+47 billion, and statistics calculate $1 Trillion over the last forty years[181]. These are monies wasted each year attempting to maintain the Lynch Effect© rather than retrain people, societies extreme recidivism rates shows that little, if any, progress made in the reversing of the Lynch Effect©. Perhaps it is simply cheaper to maintain the permanent underclass than to repair the self-inflicted cancer, infecting America.

The wild or natural state is spelled out in [LMAS8 listed on page #330], is no good for the economy in the end. Effectively, *The Establishment* reminds us that someone has to pick the cotton.

Wonder why Blacks seem to pull each other down? Force of habit. *The Establishment* perpetuates selfishness[17] in the Black community. Horses learn to pull against each other; the horse doing nothing becomes dead weight. The horse trying to get ahead simply collapses under the strain. Blacks received training for hundreds of years not to share, nor to give consideration, and to other Blacks as competition for meager crumbs. The best way for Blacks to ensure sufficiency year after year is to remove the Blacks Black competition.

What is the reason *The Establishment* pays special attention to the female and the young? It is a simple equation; the male represents the present and the female represents the future. She is responsible for controlling, feeding, nurturing, and protecting the young, especially in this unnatural environment. *The Establishment* created the scenario where there is no male in the herd. It is not by chance that the housing developments (Black Reservations)

---

[17] The only true application of any semblance to the term Nigger; Niggardliness.

bear the moniker Projects [synonyms - exploit, process, effort, task, mission, quest, exploration], and exclude all but the handicapped male.

By scaring off the males, *The Establishment* ensures perpetual dependence of the female, and the young males learn to depend on *The Establishment* for food, safety, and shelter (The Modern Welfare System). *The Establishment* failed to realize that this production system set up the devastating crippling system we now know as Welfare. Welfare is not a demon in everyone's life; but demons oversee the program. Many disenfranchised people benefit from welfare for the first generation; but when you find 3rd, 4th, and 5th generation welfare recipients, it is obvious either they don't know how to get out or there is no way out available to them to escape.

Women's Liberation on its face was a good thing. Equal pay for equal work is obviously a logical proposition. However, according to statistics one of the worst things that ever happened to Society was removing women from the home and placing them the workplace.

This may seem insulting to women because they want to work but we are speaking in terms of balance of the society and necessity of tasks. Studies show that the entrance of women into the workforce affected the society as a whole, by displacing the bedrock of family stability - the mother.

Lisa Quast cites various issues arising from increasing numbers of women in the workforce. While she cites the obvious positives such as increased economic freedom, education, and escape from abusive marriages, she also points out the down side; the side that *The Establishment* needed to enhance to protect its future.

- Less time for mothers to spend with children due to their work schedule
- Increased stress levels and changing roles
- Difficulty accessing quality child care
- Changing the school schedules of children
- Latchkey kids[182](kids left home alone after school while parents worked)

[LMAS10] - Whereas nature provides them with the natural capacity to take care of their offspring, we break that natural string of independence from them and thereby create a dependency status, so that we may be able to get from them useful production for our business and pleasure] reads like a roll call of issues plaguing the Black, poor White, and Native American communities. These are the communities hit hardest by *entrenched racism* in America, and the similarities are staggering. We all agree that the natural environment for kids is at home nurtured by two loving parents. *The Establishment's* Method absolutely needed to disrupt this scheme and replace it with its own bastardized dependency driven brand of home life.

The Establishment destroyed the relationship between Black women and men to keep the slaves in line on during slavery. After slavery, another method was needed to maintain *The Establishment*. In modern times, the media has undertaken the task by helping *The Establishment* increased the division. During slavery, Black women could not have their own men. *The Establishment* morphed this into Black women dare not have any stable man for fear of punishment.

This idiotic construct held strong until the 1960s when Women's Liberation changed the ominous into the opportune. 'I cannot have a man' changed into 'I do not need a man'. What sheer folly; women and men need each other and the kids need them both. Not even *The Establishment* foresaw the negative effect the Woman's and the 'Strong Black Woman's Movement' were to have.

TV shows played female hosts day after day telling women they did not need men, they were strong, Black and beautiful. Does this then mean that the Black mother; the same mother that hid Moses in the basket and delivered their people, were not strong, Black, and beautiful because they had men? The effect of these aberrations on the family had a devastating effect across the last hundred years, as shown in [Fig 47-50].

2019 CRIME CLOCK STATISTICS

A Violent Crime occurred every   **26.3 seconds**
One Murder every   32.1 minutes
One Rape every   3.8 minutes
One Robbery every   2.0 minutes
One Aggravated Assault every   38.5 seconds

A Property Crime occurred every   **4.6 seconds**
One Burglary every   28.3 seconds
One Larceny-theft every   6.2 seconds
One Motor Vehicle Theft every   43.8 seconds

[Fig 46]

2018 Crime rate data sex of victim

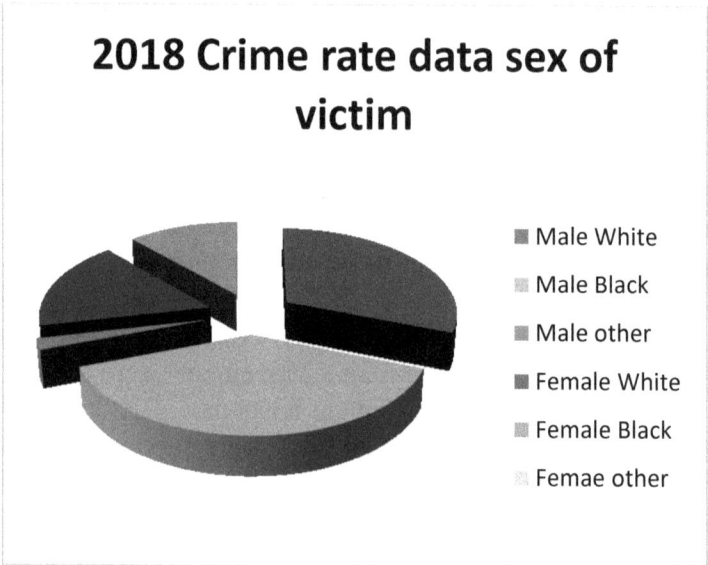

- Male White
- Male Black
- Male other
- Female White
- Female Black
- Femae other

[2018 Crime rates: Murder, Race, Sex, and Ethnicity of
Victim by Race, Sex, and Ethnicity of Offender]
[Fig 47]

[Fig 48[183]] shows that Black arrest rates lead in two of the three most heinous crime categories, not just percentage wise, but numerically.

[Fig 47[37]] shows the race, sex, ethnicity of offender and victim's rates.

These figures are not accidental; they are empirical data reports of the design. Why waste time monitoring a hostile species when you can build self-destructive, cannibalistic behavior into the model? The generational result of pitting the males against each other by age, skin tone, or for property is an unrecoverable schism: and th stats verify success.

Race of victim	Total	Race of offender				Sex of offender		
		White	Black or African American	Other[1]	Unknown	Male	Female	Unknown
White	3,315	2,677	514	61	63	2,914	383	18
Black or African American	2,925	234	2,600	17	74	2,603	291	31
Other race[1]	220	54	39	122	5	196	22	2
Unknown race	110	46	24	7	33	100	9	1

[Shows 80% White on White crime by males,
and 88% Black on Black crime by males]
[Fig 48]

Black women and children are crucial to the economy; their value to the labor force is significant. The woman needs to continue to produce good 'Negros' that will work. Those that will not work within the plantation constraints, make good ornaments to hang from the trees, pit fighting, and jail, or dragged behind a truck.

Offense charged	Total arrests						Percent distribution[1]					
	Race											
	Total	White	Black or African American	American Indian or Alaska Native	Asian	Native Hawaiian or Other Pacific Islander	Total	White	Black or African American	American Indian or Alaska Native	Asian	Native Hawaiian or Other Pacific Islander
TOTAL	7,710,900	5,319,654	2,115,381	164,430	92,737	18,698	100.0	69.0	27.4	2.1	1.2	0.2
Murder and nonnegligent manslaughter	8,957	3,953	4,778	105	94	27	100.0	44.1	53.3	1.2	1.0	0.3
Rape[2]	18,778	12,794	5,376	267	239	50	100.0	68.1	28.6	1.4	1.5	0.3
Robbery	66,799	29,025	36,187	678	641	260	100.0	43.5	54.2	1.0	1.0	0.4

[Chief offenders are male Blacks]
[Fig 49]

The Anti-nigger© is an age-old slave plantation problem; always escaping and rebelling. In 2020, the combination of bastardization, and poverty (*Establishment Styled Nurturing*©) caused people with the Anti-nigger rebellious mentality to fill the jails. Many of incarcerates are have the Anti-nigger personality, and refuse to pick cotton or conform to being tied together as mentioned in [LMAS3[as listed on page #92]]. The modern free-Black male, rebellious; although lost, is crucial to the survival of the Black species.

Sex of victim	Total	Race of offender				Sex of offender		
		White	Black or African American	Other¹	Unknown	Male	Female	Unknown
Male	4,639	1,942	2,430	133	134	4,073	521	45
Female	1,921	1,064	745	72	40	1,731	184	6
Unknown sex	10	5	2	2	1	9	0	1

[Arrests by race and ethnicity, 2018. [12,212 agencies]
[Fig 50]

In the article <u>Fact Check: Was Planned Parenthood Started to 'Control' the Black Population?</u>[184], an interesting usage of familiar terms rears its ugly head. Two statements stand out from the article.

1. "Did Margaret Sanger believe in eugenics? Yes, but not in the way Carson implied. Eugenics was a discipline, championed by prominent scientists but now widely debunked, that promoted "good" breeding and aimed to prevent 'poor' breeding. The idea was that the human race could be improved through encouraging people with traits like intelligence, hard work, cleanliness (thought to be genetic) to reproduce.

2. In the United States, eugenics intersected with the birth control movement in the 1920s, and Sanger reportedly spoke at eugenics conferences. She also talked about using birth control to facilitate, "The process of weeding out the unfit [and] of preventing the birth of defectives."

No one in their right mind after reading these words can discern anything but contempt for certain humans regardless of condition. The Machiavellian and macabre nature of Planned Parenthood's killing of the unfit to better the human race, begs the questions;

1. What is Planned Parenthood's definition of unfit?

2. Who gets to decide?

Obviously, *The Establishment* did not establish Planned Parenthood, but instead capitalized on the myth of the Shiftless Negro and Selective Breeding. What self-respecting White person seeing the poorly educated, poorly clad Negros shuffle aimless about the city as maids, and other menial tasks would believe them to be fit, or a good choice to clone?

The danger of entrenched racism is that it slips and slides effortlessly into any shape or orifice it can adorn. Any human that thinks they can develop a better human, is not only a demi-god, but also an insane demi-god. The adage, "Whom the gods wish to destroy they first make mad," has never been truer of;

- Margeret Sanger - nurse and educator
- Ethel Byrnea - registered nurse
- Fania Mindell - a volunteer that spoke three languages
- Elizabeth Stuyvesant - social worker

These 'humanitarians' easily justified their vehemence: after all Negros were likened unto horses and apes; not humans. When you look at the credentials of these women, classical trained to preserve life, apparently just White lives apparently.

I watched the chief prosecutor from Nuremberg give a lecture on C-Span not too long ago. Interestingly enough he reminded the hearers that many of the men that signed the orders for mass murder and eugenics were MDs and double PhDs. Look at the credentials of the four Planned Parenthood croons; who better to study human history and understand the implications of entrenched hatred, and bias than students of human nature.

Since 1920 Planned Parenthood has not been just facilitated population control, Planned Parenthood fills its function as a Product Control Mechanism©.

11.4 Black Cotton

The Cotton Belt is the collective name given to the cotton growing southern states from Virginia to California. Cotton is a major crop in 14 of the United States. It has the longest growing season of planted crops in the country 150 to 180 days. The cotton fiber is still used to manufacture textiles. Today, the world uses more cotton in manufacturing than any other fiber and it is still a leading cash crop in the India, China, United States, Brazil, Pakistan, Turkey, Usbekistan, Mexico, Australia and Mali.

The article 7 Events that enraged Colonists and led to the American Revolution[185], indicates money was the underlying issue in the U.S. for (Financial) Independence.

- The Stamp Act (March 1765)
- The Townshend Acts (June-July 1767)
- The Boston Massacre (March 1770)
- The Boston Tea Party (December 1773)
- The Coercive Acts (March-June 1774)
- Lexington and Concord (April 1775)
- British attacks on coastal towns

The Declaration of Causes of Seceding States[186], replete with disparaging language also cite the same underlying financial reason for Seceding from the Union.

- [Georgia] - "They have endeavored to weaken our security, to disturb our domestic peace and tranquility...The question of slavery was the great difficulty in the way of the formation of the Constitution[18]. **While the subordination and the political and social inequality of the African race was fully conceded by all**...Because by

---

[18] It is clear that this is the reason the 13th, 14th, and 15th Amendments ('The Civil War Amendments') had to be enacted by a change in the Constitution. The original framing made no allowances for the Africans - they were officially African'ts by Legislation.

their declared principles and policy they have outlawed $3,000,000,000 of our property..."

- [Mississippi] - "Our position is thoroughly identified with the institution of slavery-- the greatest material interest of the world. Its labor supplies the product, which constitutes by far the largest and most important portions of commerce of the earth. These products are peculiar to the climate verging on the tropical regions, and by an imperious law of nature, none but the Black race can bear exposure to the tropical sun. These products have become necessities of the world, and a blow at slavery is a blow at commerce and civilization. That blow has been long aimed at the *Establishment*, and was at the point of reaching its consummation."

- [South Carolina] - "The ends for which the Constitution was framed are declared by itself to be 'to form a more perfect union, establish justice, ensure domestic tranquility, provide for the common defense, promote the general welfare, and secure the blessings of liberty to ourselves and to our posterity.'

These ends endeavored to accomplish, by a Federal Government, that each State was recognized as an equal, and had separate control over its own institutions. The right of property in slaves was recognized by giving to free persons, distinct political rights, by giving them the right to represent, and thus burdening them with direct taxes for three-fifths of their slaves; by authorizing the importation of slaves for twenty years; and by stipulating the rendition of fugitives from labor.

A geographical line has been drawn across the Union, and all the States north of that line have united in the election of a man to the high office of President of the United States, whose opinions and purposes are hostile to slavery. He is to be entrusted with the administration of the common Government, because he has declared, "Government cannot endure permanently half slave, half free," and that the public mind must rest in the belief that slavery is in the course of ultimate extinction.

This sectional combination for the submersion of the Constitution, has been aided in some of the States by elevating to citizenship, persons who, by the supreme law of the land, are incapable of becoming citizens; and their votes have been used to inaugurate a new policy, hostile to the South, and destructive of its beliefs and safety."

- [Texas] - "Texas abandoned her separate national existence and consented to become one of the Confederated Union to promote her welfare, insure domestic tranquility and secure more substantially the blessings of peace and liberty to her people. She was received into the confederacy with her own constitution, under the guarantee of the federal constitution and the impact of annexation, that she should enjoy these blessings. She was received as part of the common holding, maintaining, and protecting the institution known as Negro slavery - the servitude of the African to the White race within her limits - a relation that had existed from the first settlement of her wilderness by the White race, and which her people intended should exist in all future time."

- [Virginia] - "...that the powers granted under the said Constitution were derived from the people of the United States, and might be resumed whenever the same should be perverted to their injury and oppression; and the Federal Government, having perverted said powers, not only to the injury of the people of Virginia, but to the oppression of the Southern Slaveholding States."

Georgia points out the most interesting *'Willi'ism'* of all the dissenting states when it points out that Slavery was agreed to by **all** after discussion at the framing of the Constitution of America. Their argument: We **All** declared these people to be American'ts; you cannot discard that acknowledgement without reframing the Constitution. This was not just a financial argument; the peace, tranquility and according to South Carolina a more perfect union was framed with an understanding unilaterally which perpetually excluded Negros.

The Establishment forged a way, because economics are a morality unto themselves. When America fled

Britain's tyranny, their intention was not a moral freedom but a fiscal freedom; which required an economic base. America wanted to become an Empire; and no Empire in history existed, thrived, or survived without slaves.

The modern crop in America is Black Cotton. Statistically it appears that Black Americans progressed from picking the Cotton plant to being a crop of Human Cotton; Black Human Cotton.

11.5 The Black Cotton Gin©

Eli Whitney is famous for patenting the Cotton Gin; a machine that mechanized the production of cotton by automating the process of removing seeds from cotton fiber. The modern Cotton Gin known as the Criminal Justice System, does the same thing, it mechanizes and encapsulates the proverbial seeds (Black males) from the Black Cotton.

The purpose of the Black Cotton Gin is to function as a financial machine to maintain a strong economic base. Black Cotton is just a Fiat System[19] predicated on allowing indentured servant-hood to be the Neo-Colonial Slavery©. If you do not own land, your wealth just flows through your hands, it is not your own.

- $1 Trillion in consumer spending per year[26]
- A disproportionate percentage of $182 billion per year[20] spent on incarceration
- An untold percentage of the $1 Trillion spent over 40 years of the Drug Wars[21]
- $150⁺ Billion in revenue[187]

---

[19]A Fiat System is a System using paper money as required by government regulation, but that paper money has no intrinsic value. Fiat money does not have use value, and has value only because a government by restriction controls its value, or because parties engaging in exchange (Federal Reserve) agree on its value.

- Whites own 70.9 % of all U.S. businesses, 88 % of the overall sales, and control 86.5 % of U.S. employment[28] Blacks own 9.5 %
- Over 90 % of Latino and Black firms do not have even one employee other than the owners[188]
- According to the USDA Blacks own less than 1 percent of rural land, 98% being owned by White[189]

Even the small business owner is just another type of sharecropping taxpayer. It is not by accident that Title 26 of the United States Code (U.S. Tax Codes) is such a lengthy document. Several thousand pages of rhetoric exist to maintain the Republic's Economic strength. I think African American'ts do not understand that Title 26 was not written with them in mind.

11.6 The Black Messiah

At the time of his death he was no longer Malcolm X, preaching to Black urban ghettos, but Malcolm the global revolutionary, who had brought together an alliance of African and Middle Eastern leaders in support of his new Organization of Afro-American Unity, and who was intent on pressing his human rights claims against the U.S. government at the United Nations[190/191]."

By far the most feared African American't in American history was the individual born Malcolm Little. This average, uneducated individual, who dropped out of school because his teacher told him he would be better off trying to be a carpenter because he could not be a lawyer (American'tism), spent a lot of his life in jail. Rather than become Black Cotton however, with the help of a man who cleaned himself up he learned;

- To think for himself

- To read, write and express himself
- A religion unlike the one he had seen and heard was about freedom but had been used to keep hi people in chains

Inspired, Malcolm Little did something that nobody else had really been successful at doing in a public forum. Malcolm was not the first Blackman to stand up and have his voice heard, but Malcolm pioneered the public application of a concept that people heard growing up referred to as Black-White people.

BWP are Black people who were not afraid to stand eye-to-eye with White people and argue they were not afraid to read books in public, they were not afraid to have their voice heard and to stand up for themselves and to stand for anybody else that was being abused, overlooked or downtrodden in their presence.

Black-White people became nauseating because they were not the Blacks *The Establishment* wanted for the plantation. Black people were not interested in stepping and fetching any longer; they were not interested in bowing their heads when they spoke to White people and they were not interested in looking to future that does not hold something for them; mentally Blacks had started to return to their pre-slave nature - PROUD.

Bob Marley (another free-d African't) wrote a line in one of his songs, "Emancipate yourself from mental slavery, none but ourselves can free our minds." To this, Malcolm spoke often. Both men realized that poverty was unpleasant, but mental impoverishment imposed by an oppressor is a far more reprehensible existence.

To *The Establishment* Malcolm was a radical Black troublemaker monitored and constantly feared. J.D Edgar Hoover termed Malcolm 'The Black Messiah'.

White people did not dread Malcolm until other 'slaves' started to follow him off the plantation. These Blacks did not want to just escape into the swamps (about which *The Establishment* would not have cared). These slaves did something that *The Establishment* never anticipated.

The Establishment had assured White people that if they abused Blacks long enough, Black people would perpetuate ignorance and self-destruction. *The Establishment* never expected to see a slave turn around and tell other slaves to go back home, stop abusing Black females, take responsibility and care of Black children, stop using drugs, stop using liquor, and stop gambling. In other words, this uppity Nigger, was helping other niggers become uppity, and undoing the effects of racial institutionalization. What happens to a plantation, which no longer had plowers, mules, and cotton pickers, instead had men and families together, unifying, becoming healthy and strong; they would lose their economic golden eggs.

Travelling to Mecca sealed Malcolm's fate. Going to Mecca and making friends with people that looked like Malcolm and shared Malcolm's religion and happened to control oil, Malcolm became a threat to *The Establishment*.

Initially, the FBI monitored Elijah Mohammed more than Malcolm because he had thousands of dedicated followers. Malcolm however was political and more so than Elijah leading the people's souls; Malcolm motivated Black people's hearts, minds and actions.

When Malcolm came back to the USA, he disassociated himself with the government sanctioned nonprofit organization the Nation of Islam and incorporated his own mosque, American Mosque Inc., to which he said White people could support but they could not be members. Malcolm then became more than a White-Black person, he transformed himself into an American; and other Blacks were watching.

Malcolm garnered a seat near the table because of his International standing not because White people respected him but they respected the friends he had made. Malcolm had to go. *The Establishment* did not have enough space or time to allow everybody under their control to either be free, return to Africa or be equals. Green Cotton depends on Black Cotton to survive. Malcolm was the greatest threat to Green Cotton.

The Establishment reverted to edicts from days gone by. Instead of marching in and gunning Malcolm down or even using somebody White to kill him, they chose to use people that looked like him and were of the same religion as Malcolm. This action achieved several things:

- Caused distrust among the Nation of Islam
- Caused distrust among Black people
- Cause distrust male-to-male

there by throwing and thrusting Black people back into the confusion that *The Establishment* requires for survival. In order to stop this Black Messiah from producing free 'colts'; Malcolm was gelded via shotgun. However, they left his wife alive to create potential products. Perhaps hoping she would revert to niggerism up his death.

11.7 The Black Cloud©

Oscar Wilde said, "An idea that is not dangerous is unworthy of being called an idea at all." The Black Cloud is what I refer to as the ideation that there is a potential for integrating ideas and lifestyles between White people and Black people. In other words, it was not that White people were as afraid of Black people contaminating them physically as they were of other White people liberating Blacks. This Black Cloud became the impetus for enhanced Whiteness.

The purpose of a uniform for soldiers in the military (other than camouflage) is to distinguish one set of soldiers from the other. This is more important than you realize. Friendly Fire accounts for a great deal of casualties in war efforts. In the heat of battle the last thing you were trying to figure out is which one of the people jumping through the bushes beside you is on your team. The necessity for color coordination became imperative. *The Establishment* understands this, having survived the Civil War and realizing in the Civil War that one of the things that worked against them was that White people all look alike. They did not have big ears or big noses or any of that stereotypical ignorance, they all look alike in that how could you look at the skin of a White man and tell if he was Northern or Southern. The social-uniform against African American'ts became Whiteness.

The Establishment utilized ignorance and mis-education, to convince White people that the thing that unified them and ensured their safety was the color of their skin. According to Supreme Court, the Negro (an archenemy by design), bears the indelible marks of race and color. It is no wonder then that North African people, Latino people and even dark skin people from East India readily accept their demographic categorization as 'White'. After all who would want to be the enemy of *The Establishment*?

How then did the White House survive eight years of a unified Black family sitting at the helm? What must have gone through the minds of *The Establishment's* Guardians when they realized that they would have to give internal controls and the internal command structure to somebody that as far as they were concerned was an American't. Perhaps this is why so much time and effort was put into trying to negate Obama's citizenship. The whole point of African American'tism is to prohibit just such a thing as a Black president.

Obama did not happen overnight. It took decades, Amendments to the Constitution, lynchings, and beatings by the police disenfranchisement, voter fraud, Jim Crow, Grandfather Clause, and everything else that *The Establishment* could think of at the time, to stop Black people's ability to self-control and self-determine in America.

Unforeseen, was that there would even be White people who when looking at this African-American't in a suit and a tie with a wife darker than he was, articulating himself, believed that he was not a threat to their Whiteness. The Lynch Letters called decent, non-racist White people who truly believe all men and women deserve equal treatment "future misunderstanding generations". Decent people broke another of *The Establishment's* rules, when they elected; not once, but twice, a Black man and woman to sit in the Oval Office - while they slept restfully.

[Fig[192] 51]

This does not mean that Obama was a sell-out or turncoat; it just means that his polish, poise, and elocution were not what they expected from a free-d underling. He did not leap from the rafters with the rhetoric about killing Whitey, we are getting even, or even rhetoric about what White people had done against Black people. He said now that I am here now that I sit in this office, I will do what should have been done in the first place; treating all citizens of this country the same.

The Establishment predicted change but never perfected a permanent method to prevent Black progress. De in large to White people of good conscience, the Dark Cloud shifted and once White people started to accept that Black people were equal, *The Establishment* had an enemy far greater than Martin Luther King Jr. ever could have been.

The Establishment's greatest enemy is White people who cling to the idea that the country was founded upon; Fortunately, Christians and Abolitionists still exist. For now the African American'ts were going to be included and they were going to be accepted as African Americans.

When Obama said he would listen when we disagree he reiterated one of the founding principles of America; that all men and women were created equal. Obama's appeal to common decency engendered support from White men, White women, Black men, Black women, Latin men and women, Asian men and women, gay men and women, East Indian men and women, North African men and women, men and women from Alaska.

Peniel Joseph in his article, <u>Obama's effort to heal racial divisions and uplift Black America</u>[193] sites the following responses in America both entrenched racists or not;

- Obama's presidency signaled a "post-racial" America at first, but the racial conflict followed disproved that
- The Obama victory helped fulfill one of the great ambitions of the civil rights struggle
- Obama's, extended this reimagining of Black American life by providing a conspicuous vision of **a healthy, loving and thriving African American family that defies still-prevalent racist stereotypes**
- Almost immediately, the Obama presidency unleashed racial furies that have only multiplied over time
- The national racial climate grew more, and not less, fraught

The election of the African-American't sadly was even more divisive than the nation cared to admit. President Lyndon B. Johnson after signing the Civil Rights Bill into law is credited as saying, "We have lost the South for a generation." His math was wrong.

11.8 White Flight

White Flight or the White Exodus were terms applied to the 1950s and 1960s large-scale migration of

White people from racially diverse neighborhoods to less diversified suburban or exurban regions. Housing laws and discriminative mortgage lending helped facilitate the trend.

11.9 White Slight©

The White Slight reared its ugly head when Obama won his first and second election. Statistically, Black anger and resentment was joined at a rapid, increasing pace by White anger and fear; this I call the White Slight.

America did not just happen to fall into this chaotic period that it finds itself currently, this was 250 years in the making. I believe that the QUAD^E- America Paradigm© is at work in 2021.

After years and years of abusing people that did not look like them, suddenly one of the peoples they abused was at the helm. They did not know what they were in for, in many of their minds Toussaint L'Ouverture returned from the dead.

QUAD^E-USA

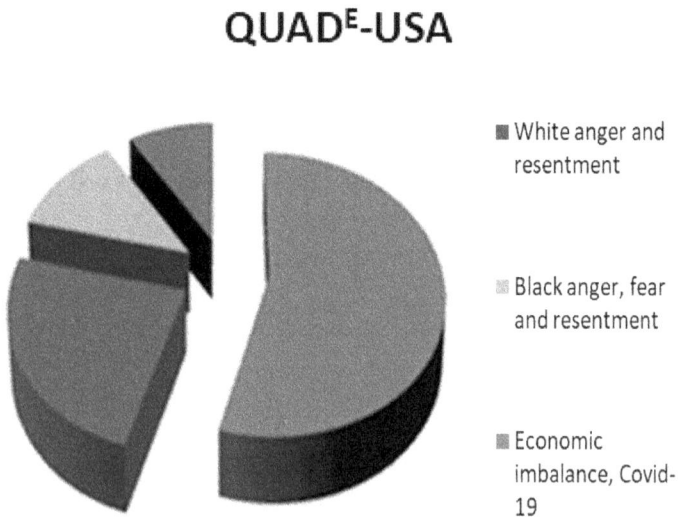

- White anger and resentment
- Black anger, fear and resentment
- Economic imbalance, Covid-19

[Fig 52]

Jennifer Agiesta a CNN Polling Director in the article, Most say race relations worsened under Obama, poll finds[194], sites 54%　of Americans say relations between Blacks and White got worse when Obama became president, including 57% of White and 40% of Blacks.

QUAD^E (Emotions) is an accounting of anger on both sides. Black people are angry about hundreds of years of oppression and abuse. White people are marginally angry about the change to their ecosystem with Civil Rights. White people's anxiety spiked in the Obama Administration.

The Obama Administration fostered anger amongst the entrenched racists and engendered new comers to the rank of the entrenched that stood on the line called bias because there were many who resented having a Black person tell them what to do; it is blue in the face of more than 250 years of White privilege.

The Establishment sought to destroy the Black-nature, and even override God for the chance to create wealth. While the world watched what *The Establishment* set in motion against the U.S. Black male, no one paid attention to the greater goal it sought: A perpetual wealth crop system

I fear however, QUAD^E will soon be replaced by QUAD$^{N©}$; Wherein the N stands for numbers. The rage and reckless chaotic behavior associated with the BLM movement caused some quivering in the support of the numerous White businesses and industry that had previously been ardent supporters of the movement.

Remember, politics is a game dominated by the voting masses. No matter how many Black people vote numerically we are outnumbered.

QUAD^N-USA

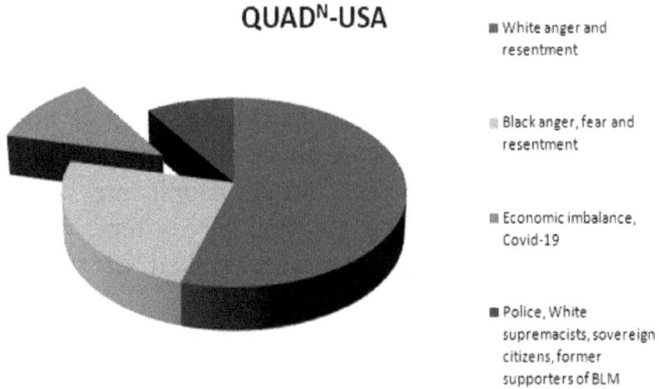

- White anger and resentment
- Black anger, fear and resentment
- Economic imbalance, Covid-19
- Police, White supremacists, sovereign citizens, former supporters of BLM

[Fig 53]

I feel it if Blacks continue in this reckless violence, the attacks on the police, random attacks on White people, allowing White people to attack White people and riot on our behalf in an effort to force equality, I fear that one day Blacks will wake up and be out of the word that Admiral Yamamoto famously quoted "I fear all we have done is to awaken a sleeping giant and fill him with a terrible resolve."

Blacks did not win The Civil Rights Movement. Blacks did not end Slavery. The White efforts made Blacks victorious. These movements, even though championed to and by Blacks, required the support of White people.

If Blacks end up randomly killing White people, attacking the defenders of the White way of life, the police; Blacks make Whites afraid. Then it will just be White against Black, White in which case Blacks are outnumbered.

I think we learned in the response to MOVE in Philadelphia that if Blacks use violence and push White too hard, when Whites push back, scorched-earth is to be the result.

12.0

What Role

Does

Education

Play?

"Invariably, knowledge dictates life, liberty, and death, but those who have historically occupied the seats of power not only dictate what is defined as knowledge but also dictate what's included, what's excluded, and how it is filtered to society vis-à-vis America's major institutions . . . particularly the educational system; ultimately, shaping the very essence of life [Martin Guevara Urbina]."

12.1
What Role Does Education Play

"The only thing that interferes with my
Learning is my education[Albert Einstein]."

—❧—

The Establishment, as do all houses of higher learning requires teachers. A college degree is not granted, it is conferred. Upon completing academic requirements, and paying the library dues, the university confers the degree announcing to the world that the candidate completed the initiation and is now eligible to join the 'Republic'. The degree is not just a measure of education; it is recognition of indoctrination and conformity. Using a controlled educational format has long since been a Colonial tactic.

A common reading of the phrase 'What do we need?' in the Lynch Letters creates a contextual error. It is not so much a query as it is a listing of exactly what *The Establishment* needs to craft to make this right. *The Establishment* did not reinvent the wheel; they just determined a different use for it. What they needed was a mule; a strong, pet they could control. The slavers wanted Blacks; disdained by other slaves and the Whites, and comfortable nowhere but at work for Massa. "The exact origin of the first mule is unknown, but we do know that the mule was deliberately bred by man in ancient times. The breeding of a jackass (male donkey) with a female horse (mare) is the most common and oldest known man made hybrid[195]." The donkey was too stubborn (Kunta-Kinte) and the horse too fast and independent (Malcolm X). Perhaps Toussaint had valid reasons for killing the 'Mulatto' (slaver-slave crossbred children). Perhaps the Administrators of *The Establishment still* have *Cauchemars* (Nightmares) about Toussaint[20].

---

[20]{[LMAS7] What do we need?

[LMAS8]First of all we need a Black nigger man, a pregnant nigger woman and her baby nigger boy.
[LMAS9]Second, we will use the same basic principle that we use in breaking a horse, combined with some more sustaining factors. What we do with horses is that we break them from one form of life to another, that is we reduce them from their natural state in nature.
[LMAS10]Whereas nature provides them with the natural capacity to take care of their offspring, we break that natural string of independence from them and thereby create a dependency status, so that we may be able to get from them useful production for our business and pleasure.
[CPMN6]Both must be taught to respond to a peculiar new language.
[CPMN7]Psychological and physical instruction of containment must be created for both.
[CPMN8]We hold the six cardinal principles as truth to be self-evident, based upon the following the discourse concerning the economics of reeking and tying the horse and the nigger together, all inclusive of the six principles laid down about. NOTE: Neither principle alone will suffice for good economics.
[CPMN9]All principles must be employed for orderly good of the nation.
[CPMN10]Accordingly, both a wild horse and a wild or nature nigger are dangerous even if captured, for they will have the tendency to seek their customary freedom, and in doing so, might kill you in your sleep.
[CPMN11]You cannot rest. They sleep while you are awake, and are awake while you are asleep.
[CPMN12]They are dangerous near the family house and it requires too much labor to watch them away from the house.
[CPMN13]Above all, you cannot get them to work in this natural state. Hence, both the horse and the nigger must be broken; that is breaking them from one form of mental life to another. Keep the body, take the mind! In other words, break the will to resist. Now the breaking process is the same for both the horse and the nigger, only slightly varying in degrees. But as we said before, there is an art in long range economic planning. You

must keep your eye and thoughts on the female and the offspring of the horse and the nigger.

[CPMN16]Therefore, if you break the female mother, she will break the offspring in its early years of development, and when the offspring is old enough to work, she will deliver it up to you, for her normal female protective tendencies will have been lost in the original breaking process.

[PIN1]Earlier we talked about the non-economic good of the horse and the nigger in their wild or natural state; we talked out the principle of breaking and tying them together for orderly production. Furthermore, we talked about paying particular attention to the female savage and her offspring for orderly future planning, then more recently we stated that, by reversing the positions of the male and female savages, we created an orbiting cycle that turns on its own axis forever unless a phenomenon occurred and resift and positions of the male and female savages. Our experts warned us about the possibility of this phenomenon occurring, for they say that the mind has a strong drive to correct and re-correct itself over a period of time if I can touch some substantial original historical base, and they advised us that the best way to deal with the phenomenon is to shave off the brute's mental history and create a multiplicity of phenomena of illusions, so that each illusion will twirl in its own orbit, something similar to floating balls in a vacuum.

[PIN2]This creation of multiplicity of phenomena of illusions entails the principle of crossbreeding the nigger and the horse as we stated above, the purpose of which is to create a diversified division of labor thereby creating different levels of labor and different values of illusion at each connecting level of labor. The results of which is the severance of the points of original beginnings for each sphere illusion. Since we feel that the subject matter may get more complicated as we proceed in laying down our economic plan concerning the purpose, reason, and effect of crossbreeding horses and nigger, we shall lay down the following definition terms for future generations. Orbiting cycle means a thing turning in a given path. Axis means upon which or around which a body turns. Phenomenon means something beyond ordinary conception and inspires awe and wonder. Multiplicity means a great number. Sphere means a globe.   Cross breeding a horse means taking a horse and breeding it with an ass and you get a dumb backward ass long headed mule that is neither reproductive nor productive by itself.

[PIN3]Crossbreeding niggers mean taking so many drops of good White blood and putting them into as many nigger women as possible, varying the drops by the various tones that you want, and then letting them breed with each other until another cycle of color appears as you desire.

[PIN4]What this means is; put the niggers and the horse in a breeding pot, mix some assess and some good White blood and what do you get?   You got a multiplicity of colors of ass backward, unusual niggers, running, tied to a backward ass long headed mule, the one productive of itself, the other sterile. (The one constant, the other dying, we keep the nigger constant for we may replace the mules for another tool) both mule and nigger tied to each other, neither knowing where the other came from and neither productive for itself, nor without each other.

[CTL1]Crossbreeding completed, for further severance from their original beginning, we must completely annihilate the mother tongue of both the new nigger and the new mule and institute a new language that involves the new life's work of both.

[CTL2]You know language is a peculiar institution. It leads to the heart of a people.   The more a foreigner knows about the language of another country the more he is able to move through all levels of that society.

[CTL3][ES]Therefore, if the foreigner is an enemy of the country, to the extent that he knows the body of the language, to that extent is the country vulnerable to attack or invasion of a foreign culture. For example, if you take a slave, if you teach him all about your language, he will know all your secrets, and he is then no more a slave, for you cannot fool him any longer. For example, if you told a slave that he must perform in getting out "our crops" and he knows the language well, he would know that "our crops" didn't mean "our crops" and the slavery system would break down, for he would relate on the basis of what "our crops" really meant. So you have to be careful in setting up the new language for the slaves would soon be in

The Establishment declared war on the fabric of Black society. The dissection of the family guaranteed discord in America; indefinitely[196]. In order to control the environment and the slaves' way of interacting, they needed to control familial bonds[197];

- Destroying confidence, removing positive ways to interact with others
- Destroying emotional well-being
- Destroying propensity for higher levels of education
- Contributing to a decrease in behavioral problems
- Removing the safe and supportive environment develops self-confidence
- Destroying Moral influence
- Distorting parenting skills
- Distorting gender roles

Here is where the selectivity and Darwinian motif begins. My father owned and raced horses and my siblings and I enjoyed years of Equestrian activity. Horses are peculiar, their strength, speed, and stamina rivaled only by

---

your house, talking to you "man to man" and that is death to our economic system.

[CTL4]In addition, the definitions of words or terms are only a minute part of the process. Values are created and transported by communication through the body of the language.

[CTL5]A total society has many interconnected value systems. All the values in the society have bridges of language to connect them for orderly working in the society. But for these language bridges, these many value systems would sharply clash and cause internal strife or civil war, the degree of the conflict being determined by the magnitude of the issues or relative opposing strength in whatever form. For example, if you put a slave in a hog pen and train him to live there and incorporate in him to value it as a way of life completely, the biggest problem you would have out of him is that he would worry you about provisions to keep the hog pen clean, or the same hog pen and make a slip and incorporate something in his language whereby he comes to value a house more than he does his hog pen, you got a problem. He will soon be in your house}.

their stubbornness. The same power to carry a man at full gallop over miles easily and readily turns against the rider when desired. One of the ways to control a stallion is to Geld (castrate) him. He is then docile, and controllable. However, the gelding cannot reproduce. Therefore, the Nigger needed his mind broken, not his fertility. Take away his desire for his mare (the Black woman) by reminding him that she is property and belongs to another. In doing so, the male runs the risk of the enhanced punishment for damaging the owner's property. In time, the mare changes from a desirable thing to a simple broodmare: Just a tool to produce little slaves with the Black men, and a toy for White men.

Look at the list of benefits listed in [LMAS8 found on page #330], and then reflect upon the state of the Black family in America. *The Establishment* studied both sets of family long and hard, both sets of family and determined that a removal of healthy productive family environment, replacing same with a toxic or at minimal stagnant environment would have devastating, permanent effects on their Crop-nigger© herd.

12.2 Crop-Niggers©

In 1866, many U.S. States leased convicts as cheap labor. Peonage made arresting Blacks lucrative, and engendered a need for larger and more powerful police agencies.

Police agencies primary responsibility during Peonage was to search out and arrest Blacks who were in violation of Black Codes. Once arrested, these men, women and children were made available to plantations to harvest cotton, tobacco, coal or service the railroad. The owners of these businesses paid the state a 'tax' for prison laborers Peonage ended around 1940.

This Peon-indoctrination undoubtedly is what we suffer from in modern, socially conflicted America. So many traditions and ignorance's from previous eras continue today. Many people still work the machinery of the antiquated entrenched factories ignorant to their origin.

Peon-indoctrination left its stain, evidenced by similarities in modern improprieties in the Law enforcement System.

Sadly The 13th Amendment; the landmark legislation benefitting Blacks declared that "Neither slavery nor involuntary servitude, except as a punishment for crime whereof the party shall have been duly convicted, shall exist within the United States, or any place subject to their jurisdiction." The obvious loophole to the Amendment was to find a reason to lock up Black people.

When people ask why the number of Blacks incarcerates is inexplicable, maybe its because no one wants to simply say, 'Because we have done it this way for so long.' It is an inescapable extrapolation, that the same economic undertone, considering Blacks as 'crop-materials', exhibiting itself in 2021 as indiscriminate arrests, and systemic brutality by the Law Enforcement profession. Maybe to this, the term Robot-gunslinger again bears some credence.

Black Cotton is a multi-billion dollar crop, but it is not without its drawbacks. "Picking cotton is hot, dirty, back-breaking, monotonous work. That work chewed up millions of lives from Ely Whitney's invention of the modern mechanical cotton gin in 1793 well into the 20th century. To pick the cotton, a worker would pull the White, fluffy lint from the boll, trying to not cut his hands on the sharp ends of the boll.

In a typical day, a good worker could pick 300 pounds of cotton or more, meaning that, in any given day, a typical picker would carry a substantial amount of weight, even if he emptied his sack several times.

Farm workers and cotton pickers are exposed to residual impacts of pesticide use in cotton production, in addition to dust, ultraviolet radiation. Cotton picking causes various health hazards among cotton pickers with varied health cost[198]."

The product of the Black Cotton Gin is the Crop-Nigger; the Black Cotton. The Crop-Nigger product differs from the freed African American'ts in several potentially toxic ways:

- Lacking in confidence, far fewer positive interactions with others
- Prone to dangerous activities
- Unstable emotionally
- Indifference towards higher levels of education
- Increased behavioral problems especially violence
- Unbalanced early onset of adult problems
- Survival oriented versus moral influence
- Poor health
- Poor parenting skills

12.3 Cotton Speak©

Cotton Speak is not an actual language; it is the term I use to describe the new language the slaves learned to speak. In order to maintain as much possible confusion, the mis-education of the Negro[199] began as soon as the slave traders corralled slaves for debarkation. The slavers separated tribes and groups before departing Africa. Once ripped from the shores of a familiar place, language, food, music, and faces, the horror began. Imagine a three-month journey consisting of whipping, yelling, and starvation; and you have no idea what the White creatures were saying.

Cotton Speak is the language of brutality, rape, depredation, humiliation, dehumanization, fear, and rage. *The Establishment* studied history well. Former colonists were well acquainted with the Colonial heritage of Britain. *The Establishment* also reasoned that the more horrendous the captivity experience, the longer indoctrination lasted.

Until they became Green Cotton© the slave was relegated to the level of a dog, responding only to tonality and pitch. The White words meant nothing. Once they learned English, they had to question their new religion, which even made God seem to hate Blacks.

After Blacks learned to question religion, they learned to question the Law and the police. After all, it was the law and the police that hunted the free (escaped) man and women down and returned them to slavery, and also enforced the new religion.

Someone then came along and shared buzz-words like freedom, equality, inalienable rights, democracy, voting, and emancipation. These words turned out to be false or at least not applicable to African American'ts. Neither of the words in the languages applied to the Black community. Blacks were after all neither White, nor apparently human, at least not according to the application of language. In the hundreds of years of the Western Black experience, the language of the slaver - English; and Cotton Economics aligned closely.

Fellini[200] said, "A different language is a different vision of life." Wittgenstein[201] commented, "The limits of my language mean the limits of my world." Moreover, of language Woodson says, "The oppressor has always indoctrinated the weak with his interpretation of the crimes of the strong[202]." These quotes remind us of the dangerous and manipulative effect of language. Farrakhan makes a fair assertion in that is people do not see themselves in the education; they do not see a purpose to absorb the education. Decades of Whites only education, fostered indifference within the African't community as Blacks saw no future for them even with an education.

There is no more concise definition of both slavery and *entrenched racism* than 'psychological and physical containment'. *The Establishment,* the sinister genius, wanted to go further than any other regime creating a dynasty of terror and exploitation. More than an overseer, *The Establishment* was more like Pharaoh in that it built monuments to self, using the available human resources.

The Establishment knew that physically containing slaves would never support a dynasty, it needed the slaves to believe they did not deserve better. The best way to ensure that the slaves did not think they deserved anything better was to never allow them to see any other Blacks succeed. The best way to make this policy was to ensure that no Blacks succeeded.

The Grandfather Clause, Jim Crow, Segregation, Poll Taxes, and U.S. Constitution Article 1 Section 9 are examples of perpetuation of the containment both psychologically and physically, ongoing efforts to ensure no Blacks succeed. *The Establishment's* primary concern is economics and its perpetuation.

The terms *Nation* and *We the People* obviously only meant White people to *The Establishment.* Sometimes, it seems like this mentality never changed. *The Establishment* however, fully intended to include all White people in the profits engendered from oppression.

The police stand between the Horse and his Master. Reinforcing why Whites fear Blacks, and why the police are such important factors in the equation: The horse, not so tame now, has grown tired of the whip. Were it not for the overseers, not even White Flight (now called urbanization), or re-gentrification (where they relocate Blacks) might keep the peace.

The Establishment warns and urges simultaneously. The continuing warning is that beneficiaries of *The Establishment* should be wary in closing their eyes and sleeping, lest they wake up staring into the face of L'Ouverture and his Flames of Liberty. *The Establishment* urging is a reminder to be vigilant. *The Establishment* cannot rest; it cannot afford loopholes through which Blacks might develop hope. *The Establishment* lets Blacks sing about home, family, and being happy. Blacks can sing about heaven all they want, that just means they know what this life has to offer them, and heaven is the only peace they will know. DO NOT UNDERESTIMATE THE HELL *The Establishment* CREATED WITHIN THE BLACK SPIRIT.

Anyone familiar with horses knows they have a unique way to contend with the rider or bridle, whichever pisses them off first. Bucking is only one of the tools horses have in their arsenal. If they cannot buck you off they will charge into bushes trying to find some way to knock you off. If that does not work, they simply stop, drop, and roll crushing you if they can. No one except other horses pass on this information.

Keeping wild animals is difficult; taming them diminishes their work capacity. *The Establishment* warns about collateral loss of property due to revolts, uprising, and the increasing amount of violence required to control the males, and females. No matter the tribe, the whipped back finds a friend with another torn back, and together they hate the whip master in silence: or his delegates with badges.

The insidious nature of *The Establishment's* plan has many authors on the topic of racial insensitivity, many of them Black; erroneously cite that the war is against Black men. A careful reading of *The Establishment's* methods, set about the understanding that **the Black male is NOT the target, he is manufactured goods**. The actual target is the Black woman, more to the point, the sphere and influence of the Black woman - her kids.

In her article Kay S. Hymowitz[203] cites, "Almost 70 percent of Black children are born to single mothers." *The Establishment* plan was never against the male, it removed the man because he was in the way of *The Establishment's* crop-nigger yield.

Hymowitz continues, "The truth is that we are now a two-family nation, separate, and unequal; one thriving and intact, and the other struggling, broken, and far too often African-American." Within the article, she references the Moynihan Scissors Effect, which heralded that, while more Black men - were getting jobs; more Black women were joining the welfare rolls[204]. *The Establishment's* effect was recognized but misdiagnosed.

"More than most social scientists, Moynihan, steeped in history and anthropology, understood what families do. They "shape their children's character and ability," he wrote. "By and large, adult conduct in society is learned as a child." What children learned in the "disorganized home[s]" of the ghetto, as he described through his forest of graphs, was that adults do not finish school, get jobs, or, in the case of men, take care of their children or obey the law." There was no need for *The Establishment to* war against Black men; Black men were removing themselves from the equation per the plan.

The true war against the Black man occurred before and during the Middle Passage. Once Kunta became Toby, he was effectively neutralized. *The Establishment Castle*©

did for *The Establishment* the same thing castling does in Chess. It moved the king into a safer position from which to control the board.

From the ramparts of the castle, we see that the planned effect continues from 1712 to the current date. Surely, the success of *The Establishment's* method is irrefutable. The irrefutability of *The Establishment's* method invalidates (forever) anyone's ability to dismiss the effect slavery has on the Black population in America. We see the effects throughout the Black community, but the Establishment flees acknowledgment of the cause. {A brief discourse in offspring development will shed light on the key to sound economic principles[CPN14]}. According to Economists, there are 5 governing economic principles;

- Opportunity Cost - What has racism cost Blacks
- Marginal Principle - Look how many costs are associated with *entrenched racism*
- Law of Diminishing Returns - (The American Systemic disregard for the poor and minorities has brought her to a point at which the level of profits or benefits gained is less than the amount of money or energy invested)
- Principle of Voluntary Returns - (Consumers and producers acting in their self-interest is the basis for a healthy economy. Slavery and discrimination make for a steady economy, but lower levels of innovation and growth. Trumps' rally cry of making America great can only come true in a country where productivity and ingenuity are a voluntary return for fair, valued, equal treatment)
- Real/Nominal Principle - (People without money have no value. It is a sad statement, but true. Indentured servitude was replaced by the Modern Credit System in 1950. In an effort to control the environment yet and still, everyone entered the MCS[205] and discriminatory lending and practices came on line to ensure dominance of the *Establishment's* Graduates)

Universities and High Schools as the academic wings of *The Establishment* decided to wage a fundamentally exclusionary war on education in the Black community since the near mis-hap of the 60s integration.

Abundant amounts of data show that Blacks and Native Americans consistently achieve the lowest collegiate graduation rates. Obviously, socio-economics plays its part, but *The Establishment*, environmental infusion of ignorance and toxic matter into these two communities also takes their toll. Priscilla Tacujan quotes Rorty in terms of the absurd amount of wealth lost and or squandered due to racism. "Richard Rorty believed that the 'moral and social order' bestowed to Americans by the Founders eventually became 'an economic system which starves and mutilates the great majority of the population.' Such is the 'selfishness' of an 'unreformed capitalist economy.' For this reason, there is 'a constant need for new laws and new bureaucratic initiatives which would redistribute the wealth produced by the capitalist system[206]."

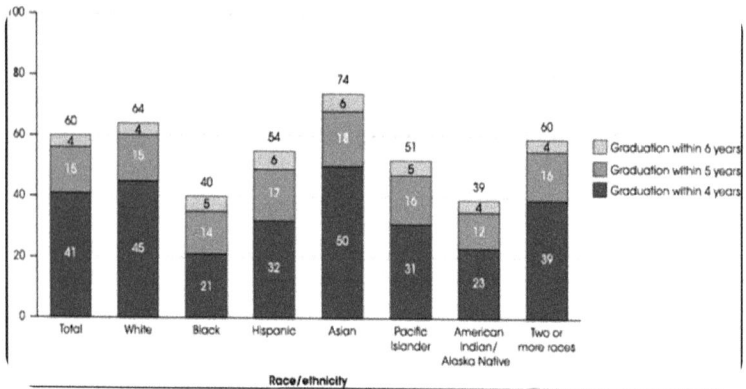

[Graduation rates from first institution attended for first-time, full-time bachelor's degree-seeking students at 4-year postsecondary institutions, by race/ethnicity and time to completion[207]].

[Fig 54]

While assisting a doctoral candidate, I learned an interesting fact. The student was studying scholastic failure rates between races. During the research, we chanced upon some interesting studies. The studies indicated that poor language skills were the underlying issue causing unilateral academic failure. After all, all test instructions and homework assignments are assigned to the students in English; written prose, not conversation prose or Emojis. However, if the child's language or reading are deficient (Cotton Speak), they cannot understand the assignment.

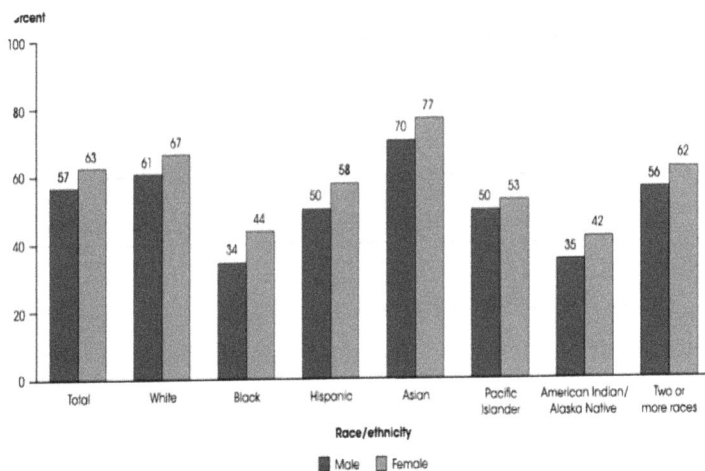

[Graduation rates from first institution attended for first-time, full-time bachelor's degree-seeking students at 4-year postsecondary institutions, by race/ethnicity and time to completion[208]].

[Fig 55[209]]

Performance is not the issue, it is comprehension, "...the vast majority of young children learn language (an inborn drive), but whether they learn Black English or Standard English depends on their experiences in their language communities. So, a child's language acquisition reflects individual and human biological potential, but also it reflects the linguistic characteristics of a particular cultural community.

Spoken grammar is flexible in its word order...Spoken grammar is much less strict than written. The 100 most common words in written grammar are prepositions, pronouns, and articles - the small words which give correct grammatical structure to sentences. In spoken English, many of the top 100 words are verbs.[210]"

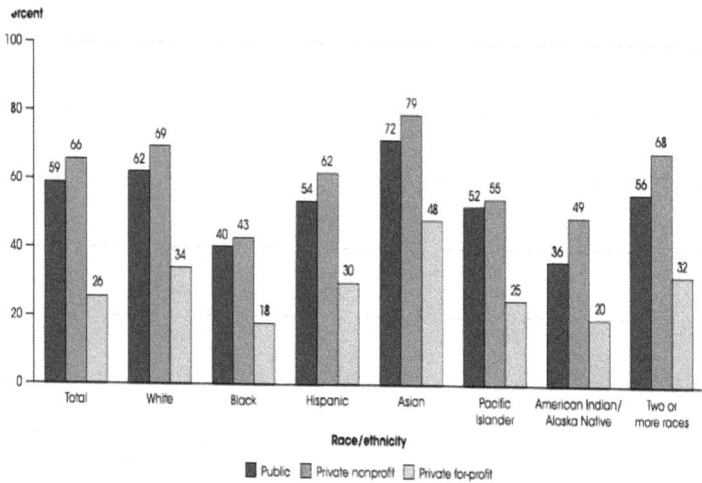

[Graduation rates from first institution attended for first-time, full-time bachelor's degree-seeking students at 4-year postsecondary institutions, by race/ethnicity and time to completion[211]]

[Fig 56[26]]

It is a simple equation; because there is so little reading among today's youth, written prose is unfamiliar to this Cell phone driven generation. In short, many of the kids do not understand what the hell is being asked of them?

{Pay little attention to the generation of original breaking, but concentrate on future generations[CPMN15].} The Generation of Original Breaking is an anathematic phrase. Its incendiary implication is that slavery **was not the** launch point, it was **A** launch point. *The Establishment* is a franchise operation.

Governor Wallace was doing the right thing to preserve the *Nation* Wallace and *The Establishment* wanted to perpetuate. The fear was not of the Blacks entering the educational system; it was of the Blacks learning their Entrenched Racial and Discriminatory Systems. As Minister Farrakhan said, "White people taught us about business, but they did not teach Blacks about White business." Education is the same, do you think HBCU's[212] came about because of generosity? 89% of all HBCUs are in the southern region of the United States, the re-education of the Negro brought about a racial upheaval, even *The Establishment* did not foresee.

In my humble opinion, Desegregation was just furthering of maintenance of *The Establishment*; Blacks lost more than they gained. Whites invited Blacks to dinner after desegregation and to the counters but for the same purpose as before; to clean them. However, after desegregation the Black educational reformation of doctors, lawyers, teachers and politicians died off. Never again, to reach the epoch that it did in the 60s.

An article written June 2020, <u>Where are the African American leaders</u>[213]? Echoes the cry in the darkness, where are the Black stallions; our strong Black men? "African-American women continue to face long odds to succeed more than five decades after the height of the civil rights movement… and are still more likely to be mired in poverty due to working in low-wage jobs, and are incarcerated at twice the rate as White women[214]." The rearing of the Black child in America has been marred by stress, abusive languages, abuse (physical, sexual, mental) and criminal exposure. The lack of family and leadership engendered and strengthened the hold of Gangs in the Black community.

The financially struggling Black female found herself in the struggle between her two men; the colt pulling to the left, the stud pulling right. *The Establishment's* effect reached a glorious low within this part of the struggle. By design, the young colt replaced the stallion in value and need.

Just such an illusion is the American Dream; the imagery is enticing yet deceptive. *Establishment* programs require the removal of any reference to both home and history, and leave the subject floundering.

The illusive American Dream is a dream for everyone that is an American. There are two types of people that do not seem to be welcome to share the American dream; The Native American't and the African-American't. Although most immigrants to the USA arrived more than 250 years ago, these two step-kids have never been welcomed at the table. The Braves from both tribes though scourged, brutalized and murdered systematically, still evoke fear responses in the sleepless nights of *The Establishment*. Otherwise why continue to oppress and disenfranchise them?

The history of these tribes, even in America is downplayed and they are branded as miscreants, divisive, and dangerous; to *The Establishment*. These tribes pose a lesser threat to the people of the country and more to *The Establishment* they rely on to maintain a balanced economy.

Victor Hugo reminds us, "He who opens a school door, closes a prison." The lack of positive role models, the history of the slave, steppin' and fetching, the spook, the darkie, Rosewood, Amistad, Brown vs. The Board of Education, when will Black leadership stop trying to place blame, and offer solutions. Even the dumbest redneck knows of the horrible effect the treatment of Black people caused. However, we are fighting in a vacuum. If we know that we need to get off a boat prior to the waterfall, yet continue to ride - the battle is already lost before we drown.

Prima Nocta is the ancient policy of sleeping with a bride on her wedding night, and implanting a seed other than her husband's. This policy was not only to selectively dilute the bride's tribe's bloodline; its intention is to make the impending reprise or revolution from the bride's tribe less bloody. This is what Toussaint reversed in the Caribbean, by also killing the Mulattos. To this day, Haitians remain unforgiven by *The Establishment* for their revolution. In the predominantly Black Caribbean, Haitians are less welcome by the other former slave colonies that joined the commonwealth, or at least accepted British rule.

Some dim-witted educators postulated the use of Idiot Speak; they called it Ebonics. Ebonics was rumored to be a sort of Black English[215]. The reasoning behind the introduction of Ebonics was to level the playing field for Black kids in scholastic settings, as well as develop civic pride in their culture. There are innumerable flaws in this reasoning.

- Many Blacks cannot successfully trace their ancestry tribe, and language. Many of the source tribes no longer exist
- Regardless of which part of The Continent Blacks came from, they now live in the New World
- Since the American School system is English based, Ebonics creates even more of a disadvantage. No matter the culture in America, kids learn in English, it is necessary for the smooth operation of the society
- The Blacks in this country are the result of a diabolic attempt to make them a permanent subculture; all Cotton Speak linguistics should be eradicated, there is nothing in it to be proud of, why foster the language of slavery. In America, Whites speak English. Those that wish to excel need to either learn to make use of *The Establishment*s lingo and glyphs, or contend with sub-lingo (White) lifestyles
- *The Establishment* is not going to pay for Ebonics test books and tests etc.
- Once schooled in Ebonics, the student still has to function within the English framework used in mainstream society.

If language truly reflects the heart of a people, then Black inner city slang speaks volumes. Terms like 'my nigga, my dog, my peoples, road dog, or my pardna', do not imply respect or endearment, they imply isolation from the mainstream, and a disassociation with the language not commonly used in the street.

Promulgators of Black English, endeavor to equalize the past, at the cost of the future. In Chinese, Latino, or African parts of town, they speak their mother tongue, for those, English is more of a *Lingua Franca* or trade language. These cultures teach their kids their mother tongue, hoewver for business and school, it is English. Does this not fly in the face of common sense, that every other color kid can understand Dick and Jane, but the little Black kids cannot. In Africa; to this day, missionaries teach the children how to read and write English, after all it is a common language[216].

I grew up speaking slang, and I went to Private School where we spoke only 'proper' English. At home, my father did not allow the use of slang. My father was not ashamed of the culture; on the contrary, he is still proud of his heritage, yet the places I was to travel to, high school, college, industry did not use slang, and therefore learning fluidity in where I was headed made more sense than preparing to live where I was.

Pragmatism is not shame; I do not see Asians hang their head when they speak English. They make no bones about their preference, but communication is more important than ideology when it comes to survival, and success.

No matter how we came to this country, we are here now, in America. Unless you are two hundred years old, you have no country to go back to, no one to visit for Christmas, unless you are lucky.

Two term President Obama could have spent more time *hollering* at us speaking Black English, yet he chose to master the language, edit the journals and in time, sign his name above the words, '*President of the United States of America*'.

I do not know what type of clearance Obama had, but he had all the nuclear codes, NSA, CIA, NASA, DIA, FBI, JCS and a host of other alphabet Agencies reporting to him daily. Slavery can eventually be reversed, but in order to be free from a system, you must first understand *The Establishment*.

As discussed previously, keeping Blacks out of the education system aimed to deprive them of the ability to tie into *The Establishment*. One method to achieve this exclusionary task is the use of inexplicably high costs for higher education. [Figs 54-59] show attrition rates between races from college. Fiscal difficulties are the primary cause of college attrition.

Why does *The Establishment* want to keep Blacks away from of its inner teachings? The Black lawyers could understand and change the law, Black doctors could fix what *The Establishment* broke, and Black teachers could remind the children of what they lost, and how to access and benefit from what they have.

No longer is the use of proper English language the mark of the Uncle Tom, mulatto, or the house Nigger, it is the language spoken by Americans. In America, American-English imparts the values and ideology of the country, no disrespect to my learned colleges but if you refuse to become part of the ideology, why would you accept to be accepted into or succeed within *The Establishment*? Yes, *The Establishment* is the moral cousin of the *Institute*. It has flaws but is no way as nefarious as the Plantation.

- Clarence Thomas
- AdamClayton Powel
- Colin Powell
- Condoleezza Rice
- Shirley Jackson
- Lewis Latimer
- Marie Van Brittan Brown
- Otis Boykin
- Lonnie G Johnson
- George Washington Carver
- Charles Drew
- Madame C.J. Walker
- Marian R Croak
- Lisa Gelobter
- Gulion Bluford
- Mae Johnson
- Bernard Harris
- James M Smith
- Macon B Allen
- Barack Obama

If the above listed people are sell outs, or race-traders because they mastered English and achieved success in *The Establishment*, then I ask you; what did you invent or contribute?

13.0

Who are the Useless Eaters?

...Cause by means of limited wars in the advanced countries, and by means of starvation and diseases in Third World countries, the death of 3 billion people by the year 2000, people they call "useless eaters." The Committee of 300 commissioned Cyrus Vance to write a paper on this subject of how best to bring about such genocide[217]."

13.1
Who Are the Useless Eaters?

"We cannot run society for the privileged and allow a significant portion of the population to be marginalized. It impacts the quality of life for all of us if we have to 'throw away' people. A justice system which tolerates injustice is doomed to collapse{Leonard Noisette},"

It is hard to believe that these words were uttered by somebody in an official report to the President of the United States of America. The brashness and candor of this terminology shows not only a complete indifference by the author, but a belief that this would not be egregious and offensive, when read by the President.

If a president does not find these notes to be disgusting and does not immediately terminate the author and the researcher of the same then the question becomes what does the president think of the citizens of the country over which they preside?

What is a useless eater? Would a useless eater be somebody that takes from society and puts nothing back? The Nazis started with mentally disabled persons and the elderly. If however you look at Planned Parenthood's criteria for useless people; it would also be people of African-American heritage who *The Establishment* does not want to maintain, foster, grow, interact with, or have to protect. This sounds absurd, and it is, but it does not make it false.

My Black Side

One of the most common and unintelligent arguments against the existence of *entrenched racism* is show me examples. Examples appear every day that we have sighted; Criminal Justice System inequities, Planned Parenthood, traffic stop rates for different ethnicities, violence against a variety of different ethnicities, which are not White.

What is most irritating is that people who argue against the idea of racism themselves may not be practitioners of racism and therefore they do not believe it exists. This naiveté causes anger to victims of oppression and systemic racism, when they are trying to explain that they are pointing out how they have been treated; not what they believe. Because you do not think you have ever participated in an *deep-rooted racial event*, saying that you do not think people are *victimized* is just ignorant.

You may disagree with my perception, but you cannot disagree with an occurrence or an event. If a house burns down it burnt down. Do not say that the house did not actually burn down, it just caught a blaze and then collapsed: that is just sheer stupidity. So when people say their rights were violated, prior to saying, 'Oh that doesn't happen,' why don't you ask them what actually happened. You do not have to agree with their assessment but only then can you give an intelligent response.

The way to move out of the category of useless eater is to;

- Become a taxpayer
- Exercise your right to vote
- Exercise your right to freedom of speech
- Talk to the news media when you have a problem with the police
- Talk to your senator talk to your congressman if you feel the police are profiling you
- Call 911
- Speak to a supervisor
- Become a part of the process that holds the police accountable do not become a part of the cheap seats that all they want to do is complain and shout absurdities and throw tomatoes good nobody wants that way

My Blue Side

If a police officer stops somebody because this individual matches the description of somebody who committed a crime; that is a legitimate stop, even if you are not the culprit. Whether you committed a crime or not, does not undo the legitimacy of the stop. If you choose to dispute the validity of a stop with a police officer, all you are doing is making the situation worse. Ask to speak to a supervisor, and request that he come to the scene. If none is available, cooperate, then file a formal complaint.

That officer has a belief and the authority to compel you to comply with what he is demanding; at the time. This DOES NOT MAKE HIM RIGHT, no **arrests in the history of mankind made the officer right.** What the arrest does is take a person into custody and allow them to be brought before a judge thereby a decision can be made. This system is not perfect, but it is the one we agreed to live within. Remember: cops do not determine incarceration; that decision comes from the court system.

If the police officer is wrong, there are remedies for that. If *The Establishment* fails to utilize the proper remedies due to a judicial issue, we have a remedy for that. If the state fails to handle it, we have a federal remedy. Every four years there is a natural remedy. If you get gunned down by a police officer trying to make a point - currently there is no remedy to fix your death.

What this system cannot afford however is for everybody in America to decide they do not want to obey the police; this does not lead to anything good. It is unsafe for the police, and it is unsafe for citizens, the only people who benefit from anarchy the criminals.

13.2 Role Models

Christie Ellis cites a 2004 Educational study where only one in nine Black students reported having a Black AP instructor. Ellis further adds a dagger by reminding us of the merits of and sinister *entrenched* exploitation of the American educational system, "a lower proportion of Black college students choosing to major in education, lower college completion rates, and lower rates of hiring and retention when compared to the statistics for White teachers[218]."

Black males MUST expand their list of role models beyond athletes, and musicians;

- Elias Bowie - the first Black NASCAR driver in history
- Thurgood Marshall - first Black to serve on the Supreme Court justice?
- Condoleezza Rice - the first female African-American Secretary of State and the first woman to serve as National Security Advisor
- Guion Stewart Bluford Jr. and Mae Jemison - first Blacks to go into space
- James McCune Smith - first Black physician
- Madam C.J. Walker - the first Black and the self-made first female millionaire in America (Guinness Book of World Records)
- Barack Obama - first Black President to the United States
- Camilla Harris - first Black and first female vice President to the United States
- Bass Reeves - the first Black deputy U.S. Marshal west of the Mississippi River
- Joan and George Johnson - the first Black-owned business on the American Stock Exchange
- Colin Powell the first Black Secretary of State and Black Chairman of the Joint Chiefs of Staff
- Joycelyn Elders - first Black and second female Surgeon General
- Adam Clayton Powell Jr - first African-American to be elected to Congress from New York

There is nothing wrong with athletes and musicians as role models but we can't all sing and play. On the above list all but two of the people listed undertook education as their pathway to both freedom and accomplishment. All of those listed learned, recited, excelled and mastered the English educational system of the Americas. Though educated they escaped indoctrination, because others showed the way. Joan and George Johnson's would never have conceived of aspiring to business heights of some former 2nd class citizen did not show the free-d method to acquire wealth with the racist, oppressive system. At some point, Blacks that acknowledge then master the rules of *The Establishment*, rise above the claws of the entrenched racial underworld set aside in America for Blacks.

Those who call successful Blacks sell outs fail to understand the importance of Black success. The first Black rebel in American history is fairly unknown. Crispus Attucks - the first **American** killed in the American Revolution did not die as an African-American; he died as an American.

I believe from the grave he too would echo the question, Are we free yet?

From the Author

"What binds us is far more powerful than
what separates us[JFK]."

Working on this book opened my eyes to many things that previously I did not give much thought to. It is not that injustice is unimportant to me, I just never believed some of the stories, and I held a blue bias against most opinions.

I still contend that the media uses the false narrative to maintain uproar, not to help with any problem. I also contend that radical solutions, and biased based solutions, lies, and hatred from either Black or Blue sides benefit no one.

The Establishment requires fodder, and it does not care where it comes from. Tomorrow, no matter the power of the BLM movement, *The Establishment's* weapon against civility is the police.

Having been tasked to raid a redneck biker bar in my zone, my squad entered the bar and proceeded to make an arrest. I was the only Black member of the squad and ended up not making arrests but fought with several individuals in a corner. The fight was not started by racial slurs or by their numerous slurs of Nigger spewed at me. One of the bikers had drugs in front. After handcuffing, it turned out that one of the arrestees served in the United States Marine Corps. When he realized that I too served in the Corps, his personality, demeanor, and the way he spoke to me changed drastically. When he was issued a citation, he took The citation from my hand and said you gave me something to remember you by here's something to remember me by; the next time you come to the bar just remember who I am.

The next time I was there making arrests, the same scenario occurred. This time when I walked in and started fighting, a voice said stop he is with me and I looked up and it was the fellow marine. He said, "I told you I remembered," and actually he got the guy to walk over to the table and we handled the corner that I was in, with civility; and then he laughed and said *Semper Fi* and walked away.

I stand proudly behind the body of law enforcement work I achieved. For people who say I am Black I should not have been a cop, my question is why? My retort is; and why weren't you a cop?

For those of you who say I should not have joined the military, I should not have become a Marine: my questions; why and why are not you?

My question to White people is: if as a Blackman I served *The Establishment* as a cop and a Marine, have earned the right to be free? Is this the only way that Black Americas can avoid persecution and oppression is to become part of *The Establishment*?

To Black people I say policing is one of the best jobs I can conceive of and being a soldier is honorable. Moreover, if you are not a part of *The Establishment* why would you ever expect to receive any benefits from *The Establishment*?

As I stated when I started this book, there is no easy solution. I will not be ashamed or embarrassed to say I personally arrested thousands of Black people, and have personally arrested hundreds of White people. The reason for the disparity is the area in which I worked. I primarily focused on drug sellers during the time. However, I identified a trend that the drug users in my area were mostly White. The violence in my area however was perpetrated by Blacks against Blacks. I do not know if Blacks are afraid to go outside of the community for fear of retaliation by White people, but for whatever reason Black on Black crime continues to escalate annually. For every Black face I put in jail, every Black person I pointed a gun at, or took a gun from, every Black prisoner I dragged out of a neighborhood kicking and screaming; I'm proud. For every Black blight removed there were at least 50 other people that looked like me and whose quality of life improved the minute I removed the blights from their surroundings. Black people were able to sit outside without constantly worrying about stray bullets, held hostage in their home, forced to hide guns and drugs in their homes, or have their kids run down by stolen speeding cars.

No matter what happens tomorrow, or the next day, in order for it to be a positive change, you have to positively be a part of that change. While protesting shows that you still have emotion and that you care; destroying property and killing each other confuses everybody. Nobody knows what you care about. If you want to make a change in law enforcement, become a cop. You want to make a change in the legal system and become a lawyer. Otherwise, remember somebody is going to have to pick/be the cotton; we get to choose which part we play.

My point is that no peoples are evil, individuals are. We can demand Whites atone for their behavior and the debauchery; and they can demand Blacks atone for the present proliferation of violent crime. They had slavery, we have armed robbery. They had murder, we have murder. Or we can look at each other, admit our faults and decide to work together for a better tomorrow. If we do not, the victimization will increase. The cops are not the enemy, they are a tool. *The Establishment* will continue to use them to control, divide, and conquer us all. Nevertheless, no matter who is in power and whatever tool they use, be weary of seeking power for power sake. Anybody can abuse power.

The only thing *The Establishment* fears, The New Abolitionists, they are needed as friends in the cause of Black equality. As with all the causes in history, a moral portion of *The Establishment* MUST support enlightenment, or the establishment simply crushes the movement. The established society may not actually be as reprehensible as *The Establishment,* but without an internal shift, *The Establishment* does not feel a necessity to change. In other words, America can never be great until **all her peoples are free**. The granting of freedom in an oppressive system can only be granted by those in charge.

I grew up a free Black man, in a free, progressive Black society. I have never had to suffer the plight of so many that look like me, I was spared this by virtue of my birth - not skill. The only thing that that I have ever done to find myself subject to racism and discrimination was being born Black.

White, Black, or Blue, "The relationship of morality and power is a very subtle one, because ultimately power without morality is no longer power[219]."

About the Author

"Being Black I not what I am trying to be it is what I am. I am running the same race and jumping the same hurdles you are so why are you tripping me up?{Carlton Banks}"

Michael Donaldson is a 20⁺ year veteran of the Metro Nashville Police Department, he retired in good standing as a Field Training Officer. The majority of his years were spent in Specialized Investigative Services.

Donaldson earned his Master's of Science Degree in Public Service Management from Cumberland University, and Bachelor's of Science Degree in Political Science from Tennessee State University. Donaldson is a member of PI Gamma Mu Int'l Honor Society in Social Science, and holds Certifications in; Executive Management, Emotional Intelligence, Ethics, and Risk Management.

As a classically trained Politologist, Donaldson's training encompassed the study and analysis of the relationships between policies, laws, government, business, and citizens. The scientific study includes the quantitative, systematic and methodological measure of; Institutions of Government, laws, political process, political and public thought, political and socio-economics, and social trends.

Donaldson successfully completed hundreds of hours of surveillance and has instructed in Undercover Tactics and Techniques to more than 5000 Law Enforcement and Armed Forces personnel. Delivered programs include career workshops which include Leadership, Train-the-Trainer, motivating personnel, coaching & mentoring, corporate staffing, teamwork, risk assessment, loss prevention, drug intervention, drug interaction, human trafficking, dealing with mentally ill persons, and dealing with high risk/stress situations. These Developmental Workshops have been successfully delivered across the United States; Department of Justice-United States Attorney's Office * Florida Department of Law Enforcement * The Supreme Court of Tennessee *Vanderbilt University Medical School* Vanderbilt Law School* Tennessee District Attorney General's Office * Metro Tennessee Public Schools System* Tennessee Department of Health Related Boards* Tennessee Law Enforcement Training Academy* Tennessee Office of Inspector General* The American Association of Pharmacy Technicians* Tennessee Airport Authority* Tennessee State University.

Awards/Accomplishments
- MNPD Police Officer Award
- MNPD Exemplary Service Award - (x2)
- MNPD Departmental Commendation - (x3)
- MNPD Efficiency Service Award
- MNPD Service Award
- FBI Outstanding service Award
- MNPD Certificate of Educational Achievement awarded for Diversity Training

"Not everything that is faced can be changed, but nothing can be changed until it is faced{James Baldwin}."

Appendices
Glossary
&
Bibliography

Appendix A
Founding Principles of America

1. Checks and Balances: Constitutional powers distributed between the branches of government limiting the power of the other branches.
2. Consent of the Governed/Popular Sovereignty: Governmental power of comes from the people.
3. Due Process: The government interacts with all people according to duly-enacted laws and applied equally to all people.
4. Equality: All individuals have the same status and rights and treatment under the law.
5. Federalism: The people delegate power to the national government, while the states retain other powers; and the people, who authorize both the states and national government, retain all freedoms not delegated to the governing bodies.
6. Freedom of contract: Freedom of individuals and corporations to make mutual agreements without arbitrary or unreasonable legal restrictions
7. Freedom of religion: The right to choose religion or form of worship, without interference; freedom of conscience
8. Freedom of speech, press, and assembly: The right to express opinions freely, orally or in writing, and the right to gather with others in groups of one's choice without arbitrary or unreasonable restrictions.
9. Liberty: Except where authorized by citizens through the Constitution, government does not have the authority to limit freedom.
10. Limited Government: Citizens are best able to pursue happiness when government is confined to those powers, which protect their life, liberty, and property.
11. Majority Rule/Minority Rights: Laws may be made with the consent of the majority, subject to the limitation that

those laws do not infringe on the inalienable rights of the minority.

12. Natural/Inalienable Rights: Rights, which belong to us by nature and can only be justly abridged through due process.

13. Private Property: The natural rights of all individuals to create, obtain, and control their possessions, beliefs, faculties, and opinions, as well as the fruits of their labor.

14. Rule of Law: Government and citizens all abide by the same laws regardless of political power.

15. Separation of Powers: A system of distinct powers, preventing an accumulation of power in one branch.

16. Civic Virtue: A set of actions and habits necessary for the safe, effective, and mutually beneficial participation in a society.

17. Civil Discourse: Reasoned and respectful sharing of ideas between individuals is the primary way people influence change in society/ government.

18. Contribution: To discover one's passions and talents, and use them to create what is beautiful and needed. To work hard to take care of oneself, one's family, and one's community.

19. Courage: The ability to take constructive action in the face of fear or danger. To stand firm as a person of character and do what is right, especially when it is unpopular or puts one at risk.

20. Honor: Demonstrating good character, integrity, and thinking and acting honestly.

21. Integrity: To tell the truth, expose untruths, and keep one's promises.

22. Justice: Upholding of what is fair, just, and right. To stand for equally applied rules that respect the rights and dignity of all, and make sure everyone obeys them.

23. Respect: Honor or admiration of someone or something. To protect one's mind and body as precious aspects of identity. To extend that protection to all other individuals.

24. Resourcefulness: Taking constructive action in difficult situations quickly and imaginatively.

25. Self-Governance: To be self-controlled, avoiding extremes, and to reject unwise influence or control by others.

26. Vigilance: Being alert and attentive, taking action to remedy possible injustices or evils.
27. Demagoguery: To lead others astray because one controls or manipulates their emotions through moving words or a deceptive vision.
28. Hubris: To have excessive pride, vanity, and arrogance that usually leads to a tragic fall.
29. Injustice: To harm others by applying unequal rules and damaging another's inalienable rights and dignity.
30. Political Intolerance: Disrespect for the different political views of others, leading one to violate their inalienable rights.

Appendix B
The Willie Lynch Letters

Greetings,

    Gentlemen, I greet you here on the bank of the James River in the year of our Lord one thousand seven hundred and twelve. First, I shall thank you, the gentlemen of the Colony of Virginia, for bringing me here. I am here to help you solve some of your problems with slaves. Your invitation reached me on my modest plantation in the West Indies, where I have experimented with some of the newest, and still the oldest, methods for control of slaves. Ancient Rome would envy us if my program is implemented. As our boat sailed south on the James River, named for our illustrious King, whose version of the Bible we cherish, I saw enough to know that your problem is not unique. While Rome used cords of wood as crosses for standing human bodies along its highways in great numbers, you are here using the tree and the rope on occasions. I caught the whiff of a dead slave hanging from a tree, a couple miles back. You are not only losing valuable stock by hangings, you are having uprisings, slaves are running away, your crops are sometimes left in the fields too long for maximum profit, you suffer occasional fires, your animals are killed.

    Gentlemen, you know what your problems are; I do not need to elaborate. I am not here to enumerate your problems; I am here to introduce you to a method of solving them. In my bag here, **I HAVE A FULL PROOF METHOD FOR CONTROLLING YOUR BLACK SLAVES**. I guarantee every one of you that, if installed correctly, **IT WILL CONTROL THE SLAVES FOR AT LEAST 300 HUNDREDS YEARS**. My method is simple. Any member of your family or your overseer can use it. **I HAVE OUTLINED A NUMBER OF DIFFERENCES AMONG THE SLAVES; AND I TAKE THESE DIFFERENCES AND MAKE THEM**

BIGGER. I USE FEAR, DISTRUST, AND ENVY FOR CONTROL PURPOSES. These methods have worked on my modest plantation in the West Indies and it will work throughout the South. Take this simple little list of differences and think about them. On top of my list is "AGE," but it is there only because it starts with an "a." The second is "COLOR" or shade. There is INTELLIGENCE, SIZE, SEX, SIZES OF PLANTATIONS, STATUS on plantations, ATTITUDE of owners, whether the slaves live in the valley, on a hill, East, West, North, South, have fine hair, course hair, or is tall or short. Now that you have a list of differences, I shall give you an outline of action, but before that, I shall assure you that DISTRUST IS STRONGER THAN TRUST AND ENVY STRONGER THAN ADULATION, RESPECT, OR ADMIRATION. The Black slaves after receiving this indoctrination shall carry on and will become self-refueling and self-generating for HUNDREDS of years, maybe THOUSANDS. Don't forget, you must pitch the OLD Black male vs. the YOUNG Black male, and the YOUNG Black male against the OLD Black male. You must use the DARK skin slaves vs. the LIGHT skin slaves, and the LIGHT skin slaves vs. the DARK skin slaves. You must use the FEMALE vs. the MALE, and the MALE vs. the FEMALE. You must also have White servants and overseers [who] distrust all Blacks. But it is NECESSARY THAT YOUR SLAVES TRUST AND DEPEND ON U.S.. THEY MUST LOVE, RESPECT AND TRUST ONLY U.S.. Gentlemen, these kits are your keys to control. Use them. Have your wives and children use them, never miss an opportunity. IF USED INTENSELY FOR ONE YEAR, THE SLAVES THEMSELVES WILL REMAIN PERPETUALLY DISTRUSTFUL. Thank you gentlemen."

B.1 Let's Make A Slave

It was the interest and business of slaveholders to study human nature, and the slave nature in particular, with a view to practical results. I and many of them attained astonishing proficiency in this direction. They had to deal not with earth, wood and stone, but with men and, by every regard they had for their own safety and prosperity, they needed to know the material on which they were to work, conscious of the injustice and wrong they were every hour perpetuating and knowing what they themselves would do. Were they the victims of such wrongs? They were constantly looking for the first signs of the dreaded retribution. They watched therefore with skilled and practiced eyes, and learned to read with great accuracy the state of mind and heart of the slave, through his sable face. Unusual sobriety, apparent abstractions, sullenness, and indifference indeed, any mood out of the common was afforded ground for suspicion and inquiry. Frederick Douglas LET'S MAKE a SLAVE is a study of the scientific process of man-breaking and slave-making. It describes the rationale and results of the Anglo Saxons' ideas and methods of insuring the master/slave relationship. **LET'S MAKE A SLAVE** "The Original and Development of a Social Being Called **'The Negro.'**" Let us make a slave. What do we need? First of all, we need a Black nigger man, a pregnant nigger woman and her baby nigger boy. Second, we will use the same basic principle that we use in breaking a horse, combined with some more sustaining factors. What we do with horses is that we break them from one form of life to another; that is, we reduce them from their natural state in nature. Whereas nature provides them with the natural capacity to take care of their offspring, we break that natural string of independence from them and thereby create a dependency status, so that we may be able to get from them useful production for our business and pleasure.

B.2 Cardinal Principles For Making A Negro

For fear that our future generations may not understand the principles of breaking both of the beasts together, the nigger and the horse. We understand that short range planning economics results in periodic economic chaos; so that to avoid turmoil in the economy, it requires us to have breadth and depth in long range comprehensive planning, articulating both skill sharp perceptions. We lay down the following principles for long range comprehensive economic planning. Both horse and niggers [are] no good to the economy in the wild or natural state. Both must be **BROKEN** and **TIED** together for orderly production. For an orderly future, special and particular attention must be paid to the **FEMALE** and the **YOUNGEST** offspring. Both must be **CROSSBRED** to produce a variety and division of labor. Both must be taught to respond to a peculiar new **LANGUAGE**. Psychological and physical instruction of **CONTAINMENT** must be created for both. We hold the six cardinal principles as truth to be self-evident, based upon following the discourse concerning the economics of breaking and tying the horse and the nigger together, all inclusive of the six principles laid down above. NOTE: Neither principle alone will suffice for good economics. All principles must be employed for orderly good of the nation. Accordingly, both a wild horse and a wild or natur[al] nigger is dangerous even if captured, for they will have the tendency to seek their customary freedom and, in doing so, might kill you in your sleep. You cannot rest. They sleep while you are awake, and are awake while you are asleep. They are **DANGEROUS** near the family house and it requires too much labor to watch them away from the house. Above all, you cannot get them to work in this natural state. Hence, both the horse and the nigger must be broken; that is breaking them from one form of mental life to another. **KEEP THE BODY, TAKE THE MIND!**In other words, break the will to resist. Now the breaking process is the same for both the horse and the nigger, only slightly varying in degrees. But, as we said before, there is an art in long range economic planning. **YOU MUST KEEP YOUR EYE AND THOUGHTS ON THE FEMALE and the OFFSPRING** of the horse and the nigger. A brief discourse in offspring development will shed light on the key to sound economic principles. Pay little attention to the generation of original breaking, but **CONCENTRATE ON FUTURE GENERATION**. Therefore, if you break the **FEMALE** mother, she will

BREAK the offspring in its early years of development; and when the offspring is old enough to work, she will deliver it up to you, for her normal female protective tendencies will have been lost in the original breaking process. For example, take the case of the wild stud horse, a female horse, and an already infant horse and compare the breaking process with two captured nigger males in their natural state, a pregnant nigger woman with her infant offspring. Take the stud horse, break him for limited containment. Completely break the female horse until she becomes very gentle, whereas you or anybody can ride her in her comfort. Breed the mare and the stud until you have the desired offspring. Then, you can turn the stud to freedom until you need him again. Train the female horse whereby she will eat out of your hand, and she will in turn train the infant horse to eat out of your hand, also. When it comes to breaking the uncivilized nigger, use the same process, but vary the degree and step up the pressure, so as to do a complete reversal of the mind. Take the meanest and most restless nigger, strip him of his clothes in front of the remaining male niggers, the female, and the nigger infant, tar and feather him, tie each leg to a different horse faced in opposite directions, set him afire and beat both horses to pull him apart in front of the remaining niggers. The next step is to take a bullwhip and beat the remaining nigger males to the point of death, in front of the female and the infant. Don't kill him, but **PUT THE FEAR OF GOD IN HIM**, for he can be useful for future breeding.

B.3 The Breaking Process Of The African Woman

Take the female and run a series of tests on her to see if she will submit to your desires willingly. Test her in every way, because she is the most important factor for good economics. If she shows any sign of resistance in submitting completely to your will, do not hesitate to use the bullwhip on her to extract that last bit of [Black] out of her. Take care not to kill her, for in doing so, you spoil good economics. When in complete submission, she will train her offsprings in the early years to submit to labor when they become of age. Understanding is the best thing.

Therefore, we shall go deeper into this area of the subject matter concerning what we have produced here in this breaking process of the female nigger. We have reversed the relationship; in her natural uncivilized state, she would have a strong dependency on the uncivilized nigger male, and she would have a limited protective tendency toward her independent male offspring and would raise male offspring to be dependent like her. Nature had provided for this type of balance. We reversed nature by burning and pulling a civilized nigger apart and bullwhipping the other to the point of death, all in her presence. By her being left alone, unprotected, with the **MALE IMAGE DESTROYED**, the ordeal caused her to move from her psychologically dependent state to a frozen, independent state. In this frozen, psychological state of independence, she will raise her **MALE** and female offspring in reversed roles. For **FEAR** of the young male's life, she will psychologically train him to be **MENTALLY WEAK** and **DEPENDENT**, but **PHYSICALLY STRONG**. Because she has become psychologically independent, she will train her **FEMALE** offspring to be psychologically independent. What have you got? You've got the nigger **WOMAN OUT FRONT AND THE** nigger **MAN BEHIND AND SCARED**. This is a perfect situation of sound sleep and economics. Before the breaking process, we had to be alertly on guard at all times. Now, we can sleep soundly, for out of frozen fear his woman stands guard for us. He cannot get past her early slave molding process. He is a good tool, now ready to be tied to the horse at a tender age. By the time a nigger boy reaches the age of sixteen, he is soundly broken in and ready for a long life of sound and efficient work and the reproduction of a unit of good labor force. Continually through the breaking of uncivilized savage niggers, by throwing the nigger female savage into a frozen psychological state of independence, by killing the protective male image, and by creating a submissive dependent mind of the nigger male slave, we have created an orbiting cycle that turns on its own axis forever, unless a phenomenon occurs and re-shifts the position of the male and female slaves. We show what we mean by example. Take the case of the two economic slave units and examine them close.

B.4 The Negro Marriage

We breed two nigger males with two nigger females. Then, we take the nigger male away from them and keep them moving and working. Say one nigger female bears a nigger female and the other bears a nigger male; both nigger females-being without influence of the nigger male image, frozen with a independent psychology-will raise their offspring into reverse positions. The one with the female offspring will teach her to be like herself, independent and negotiable (we negotiate with her, through her, by her, negotiate her at will). The one with the nigger male offspring, she being frozen subconscious fear for his life, will raise him to be mentally dependent and weak, but physically strong; in other words, body over mind. Now, in a few years when these two offspring become fertile for early reproduction, we will mate and breed them and continue the cycle. That is good, sound and long range comprehensive planning.

B.5 Warning: Possible Interloping Negatives

Earlier, we talked about the non-economic good of the horse and the nigger in their wild or natural state; we talked out the principle of breaking and tying them together for orderly production. Furthermore, we talked about paying particular attention to the female savage and her offspring for orderly future planning, and then more recently we stated that by reversing the positions of the male and female savages, we created an orbiting cycle that turns on its own axis forever unless a phenomenon occurred and reshifts positions of the male and female savages. Our experts warned us about the possibility of this phenomenon occurring, for they say that the mind has a strong drive to correct and re-correct itself over a period of time if it can touch some substantial original historical base; and they advised us that the best way to deal with the phenomenon is to shave off the brute's mental history and create a multiplicity of phenomena of illusions, so that each illusion will twirl in its own orbit, something similar to floating balls in a vacuum. This creation of multiplicity of phenomena of illusions entails the principle of crossbreeding the nigger and the horse as we stated above, the purpose of which is to create a diversified division of labor; thereby creating different levels of labor and different values of illusion at each connecting level of labor. The results of which is the severance of the points of original beginnings for each sphere illusion. Since we feel that the subject matter may get more complicated as we proceed in laying down our economic plan concerning the purpose, reason and effect of crossbreeding horses and niggers, we shall lay down the following definition terms for future generations. Orbiting cycle means a thing turning in a given path. Axis means upon which or around which a body turns. Phenomenon means something beyond ordinary conception and inspires awe and wonder. Multiplicity means a great number. It means a globe. Crossbreeding a horse means taking a horse and breeding it with an ass and you get a dumb, backward, ass long-headed mule that is neither reproductive nor productive by itself. Crossbreeding niggers mean taking so many drops of good White blood and putting them into as many nigger women as possible, varying the drops by the various tones that you want, and then letting them breed with each other until another circle of color appears as you desire. What this means is this: Put the niggers and the horse in a breeding pot, mix some asses and some good White blood and what do you get? You got a multiplicity of colors of ass backward, unusual niggers, running, tied to backward ass long-headed mules, the one productive of itself, the other sterile. (The one constant, the other dying, we keep the nigger constant for we may replace the mules for another tool) both mule and nigger tied to each other, neither knowing where the other came from and neither productive for itself, nor without each other.

B.6 Controlled Language

Crossbreeding completed, for further severance from their original beginning, **WE MUST COMPLETELY ANNIHILATE THE MOTHER TONGUE** of both the new nigger and the new mule, and institutes a new language that involves the new life's work of both. language is a peculiar entityn. It leads to the heart of a people. The more a foreigner knows about the language of another country the more he is able to move through all levels of that society. Therefore, if the foreigner is an enemy of the country, to the extent that he knows the body of the language, to that extent is the country vulnerable to attack or invasion of a foreign culture. For example, if you take a slave, if you teach him all about your language, he will know all your secrets, and he is then no more a slave, for you can't fool him any longer, and **BEING A FOOL IS ONE OF THE BASIC INGREDIENTS OF ANY INCIDENTS TO THE MAINTENANCE OF THE SLAVERY SYSTEM**. For example, if you told a slave that he must perform in getting out "our crops" and he knows the language well, he would know that "our crops" didn't mean "our crops" and the slavery system would break down, for he would relate on the basis of what "our crops" really meant. So you have to be careful in setting up the new language; for the slaves would soon be in your house, talking to you as "man to man" and that is death to our economic system. In addition, the definitions of words or terms are only a minute part of the process. Values are created and transported by communication through the body of the language. A total society has many interconnected value systems. All the values in the society have bridges of language to connect them for orderly working in the society. But for these language bridges, these many value systems would sharply clash and cause internal strife or civil war, the degree of the conflict being determined by the magnitude of the issues or relative opposing strength in whatever form.

For example, if you put a slave in a hog pen and train him to live there and incorporate in him to value it as a way of life completely, the biggest problem you would have out of him is that he would worry you about provisions to keep the hog pen clean, or the same hog pen and make a slip and incorporate something in his language whereby he comes to value a house more than he does his hog pen, you got a problem. He will soon be in your house.

Appendix C
#40 Facts About Two Parent Families

In the 1960s, for example, nearly 95 percent of babies were born to couples who were married. Today, 40 percent are born to women who are either single or living with a non-married partner.

C.1 The American Family Today

The "typical" American family has changed radically over the last 50 years. Americans today are marrying later than ever before, divorcing sooner or avoiding the institution altogether whereas married couples dominated the family structure in years past, only 30 percent of millennials feel that a successful marriage is an important part of life.

As a result, of this institutional erosion, more and more children are being born out of wedlock. In the 1960s, for example, nearly 95 percent of babies were born to couples who were married. Today, 40 percent are born to women who are either single or living with a non-married partner.

Often lost in the discussion of marital decline is a simple fact. Marriage is good for children. In fact, countless studies have shown that children born to married parents enjoy a number of socioeconomic benefits over those born to single parents.

Here are some important facts you should know.

- Today, only about 64 percent of children live in homes with two parents who are married, representing an all-time low (Pew Research Center). Trend data shows a stark and steady decline since 1960, when nearly 88 percent of children lived with married parents.

- Fifteen percent of children today are living with parents who are remarried, and seven percent are living with cohabiting parents, while 26 percent are living with one parent only.

C.2 The Effects Of Family Structure On Children

1. A solid, intact family structure can have a significantly positive impact on a child's present and future wellbeing and offers countless benefits for both adults and children.

2. Children growing up in homes with two parents who have been married continuously are less likely to experience a wide range of problems (academic, social, emotional, cognitive), not only in childhood but later on in adulthood as well (Amato; Howard & Reeves,).

3. In two parent families, for example, children typically have access to more of the economic and community resources because parents are able to pool their time, money, and energy; children tend to be more of the focus of the home.

4. Family intactness has also been shown to have a consistently positive influence on earnings for prime-age males and is one of the most important factors (or shared the place of greatest importance) for females and children in determining an area's dependence on welfare programs that targets poverty.

5. Research also shows that family intactness has a beneficial influence on reducing out of wedlock births, increasing high school and college graduation rates, and even has long-term benefits such as higher employment rates.

6. Children living with married parents are more often involved in community activities such as soccer or other sports; take part in academic pursuits in local schools and other academic institutions that can lead to college, and eventually, a career.

7. Family intactness increases high school and college graduation rates, as well as high employment rates

8. Overall, intact families tend to be more stable; parents tend to be more involved in their children's lives and are more highly invested in their children's success.

9. Fathers of intact families spend, on average, more time with their children. They also enjoy greater family cohesion than peers with adopted children or stepchildren (Lansford, et *al.*). In summary, children living with both biological parents in a low-conflict marriage tend to do better on a host of outcomes than those living in step-parent families.

10. Children living with both biological parents are 20 to 35 percent more physically healthy than children from broken homes (Dawson).

11. Research shows that family structure is related to preschool children's cognitive development skills. For example, a study by Kinard and Reinherz found that children from two parent homes had higher scores on verbal reasoning than those from single parent homes.

12. A study by Ginther and Pollack found that children growing up in intact families (traditional nuclear families) were more likely to graduate from high school and complete college compared to those who were raised in blended or single-parent homes.

13. Manning and Lamb found that adolescents in intact families had higher levels of academic achievement and were less likely to exhibit problem behaviors in school compared to peers living in homes where single mothers lived alone or with a cohabiting partner.

14. Following divorce, children are 50 percent more likely to develop health problems than two parent families.

15. In homes with stepfathers, peers were more likely to have been suspended or expelled from school, more likely to have engaged in delinquent behavior, to have problems getting along with teachers, doing homework, paying attention in school, and have lower grade point averages than those living in intact homes.

16. Children of divorce are at a greater risk of experiencing injury, headaches, speech defects, and other health concerns than children whose parents have remained married (Dawson).

17. Clearly, children do best in a stable family environment where well-adjusted parents have established consistent routines for the home. On the other hand, an environment of turmoil where continual conflict, multiple school or parental employment changes are linked to lower levels of child well-being (Teachman)

18. Being raised in a married family reduced a child's probability of living in poverty by about 82 percent.

19. The decline in two parent families has accounted for the three-fold increase in single parent homes, most often headed by single moms.

20. According to Pew Research, over half (57 percent) of those living with married parents were in households with incomes at least 200% above the poverty line, compared with just 21 percent of those living in single-parent households.

21. According to the U.S. Census, the poverty rate for single parents with children in the United States in 2009 was 37.1 percent. The rate for married couples with children was 6.8 percent. Rector called marriage one of the greatest weapons against child poverty.

C.3 Single Mother Statistics

1. According to the CDC, 4 out every 10 children are born to unwed mothers. Nearly two-thirds are born to mothers under the age of 30.

2. Today 1 in 4 children under the age of 18 - a total of about 17.4 million - are being raised without a father and nearly half (45 percent) live below the poverty line (U.S. Census Bureau).

3. Unmarried mothers generally have lower incomes, lower education levels, and are more likely to be dependent on welfare assistance compared with married mothers (Child Trends Data Bank).

4. Around 49 percent of single mothers have never married, 51 percent are either divorced, separated or widowed. Half have one child, 30 percent have two.

5. Single mothers are more likely to be poor than married couples.

6. Single mothers earn income that place them well below married mothers in the income ladder. The gap between the two groups is significant.

7. The median income for families led by a single mother in 2013 was about $26,000, one-third ($\frac{1}{3}$) the median for married couple families ($84,000). Nearly half of single mother households had an annual income of less than $25,000.

8. Single mothers often spend over half of their income on housing expenses and a third on child care.

9. Without financial aid, single mother students - a total of about 2 million - have little or no means to contribute financially to their educational expenses.

C.4 Single Father Statistics

1. While there were less than 300,000 single father households in 1960, there were more than 2.6 million in 2011. In comparison, single mother households increased more than four times that many during that same time period, up from 1.9 million in 1960 to 8.6 million in 2011.

2. Single father households differ from single mother households on several levels. For the most part, those headed by single fathers tend to be better off financially compared to those of single mothers. However, compared to men who remarry, single father households tend to be younger, less educated, and have lower incomes.

3. Pew's analysis of Decennial Census and American Community Survey data found that a record eight percent of households with minor children in the U.S. are headed by a single father, up from just over one percent in 1960.

4. According to Pew Research Center, there has been a nine-fold increase in single father households since 1960.

5. Single fathers are more likely than single mothers to be living with a cohabiting partner (41 percent versus 16 percent).

6. Single fathers tend to have higher incomes and are far less likely to be living at or below the poverty line than single mothers. Still, they fare much worse than married men.

7. Statistics show that men who become fathers outside of marriage are more likely to be poor. These men were 70 to 90 percent more likely to be poor compared to men who never had children before marriage.

8. For those living with father only, about 21 percent live in poverty. In contrast, among children living with both parents, only 13 percent are counted as poor.

9. Despite the overwhelming benefits of two parent homes, the 'stay together for the kids' axiom isn't always the right one. In fact, children are not always better off if their parents are married and living in the same home - especially if their parents are in a high conflict relationship. High conflict relationships can have disastrous effects on children, especially in children's attitudes and feelings about themselves (something that studies have shown not to be affected by living arrangement). Staying in an irretrievably broken marriage is not healthy for anyone, the parents, or the children. However, if a marriage is fixable, weighing the benefits for children may make married parents think long and hard about starting over. At the same time, unmarried parents are not all that different from married ones in terms of behavior. Marriage does not make anyone a better parent, it simply allows access to more resources and opportunities for children overall.

Glossary Of Unique Terms

- *The Entrenched Racism Abandonment System* - The Social abortion method resulting from the devastation of the bond between the Black husband and wife, and their view of family

- *American'tism* - Education, policies, laws, or media indoctrination designed to remind Blacks they are not welcome, nor able to succeed within the societal parameters

- *The Anti-Nigger* - The Black that refuses to conform to entrenched behavior and restraint

- *Badge-Side Manner* - Demeanor and deportment of the officer devoid of intention

- *Black Cloud* - An ominous theoretical area of darkness looming over whites; the fear in their minds of reprisals

- *Black Cloud* - The ideation that there is a potential for integrated wills between White people and Black people whereby Whites seek to free and empower Blacks

- *Black Cotton Economics* - The transplanted product of humans, especially minorities as economic fodder

- *Blk Cotton Gin* - Black Cotton is just a Fiat System predicated on allowing indentured servant-hood to be the Neo-Colonial Slavery

- Blue-Belief - System archaic and potentially Machiavellian Law Enforcement values

- *The Blue Fog* - Gang-like mentality wherein cops see no evil, hear no evil, and report no evil done by other cops

- *Blue Prejudice* - Arrogance and contempt for those that are not Law Enforcement

- Blue Witch Hunt© - Arrogance and contempt for those that are not Law Enforcement

- *BWP* (Black White People) - Black people who were not afraid to stand eye-to-eye with White people

- *Chapter 2 Of Birth Of Nation;* - Protocols and actions designed to *Maintaining Our Nation* maintain the Status Quo

- *Conceptual Niggerism* - Idealizing stereotypes and applying them indiscriminately

- *Crop-Numbers* - Statistical data used to quantity and validate social programs, and cotton economical values

- *Crop Niggers* - Black people within the New Cotton system, utilized and groomed to perpetuate they economic system

- *Cultivated Media Ideation* -Media indoctrination, and training designed to maintain the status quo

- *Excessive Force Subjectivity* - A Use of Force deemed reasonable at the time subjectively ruled excessive or out of policy

- *Green Cotton Economics* - A racially based capital system, applying the same mentality regarding the product Cotton to African American people

- *Lynch's Pendulum* - Systemic civic transitions which go from one extreme to the other

- *New Cotton* - The criminal justice system as a neo-economic structure

- *New Cotton Economics* - The transplanting of product for humans, not human trafficking as spoken of in terms of sex, but the exploitation of human capital nonetheless

- Nigger-ganger- A demonized ideology ascribed to Black males

- *Non-Cotton System*- Financial system not based on *of Wealth* racism, and neo-colonial slavery

- '*The Entrenched Racism Castle*'- The seasoning of Black men, emasculating them and turn them into mentally sterile, unproductive people

- *Entrenched racism Styled Nurturing* (ERSN)   - discrimination based educational and rearing used to engender pro-system behavior

- *Laws of the Cotton Field* - Rules commensurate with the repressive system you find yourself living within, i.e region, state, SES etc

- *Neo-Colonial Slavery* - Slavery that uses economics, civics, and politics to achieve the same effect as whips and chains

- *New Cotton Economics* - The criminal justice system as a neo-economic structure

- *Willie Lynch Effect* - Education and discrimination against the lack family bringing about a mental schism and fatalism

- *White Slight* - Rage, disappointment and fear amongst repressive Whites about the Obama era

- *Quad^e* (Emotions)-America - Black anger, resentment, White Paradigm anger, fear, resentment, economic imbalance and Covid 19

- *Quad^n* (Numbers) - Lack anger, resentment, White anger, fear, resentment, economic imbalance and Co-Vid 19, White supremacists, sovereign citizens, former supporters of BLM

- *Post-Traumatic Slave* - Also called the Great White Father *Syndrome* Over Me Syndrome, where Blacks systematically view themselves through oppressive denigrative eyes, looking to *The Establishment* for sustenance

- *Willie Lynch Behavior* - Stereotypical, often referred to as Ghetto behavior

- *Un-Kunta* - A freed, emancipated mind

- *2C2 Reports* - Malicious false reports by Whites designed to be injurious to Black people

- *Social-Abortion* - The use of societal authority to target and systematically control or eradicate a particular group of people. This policy requires assent from the society

- *Social-Uniform* - Disguise, moniker, marking, identification

- *United Syncretism in the Americas* - Syncretism is the merging of several originally discrete belief systems or traditions

Bibliography & Works Cited

[1] Rudyard Kipling, https://www.azquotes.com/author/8083-Rudyard_Kipling.

[2] Root Cause Analysis is a process for understanding and solving problems, determining negative events, the complex systems around those problems, and key points of failure. The Analysis also aids to, determine solutions to address those key points, or root causes.

[2] https://www.foxnews.com/transcript/bill-oreilly-president-obama-and-the-race-problem, July 22, 2013.

[4] http://www.differencebetween.net/language/difference-between-discrimination-and-racism/

[5] https://billofrightsinstitute.org/founding-documents/founding-principles/, 07/23/2020.

[6] https://www.battlefields.org/learn/primary-sources/declaration-causes-seceding-states.

[7] https://www.thevintagenews.com/2017/03/24/richard-henry-pratt-is-associated-with-the-first-recorded-use-of-the-word-racism/.

[8] Carter Godwin Woodson, The Mis-Education of the Negro.

[9] https://www.pbs.org/empires/romans/empire/slaves_freemen.html#:~:text=Slaves%20were%20often%20whipped%2C%20branded,at%20least%20be%20treated%20fairly.

[10] https://www.goodreads.com/work/quotes/235359-the-mis-education-of-the-negro.https://www.pewresearch.org/fact-tank/2019/12/12/u-s-children-more-likely-than-children-in-other-countries-to-live-with-just-one-parent/.

[1] Study finds increasing disparities in opioid overdose deaths for Black people. https://www.news-medical.net/news/20210909/Study finds increasing disparities in opioid overdose deaths for Black people (news-medical.net)

[12] Addiction Among Different Races | Alcohol & Drug Use In America. https://sunrisehouse.com/addiction-demographics/different-races/

[13] https://datacenter.kidscount.org/updates/show/264-us-foster-care-population-by-race-and-ethnicity.

[14] Jan 23, 2013 · Black Marriage in America Marriage has been a declining institution among all Americans and this decline is even more evident in the Black community. In 2016, only 29% of African Americans were married compared to 48% of all Americans. Half or 50% of African Americans have never been married compared to 33% of all Americans. BLACK MARRIAGE | BlackDemographics.com. https://blackdemographics.com/households/marriage-in--Black-america/

[15] https://theundefeated.com/features/light-skinned-vs-dark-skinned/.

[16] https://www.ncbi.nlm.nih.gov/pmc/articles/PMC4843483/.

[17] https://www.revolt.tn.news/2020/10/3/21500235/joseph-pettaway-demands-family-police-dog-mauling-footage.

[18] Faces of Power: 80% Are White, Even as U.S. Becomes More Diverse, by Denise Lu, Jon Huang, Ashwin Seshagiri, Haeyoun Park and Troy GriggsSept. 9, 2020. https://www.nytimes.com/interactive/2020/09/09/us/powerful-people-race-us.html

[19] Stokely Carmichael, Black Power: The Politics of Liberation.

[20] https://theethicalskeptic.com/2012/11/26/cultivation-of-ignorance/.

[21] Two Influential Theories of Ignorance and Philosophy's Interests in Ignoring Them, https://onlinelibrary.wiley.com/doi/full/10.1111/j.1527-2001.2006.tb01111.x. 2019.

[22] https://www.history.com/topics/Black-history/segregation-united-states.

[23] King's Last march, https://features.apmreports.org/arw/king/c1.html.

[24] https://en.wikipedia.org/wiki/Posse_Comitatus_Act, 2021.

[25] https://nypost.com/2021/01/19/cop-allegedly-caught-lying-about-being-at-us-capitol-riot/.

[26] https://nypost.com/2021/01/11/video-shows-capitol-rioter-hit-officer-with-fire-extinguisher/

[27] https://vittana.org/42-shocking-police-brutality-statistics#:~:text=The%20estimated%20cost%20of%20police%20brutality%20incidents%20in,involve%20the%20discharge%20of%20a%20weapon%20are%20men

[28] httpscopcrisis.comwp-contentuploads201504cost.jpg

[29] Top 10 U.S. Cities With Highest Murders in 2020, INSIDER MONKEY STAFF, Published on September 15, 2020.

[30] https://datausa.io/profile/geo/stockton-ca/, https://www.california-demographics.com/san-bernardino-county-demographics, https://worldpopulationreview.com/us-cities/oakland-ca-population, https://datausa.io/profile/geo/alaska, https://worldpopulationreview.com/us-cities/pueblo-co-population, https://statisticalatlas.com/place/California/Modesto/Race-and-Ethnicity, https://en.wikipedia.org/wiki/Richmond,_Virginia, https://datausa.io/profile/geo/vallejo-ca/,

https://datausa.io/profile/geo/inglewood-ca/,
https://datausa.io/profile/geo/tacoma-wa/.
[31] https://datausa.io/profile/geo/stockton-ca/.
[32]https://www.california-demographics.com/san-bernardino-county-demographics.
[33] https://worldpopulationreview.com/us-cities/oakland-ca-population.
[34] https://datausa.io/profile/geo/alaska.
[35] https://worldpopulationreview.com/us-cities/pueblo-co-population.
[36] https://statisticalatlas.com/place/California/Modesto/Race-and-Ethnicity.
[37] https://en.wikipedia.org/wiki/Richmond,_Virginia.
[38] https://datausa.io/profile/geo/vallejo-ca/.
[39] https://datausa.io/profile/geo/inglewood-ca/.
[40] https://datausa.io/profile/geo/tacoma-wa/.
[41]https://www.battlefields.org/learn/primary-sources/declaration-causes-seceding-states.
[42] Why White people keep calling the cops on Black Americans, Vesla Mae Weaver. https://www.vox.com/firstperson/2018/5/17/17362100/starbucks-racial-profiling-yale-airbnb-911.
[43] By Drew Desilver, Michael Lipka And Dalia Fahmy. https://www.pewresearch.org/fact-tank/2020/06/03/10-things-we-know-about-race-and-policing-in-the-u-s/.
[44] When Crime Is a Family Affair, Fox Butterfield. https://www.theatlantic.com/family/archive/2018/10/crime-runs-family/573394/.
[45] https://www.heritage.org/crime-and-justice/report/the-real-root-causes-violent-crime-the-breakdown-marriage-family and.
[46] Youth violence, https://www.who.int/news-room/fact-sheets/detail/youth-violence
[47] US Census bureau. https://actrochester.org/children-youth/single-parent-families-by-race-ethnicity
[48] https://gillespieshields.com/40-facts-two-parent-families/.
[49] https://www.statista.com/statistics/200476/us-poverty-rate-by-ethnic-group/
[50]https://www.washingtonpost.com/news/wonk/wp/2017/02/16/the-biggest-beneficiaries-of-the-government-safety-net-working-class-whites/.
[51] http://federalsafetynet.com/us-poverty-statistics.html
[52] https://www.usip.org/sites/default/files/SR%20294.pdf.
[53] Stephen R. Covey, The 7 Habits of Highly Effective People: Powerful Lessons in Personal Change.

[54] Here's The Simple Explanation For Why Cops Seem Arrogant, https://www.businessinsider.com/heres-the-simple-explanation-for-why-cops-seem-arrogant-2014-5.

[55] "The largest disparity noted in the U.N. report concerns Hydrocodone: Americans consume more than 99 percent of the world's supply of this opioid."https://www.washingtonpost.com/news/wonk/wp/2017/03/15/americans-use-far-more-opioids-than-anyone-else-in-the-world/.

[56] https://www.axios.com/police-diversity-george-floyd-5a712a37-9e43-4b24-985b-829abd76e56b.html.

[57] https://datausa.io/profile/soc/police-officers#demographics.

[58] https://www.pbs.org/newshour/nation/Black-men-werent-unarmed-people-killed-police-last-week.

[59] Black imprisonment rate in the U.S. has fallen by a third since 2006
By John Gramlich.https://www.pewresearch.org/fact-tank/2020/05/06/share-of-Black-White-hispanic-americans-in-prison-2018-vs-2006/. MAY 6, 2020.

[60] The Economic Costs Of The U.S. Criminal Justice System
Tara O'Neill Hayes. July 16, 2020.
https://www.americanactionforum.org/research/the-economic-costs-of-the-u-s-criminal-justice-system/#ixzz6oOopHFZI.

[61] How Black People Really Feel About The Police, Explained: Research suggests Black people want a systemic overhaul on crime reduction and inequality. Aaron Ross Coleman, June 17, 2020.

[62] https://www.colorlines.com/articles/juvenile-injustice-racial-disparities-incarceration-start-early.

[63] https://www.bet.com/news/national/2019/03/05/outrage-after-12-year-old-boy-faces-felony-charges-for-selling-c.html#!

[64] Not sure why there was no upheaval about this case with the toddler do Black Lives Matter?

[65] The word Sheriff and the duties derived from "Shire Reeve - an office held by a man of lower rank, appointed as manager of a manor and overseer of the peasants."
https://www.bing.com/search?q=shire+reve&src=IE-TopResult&FORM=IETR02&conversationid=.

[66] https://www.goodreads.com/work/quotes/235359-the-mis-education-of-the-negro.

[67] https://www.psychologytoday.com/us/blog/family-secrets/201405/psychological-slavery.

[68] https://theconversation.com/how-the-legacy-of-slavery-affects-the-mental-health-of-Black-americans-today-44642.

[69] https://digest.bps.org.uk/2018/10/12/what-are-we-like-10-psychology-findings-that-reveal-the-worst-of-human-nature/.

[70] 7 Methods of Studying Human Behavior, https://www.psychologydiscussion.net/behaviour/7-methods-of-studying-human-behaviour/540.

[71] https://www.britannica.com/biography/Toussaint-Louverture. The Spook Who Sat by the Door, by Sam Greenlee

[72] https://newpittsburghcourier.com/2013/05/03/students-show-how-willie-lynch-syndrome-still-prevalent/.

[73] List of 19 Assassinated Black Activists and Leaders in History, https://blackexcellence.com/saytheirnames-list-of-19-assassinated-Black-activists-and-leaders-in-history/.

[74] Jose Campos Torres, The perception of Black men towards the police from: The Mind of Gil Scott-Heron. Please listen to reading on YouTube, to get the full effect of the rage.

[75] The Nigger Bible, by Robert H. DeCoy.

[76] "In a deliberate process, meant to break their will power and make them totally passive and subservient, the enslaved Africans were 'seasoned'. ' This means that, for a period of two to three years, they were trained to endure their work and conditions - obey or receive the lash." On the Plantations: The Abolition of Slavery Project. Http://abolition.e2bn.org/slavery_69.html.

[77] https://www.npr.org/2017/04/26/524744989/when-la-erupted-in-anger-a-look-back-at-the-rodney-king-riots.

[78] https://www.nytimes.com/1992/12/16/us/Black-officer-is-beaten-in-a--incident.html.

[79] https://www.dailymail.co.uk/news/article-2413509/Civil-rights-icon-Ruby-Bridges-thanks-US-Marshal-protected-attend-White-school-1960.html.

[80] A scientific control is an experiment or observation designed to minimize the effects of variables other than the independent variable. This increases the reliability of the results, often through a comparison between control measurements and the other measurements.

[81] https://simple.wikipedia.org/wiki/Mind_control.

[82] The Day Philadelphia Bombed its Own People, Aug 15, 2019, Vox.com.

[83] https://www.vox.com/the-highlight/2019/8/8/20747198/philadelphia-bombing-1985-move.

[84] https://www.vox.com/the-highlight/2019/8/8/20747198/philadelphia-bombing-1985-move.

[85] https://www.ncpedia.org/anchor/wilmington-race-riot.

[86] https://www.tulsahistory.org/exhibit/1921-tulsa-race-massacre/.

[87] (December 20, 1953 - May 5, 1977).

[88] The Murder of Jose Campos Torres, Police Brutality and Injustice, https://aagroup1.weebly.com/jose-campos-torres.html.

[89] Freedom Writers, 2007.

[90] There's one epidemic we may never find a vaccine for: Fear of Black men in public spaces. https://www.cnn.com/2020/05/26/us/fear-Black-men-Blake/index.html.

[91] https://www.cnn.com/2020/05/26/us/fear-Black-men-blake/index.html.

[92] US history explains that White fear is just another way to enforce racial segregation https://qz.com/1288067/us-history-explains-that-White-fear-of-Black-people-is-just-another-tool-to-enforce-racial-segregation/.

[93] U.S.C Section 230.

[94] US murder rate jumps in 2020 to highest seen since 1990s | The Post Millennial.

[95] Domestic Violence Statistics Are Surging During The COVID-19 Pandemic (nautil.us)

[96] Experts Predict A Big Increase In High School Dropouts Is On The Horizon | HuffPost.

[97] Study reveals increased suicide rates across U.S. (wkyt.com).

[98] CDC: Drug Overdose Deaths in 2020 on Track to Break Record (nymag.com)

[99] Chief Thomas Burns -The Alienist.

[100] Mark M. Bello, Betrayal in Black.

[101] https://www.bing.com/search?q=drug+abuse+and+cops&cvid=9042ac958335 4969ae338727fc7fe951&FORM=ANAB01&PC=U531. Mar 30, 2018.

[102] https://www.newsmax.com/bernardkerik/police-shootings-crime-statistics/2019/01/22/id/899297.

[103] National Incident-Based Reporting System (NIBRS) is an incident-based reporting system used by law enforcement agencies in the United States for collecting and reporting data on crimes. Local, state, and federal agencies generate NIBRS data from their records management systems.

[104] COMPSTAT stands for Computational Statistics. Compstat is a performance management system that is used to reduce crime and achieve other police department goals. Compstat emphasizes information-sharing, responsibility and account- ability, and improving effectiveness

[105] https://www.law.umich.edu/special/exoneration/Pages/ExonerationsRaceByCrime.aspx.

[106] https://eji.org/news/record-number-of-exonerations-involved-official-misconduct/.

[107] https://wikifactum.org/hello-world-14-2/

[108] http://www.law.umich.edu/special/exoneration/Documents/Race_and_Wrongful_Convictions.pdf.

[109] https://www.fbi.gov/news/pressrel/press-releases/fbi-releases-2019-statistics-on-law-enforcement-officers-killed-in-the-line-of-duty.

[110] https://s3-us-gov-west-1.amazonaws.com/cg-d4b776d0-d898-4153-90c8-8336f86bdfec/LEOKA_INFO.pdf

[111] Mira Grant, Feed. https://www.goodreads.com/quotes/tag?utf8=%E2%9C%93&id=shooting.

[112] https://www.washingtonpost.com/nation/2019/07/03/judge-says-teen-good-family-should-not-be-tried-sexual-assault-an-adult/.

[113] https://www.theguardian.com/us-news/2016/aug/10/university-of-colorado-sexual-assault-austin-wilkerson.

[114] Fatal Force, https://www.washingtonpost.com/graphics/investigations/police-shootings-database/.

[115] Experts on Why Police Aren't Trained to Shoot to Wound - ABC News, https://abcnews.go.com/US/police-trained-shoot-wound-experts/story?id=40402933.

[116] Commission on Accreditation for Law Enforcement Agencies.

[117] The US has one of the highest: 76.6% of prisoners are re-arrested within five years. https://www.businessinsider.com/why-norways-prison-system-is-so-successful-2014-12

[118] https://www.washingtonpost.com/investigations/four-years-in-a-row-police-nationwide-fatally-shoot-nearly-1000-people/2019/02/07/0cb3b098-020f-11e9-9122-82e98f91ee6f_story.html.

[119] Ijeoma Oluo, So you want to talk about race.

[120] https://www.azquotes.com/author/11361-Blaise_Pascal.

[121] The real reason White victims of police brutality don't get enough 'outrage', Lincoln Anthony Blades.

[122] A New Report Says 90% Of Guns Used In Crime Obtained Illegally | https://newstalkkit.com/new-report-says-90-of-guns-used-in-crime-obtained-illegally/?utm_source=tsmclip&utm_medium=referral.

[123] https://www.blackpast.org/african-american-history/-sit-ins-1960/.

[124] https://www.aepscorp.com.

[125] pyramid-force-continuum.png (740×642) (ke-courses-production.s3.amazonaws.com)

[126] pyramid-force-continuum.png (740×642) (ke-courses-production.s3.amazonaws.com)

[127] https://ucr.fbi.gov/crime-in-the-u.s/2018/crime-in-the-u.s.-2018/tables/expanded-homicide-data-table-6.xls.

[128]https://www.pewresearch.org/fact-tank/2017/01/12/Black-and-White-officers-see-many-key-aspects-of-policing-differently.

[129] https://www.usnews.com/news/articles/2020-06-03/data-show-deaths-from-police-violence-disproportionately-affect-people-of-color.

[130] https://www.usnews.com/news/articles/2020-06-03/data-show-deaths-from-police-violence-disproportionately-affect-people-of-color.

[131]Abel Hermant, Le Bourgeois, 1906.

[132] Not just "a few bad apples": U.S. police kill civilians at much higher rates than other countries. https://www.prisonpolicy.org/blog/2020/06/05/policekillings.

[133]https://www.keranews.org/2020-08-06/who-is-most-at-risk-for-police-violence

[134] Pack mentality, Pack Mentality - Inpathy Bulletin.com

[135] GrantB911 on Twitter: "Well this took an unexpected turn... https://t.co/MRe6BgANhC" / Twitter.

[136] Fatal Force - Nearly 250 Women Have Been Fatally Shot By Police Since 2015, Marisa Iati, Jennifer Jenkins, Sommer Brugal. Sept. 4, 2020. https://www.washingtonpost.com/graphics/2020/investigations/police-shootings-women/.

[137] Activists: Cop's shooting of White woman treated differently, Amy Forliti. April 13, 2019. https://apnews.com/article/57b423dcf5e54bdb801d7ea564416a0a.

[138] Cariol Horne, former officer who was fired after stopping 2006 chokehold, "kept fighting" for justice - CBS News.

[139]https://www.cnn.com/2020/06/16/us/buffalo-police-officer-fired-chokehold-objection-trnd/index.html.

[140] One reason for police violence? Too many men with badges. Rosa Brooks June 18, 2020. https://www.washingtonpost.com/outlook/2020/06/18/women-police-officers-violence/.

[141] https://www.prisonpolicy.org/blog/2019/05/14/policingwomen/.

[142] https://backgroundchecks.org/us-prison-population-vs-the-world.html.

[143]Maya Schenwar, Who Do You Serve, Who Do You Protect? Police Violence and Resistance in the United States. https://www.goodreads.com/quotes/tag/police-brutality

[144] The Police Officer's Dilemma: A Decade of Research on Racial Bias in the Decision to Shoot. https://www.csun.edu/~dma/Correll,%20Hudson,%20Guillermo,%20&%20Ma%20(2014).pdf.

[145]Dr. Benjamin Spock.

[146] Study finds police officers arrested 1,100 times per year, or 3 per day, nationwide, by Tom Jackman, June 22, 2016. https://www.washingtonpost.com/news/true-crime/wp/2016/06/22/study-finds-1100-police-officers-per-year-or-3-per-day-are-arrested-nationwide/

[147] We found 85,000 cops who've been investigated for misconduct. Now you can read their records. John Kelly and Mark Nichols, USA TODAY. Jun. 11, 2020. https://www.usatoday.com/in-depth/news/investigations/2019/04/24/usa-today-revealing-misconduct-records-police-cops/3223984002/

[148] ISBN -0874776570, 9780874776577

[149] Angry Aggression Among Police Officers, Sean P. Griffin, Thomas J. Bernard. https://journals.sagepub.com/doi/abs/10.1177/1098611102250365?journalCode=pqxa#:~:text=As%20applied%20to%20police%20behavior,of%20responses%20to%20perceived%20threats.

[150] https://www.azquotes.com/quotes/topics/social-reform.html.

[151] https://www.msn.com/en-us/news/us/some-cities-facing-backlash-after-defunding-police-departments/vi-AAKkzR7?ocid=msedgdhp

[152] https://www.housleylaw.com/blawg/many-innocent-americans-jailed-year.

[153] $5 million since 1989 est mine.

[154] https://pubmed.ncbi.nlm.nih.gov/28186008/#:~:text=Abstract,third%20leading%20cause%20of%20death.

[155] $30 million since 1989 est mine.

[156] https://www.ncbi.nlm.nih.gov/pmc/articles/PMC5016741/#:~:text=Medication%20errors%20harm%20an%20estimated, (20)%20(N).

[157] "Send Social Workers Instead Of Cops!" Ends Tragically As First Social Worker Killed By A Violent Client In Seattle (secondamendmentdaily.com)

[158] Prisons No Place For the Mentally Ill | Human Rights Watch, https://www.hrw.org/news/2004/02/12/prisons-no place-mentally-ill#

[159] Overprescribed: High cost isn't America's only drug problem, https://www.statnews.com/2019/04/02/overprescribed-americas-other-drug-problem/.

[160] Abhijit Naskar.

[161] Black, Indigenous, and people of color.

[162] The harmful impacts of implicit bias and systemic racism, http://neighb.org/harmful-impacts-implicit-bias-systemic-racism.

[163] https://www.statista.com/statistics/191694/number-of-law-enforcement-officers-in-the-us/#:~:text=Number%20of%20law%20enforcement%20officers%20in%20the%20U.S.,law%20enforcement%20officers%20employed%20in%20the%20United%20States.

[164] Source Countries For Illicit Drugs, Source Countries for Illicit Drugs | Encyclopedia.com.

[165] #Police #Racial Profiling, "Cop Caught Arresting the Wrong Man in Racial Profiling Incident." May 2019.

[166]Sequencing Disadvantage: Barriers to Employment Facing Young Black and White Men with Criminal Records, https://scholar.harvard.edu/files/pager/files/annals_sequencingdisadvantage.pdf

[167] Ride or Die Project.

[168] https://don-a-d.blogspot.com/2013/02/the-true-definition-of-ride-or-die-chick.html#:~:text=According%20to%20the%20urban%20dictionary%2C%20a%20%22Ride%20or,know%20that%20she%20is%20his%20now%20and%20forever.

[169]Alex Berenson, Tell Your Children: The Truth About Marijuana, Mental Illness, and Violence.

[170] Business Insider.

[171] https://dictionary.thelaw.com/.

[172] BJS report: Drug abuse and addiction at the root of 21% of crimes https://www.prisonpolicy.org/blog/2017/06/28/drugs.

[173]https://now.org/wp-content/uploads/2018/02/Black-Women-and-Sexual-Violence-6.pdf.

[174]Sexual Exploitation of Black Women, Equal Justice Initiative. https://eji.org/news/history-racial-injustice-sexual-exploitation-Black-women/

[175]The Nature and Psychosocial Consequences of War Rape for Individuals and Communities, Kristine T. Hagen , M.Ed. International Journal of Psychological Studies. 2010.

[176]https://en.wikipedia.org/wiki/List_of_lynching_victims_in_the_United_State.

[177] https://www.fbi.gov/history/famous-cases/medgar-evers.

[178]Cool Pose, Richard Majors and Janet Mancini Billson. Touchstone Books. 1993.

[179]https://ujimacommunity.org/wp-content/uploads/2018/12/Intimate-Partner-Violence-IPV-v9.4.pdf.

[180]Mass Incarceration Costs $182 Billion Every Year, Without Adding Much to Public Safety, https://eji.org/news/mass-incarceration-costs-182-billion-annually/.

[181]How Much Does the War on Drugs Cost?, https://www.monarchshores.com/drug-addiction/how-much-does-the-war-on-drugs-cost/

[182]Causes and Consequences of the Increasing Numbers of Women in the Workforce, https://www.forbes.com/sites/lisaquast/2011/02/14/causes-and-consequences-of-the-increasing-numbers-of-women-in-the-workforce/#3e07fe7f728c.

[183] https://ucr.fbi.gov/crime-in-the-u.s/2018/crime-in-the-u.s.-2018/topic-pages/tables/table-43.

[184] Amita Kelly, https://www.npr.org/sections/itsallpolitics/2015/08/14/432080520/fact-check-was-planned-parenthood-started-to-control-the-Black-population.

[185] https://www.history.com/news/american-revolution-causes.

[186] https://www.battlefields.org/learn/primary-sources/declaration-causes-seceding-states.

[187] https://aeoworks.org/images/uploads/fact_sheets/AEO_Black_Owned_Business_Report_02_16_17_FOR_WEB.pdf.

[188] Are We There Yet? – The State of Black Business and The Path to Wealth. http://blndedmedia.com/are-we-there-yet/.

[189] Who Owns Almost All America's Land?, by Antonio Moore. https://inequality.org/research/owns-land/#:~:text=African%20Americans%2C%20despite%20making%20up,worth%20of%20over%20%241%20trillion.

[190] https://yaqeeninstitute.org/malcolm-x-vanguards-of-justice-scholarship/.

[191] Why Malcolm X Is Getting Written Out Of History, https://www.newsweek.com/2015/02/27/i-worry-my-father-being-written-out-history-307941.html. Karen Bartlett 02/20/15 (Newsweek).

[192] Dreams from My Father: A Story of Race and Inheritance, Barack Obama.

[193] https://www.washingtonpost.com/graphics/national/obama-legacy/racism-during-presidency.html.

[194] https://www.cnn.com/2016/10/05/politics/obama-race-relations-poll/index.html.

[195] https://www.mulemuseum.org/history-of-the-mule.html.

[196] The Black Family in the Age of Mass Incarceration, Ta-Nehisi Coates. https://www.theatlantic.com/magazine/archive/2015/10/the-Black-family-in-the-age-of-mass-incarceration/403246/.

[197] 10 Benefits of Family Time, https://fortmagic.com/10-benefits-family-time/#:~:text=Family%20bonding%20time%20builds%20confidence,lasting%20connections%20between%20family%20members.

[198] Occupational hazards and health cost of women cotton pickers in Pakistani Punjab, https://www.ncbi.nlm.nih.gov/pmc/articles/PMC5020534/#:~:text=Farm%20workers%20and%20female%20cotton,pickers%20with%20varied%20health%20cost. Hell on Earth: What it Was Like to Pick Cotton, https://timespelunking.wordpress.com/2012/11/08/hell-on-earth-what-it-was-like-to-pick-cotton/.

[199] "As another has well said, to handicap a student by teaching him that his blacks face is a curse and that his struggle to change his condition is hopeless is the worst sort of lynching. It kills one's aspirations and dooms him to vagabondage and crime." Carter G Woodson.

[200] Federico Fellini, https://www.babbel.com/en/magazine/language-quotes-01.

[201] Ludwig Wittgenstein, https://www.babbel.com/en/magazine/language-quotes-01.

[202] Carter Woodson, The Miseducation of the Negro.

[203] https://www.city-journal.org/html/Black-family-40-years-lies-12872.html.

[204] https://www.mormondialogue.org/topic/65072-moynihans-scissors-the-importance-of-two-parents/.

[205] College expenses are one of the major examples of MCS bondage, it is cited as the third leading cause. https://www.wisebread.com/8-common-causes-of-debt-and-how-to-avoid-them.

[206] The Economic Principles of America's Founders: Property Rights, Free Markets, and Sound Money, https://www.aier.org/article/the-economic-principles-of-americas-founders-property-rights-free-markets-and-sound-money-hf/.

[207] Status and Trends in the Education of Racial and Ethnic Groups, National Center for Education Statistics. https://nces.ed.gov/programs/raceindicators/indicator_red.asp#:~:text=The%20150%20percent%20graduation%20rate,Black%20students%20(23%20percent). 2019.

[208] Status and Trends in the Education of Racial and Ethnic Groups, National Center for Education Statistics. https://nces.ed.gov/programs/raceindicators/indicator_red.asp#:~:text=The%20150%20percent%20graduation%20rate,Black%20students%20(23%20percent). 2019.

[209] Graduation rate within 6 years (150 percent of normal time) for degree completion from first institution attended for first-time, full-time bachelor's degree-seeking students at 4-year postsecondary institutions, by race/ethnicity and sex.

[210] http://worldteacher-andrea.blogspot.com/2012/11/the-difference-between-written-grammar.html. 2014.

[211] Status and Trends in the Education of Racial and Ethnic Groups, National Center for Education Statistics. https://nces.ed.gov/programs/raceindicators/indicator_red.asp#:~:text=The%20150%20percent%20graduation%20rate,Black%20students%20(23%20percent). 2019.

[212] https://www.tmcf.org/history-of-hbcus/#:~:text=During%20the%201850s%2C%20three%20more,HBCU%20operated%20by%20African%20Americans.

[213] https://theconversation.com/where-are-the-african-american-leaders-131282.

[214] President Obama, https://www.grantmakersforgirlsofcolor.org/resources-item/obama-speech-focuses-on-plight-of-us-Black-women/.

[215] Why America Needs Ebonics Now, Michael Hobbes. Huffington Post 2017.

[216] [79 million speak English / 1268 billon speak Mandarin Chinese / 1120 Billion speak Hindi / 637 million speak Spanish / 538 million speak French / 277 million speak standard Arabic / 274 million speak Bengali] https://www.ethnologue.com/guides/ethnologue200.

[217] "Too Many "Useless Eaters Dr. Kissinger?,https://tabublog.com/2014/01/19/too-many-useless-eaters-dr-kissinger/.

[218] The powerful impact of Black role models, Christie Ellis, July 23, 2020. https://www.nctq.org/blog/The-powerful-impact-of-Black-role-models.

[219] James Baldwin.

www.ingramcontent.com/pod-product-compliance
Lightning Source LLC
Chambersburg PA
CBHW060305030426
42336CB00011B/944